Bloom's Modern Critical Interpretations

Bloom's Modern Critical Interpretations

Toni Morrison's
Beloved
New Edition

Edited and with an introduction by
Harold Bloom
Sterling Professor of the Humanities
Yale University

BLOOM'S
LITERARY CRITICISM
An imprint of Infobase Publishing

**Bloom's Modern Critical Interpretations:
Toni Morrison's *Beloved*—New Edition**

Copyright © 2009 by Infobase Publishing

Introduction © 2009 by Harold Bloom

Bloom's Literary Criticism
An imprint of Infobase Publishing
132 West 31st Street
New York NY 10001

Library of Congress Cataloging-in-Publication Data

Toni Morrison's *Beloved*/edited and with an introduction by Harold Bloom—New ed.
    p. cm.—(Bloom's Modern Critical Interpretations)
Includes bibliographical references and index.
ISBN 978-1-60413-184-0 (hardcover: alk. paper) 1. Morrison, Toni. Beloved. 2.
Historical fiction, American—History and criticism. 3. African American women in literature. 4. Infanticide in literature. 5. Slavery in literature. 6. Ohio—In literature. I. Bloom, Harold. II. Title: Beloved.

PS3563.O8749B4378 2009
813'.54—dc22
                                        2009009816

Bloom's Literary Criticism books are available at special discounts when purchased in bulk quantities for businesses, associations, institutions, or sales promotions. Please call our Special Sales Department in New York at (212) 967-8800 or (800) 322-8755.

You can find Bloom's Literary Criticism on the World Wide Web at
http://www.chelseahouse.com.

Cover design by Ben Peterson

Printed in the United States of America
MP BCL 10 9 8 7 6 5 4 3 2 1

Contents

Editor's Note

My introduction suggests some aesthetic limitations that *Beloved* manifests, despite its all-but-universal esteem. The dozen critical essays included in this volume are part of that chorus of praise.

Structure is emphasized by Steven V. Daniels, while Nancy Kang explores the problematics of black masculinity as being crucial to the novel.

Teresa N. Washington meditates on the mother-daughter conflict, after which Jeffrey Andrew Weinstock argues that all of *Beloved* is an epitaph.

The sorrows of black womanhood are set forth by Reginald Watson, while Dean Franco invokes a dialectic of trauma and body, and Lars Eckstein a jazzy perspective.

Christopher Peterson brings up theory's heavy hitters, Derrida and Levinas, after which Morrison's own role is highlighted by Anita Durkin. Cynthia Lyles-Scott closes this volume with the theme of naming.

HAROLD BLOOM

Introduction

TONI MORRISON'S *BELOVED*

The cultural importance of Toni Morrison's most popular novel, *Beloved* (1987) hardly can be overstressed. Of all Morrison's novels, it puzzles me most: the style is remarkably adroit, baroque in its splendor, and the authority of the narrative is firmly established. The characters are problematic, for me; unlike the protagonists of Morrison's earlier novels, they suggest ideograms. I think that it is because *Beloved* is a powerfully tendentious romance; it has too clear a design upon its readers, of whatever race and gender. The storyteller of *Sula* (1975) and of *Song of Solomon* (1977) has been replaced by a formidable ideologue, who perhaps knows too well what she wishes her book to accomplish.

Morrison strongly insists that her literary context is essentially African American, and *Beloved* overtly invokes slave narratives as it precursors. I hardly doubt that the novel's stance is African-American feminist Marxist, as most of the exegetes reprinted in this volume proclaim. And yet the style and narrative procedures have more of a literary relationship to William Faulkner and Virginia Woolf, than to any African-American writers. I am aware that such an assertion risks going against Morrison's own warning "that finding or imposing Western influences in/on Afro-American literature had value provided the valued process does not become self-anointing." I mildly observe (since both my personal and critical esteem for Morrison is enormous) that "finding *or* imposing" (italics mine of course) is a very shrewd equivocation. Morrison, both in prose style and in narrative mode, has a complex and permanent relationship to Faulkner and to Woolf. *Beloved*, in a long perspective, is a child of Faulkner's masterpiece, *As I Lay Dying*, while the heroine, Sethe, has more in common with Lena Grove of

1

Light in August than with any female character of African-American fiction. This is anything but a limitation, aesthetically considered, but is rejected by Morrison and her critical disciples alike. Ideology aside, Morrison's fierce assertion of independence is the norm for any strong writer, but I do not think that this denial of a swerve from indubitable literary origins can be a critical value in itself.

None of this would matter if the ideologies of political correctness were not so deeply embedded in *Beloved* as to make Sethe a less persuasive representation of a possible human being that she might have been. Trauma has much less to do with Sethe's more-than-Faulknerian sense of guilt that the novel's exegetes have argued. The guilt of being a survivor is not unique to any oppressed people; programs in guilt are an almost universal temptation. *Beloved* is a calculated series of shocks; whether the memory of shock is aesthetically persuasive has to seem secondary in a novel dedicated to the innumerable victims of American slavery. One steps very warily in raising the aesthetic issue in regard to a book whose moral and social value is beyond dissent. Still, Sethe is a character in a visionary romance that also insists upon its realistic and historical veracity. A literary character has to be judged finally upon the basis of literary criteria, which simply are not "patriarchal" or "capitalistic" or "Western imperialist." Morrison, whose earlier novels were not as over-determined by ideological considerations as *Beloved* is, may have sacrificed much of her art upon the altar of a politics perhaps admirable in itself, but not necessarily in the service of high literature (if one is willing to grant that such an entity still exists).

The terrors depicted in *Beloved* may be beyond the capacity of literary representation itself, which is an enigma that has crippled every attempt to portray the Nazi slaughter of European Jewry. The African-American critic Stanley Crouch has been much condemned for expressing his disdain in regard to *Beloved*. Crouch, I think, underestimated the book's stylistic achievement, but his healthy distrust of ideologies is alas germane to aspects of *Beloved*. Sentimentalism is not in one sense relevant to *Beloved:* how can any emotions be in excess of its object, when slavery is the subject? And yet the novel's final passage about Sethe could prove, some day, to be a kind of period piece:

> He is staring at the quilt but he is thinking about her wrought-iron back; the delicious mouth still puffy at the corner from Ella's fist. The mean black eyes. The wet dress steaming before the fire. Her tenderness about his neck jewelry—its three wands, like attentive baby rattlers, curving two feet into the air. How she never mentioned or looked at it, so he did not have to feel the shame of being collared like a beast. Only this woman Sethe could

have left him his manhood like that. He wants to put his story next to hers.

"Sethe," he says, "me and you, we got more yesterday than anybody. We need some kind of tomorrow."

He leans over and takes her hand. With the other he touches her face. "You your best thing Sethe. You are." His holding fingers are holding hers.

"Me? Me?"

The pathos is admirable, rather too much so. Sethe is given the explicit tribute that the entire book has sought to constitute. She is the heroic African-American mother, who has survived terrors both natural and supernatural, and has maintained her integrity and her humanity. Morrison's design has been fulfilled, but is Sethe a person or an abstraction? Time will sift this matter out; cultural politics do not answer such a question. Morrison must be judged finally, in *Beloved*, against *As I Lay Dying* and *Mrs. Dalloway*, rather than against Harriet Jacob's *Incidents in the Life of a Slave Girl* (1861). The canonical novelist of *Song of Solomon* deserves no less.

STEVEN V. DANIELS

Putting "His Story Next to Hers": Choice, Agency, and the Structure of Beloved

When, near the end of *Beloved*, Paul D "wants to put his story next to" Sethe's (273), his desire points the reader toward the structural and, perhaps, thematic core of Toni Morrison's intense and challenging narrative of slavery's effects and aftereffects. Paul D's statement has been cited often in published criticism of the novel, but its suggestiveness has not actually been much explored.[1] Putting Paul D's story and Sethe's side by side can, however, restore a rich parallelism that is obscured by the shifting points of view and multiple pasts of the narrative. It also can serve to restore Paul D to a position of importance in the novel often denied him and to give particular prominence to the choices Morrison presents to and through her characters, mostly, ironically, while they are subject to and subjects of slavery and therefore ostensibly without autonomy.[2] The most important of these choices comes in the implicit juxtaposition of Sethe's choice of death for her children and herself, rather than return to slavery, with Paul D's choice of life when he finds himself in circumstances that present him with the same options.

The juxtaposition of stories is a task left to the reader, already tested by the choice of whether to proceed through the bewilderments of the novel's beginning and by the problem of how to emerge at the end from the emotional and thematic ambivalences of the passing of Beloved and concurrent

Texas Studies in Literature and Language, Volume 44, Number 4 (Winter 2002): pp. 349–367.

5

questions of whether the tale told is "a story to pass on" (274–275).[3] The jux-taposition will not answer all, perhaps not any, of these questions, but it aligns the novel with the view that Morrison forcefully affirms in "Unspeakable Things Unspoken," her most substantial discussion of African American liter-ature: "We are not Isak Dinesen's 'aspects of nature,' nor Conrad's unspeaking. We are the subjects of our own experience, and, in no way coincidentally, in the experience of those with whom we have come in contact. We are not, in fact, 'other.' We are choices" (208). "You got to choose," Stamp Paid tells Paul D late in the novel (231), at a moment that hardly warrants the urgency the statement appears to have. All that is at stake here are the options for relief from the cold and damp church basement in which Paul D has sought shelter after fleeing 124 Bluestone Road. But the remark is a reminder, and its burden is Morrison's best means of constructing and conveying the human dignity she wishes her characters to have. Both Sethe and Paul D "got to choose," and in their subsequent lives they are haunted by the choices they made. But in their suffering, their acceptance of responsibility for their opposing choices, lies the measure of their dignity.

If we take events in their narrated (rather than chronological) sequence, there is for both Sethe and Paul D an escape attempt, indeed a richly report-ed heroic escape, before the account of their crucial choices. Sethe's solitary march to free Ohio may be compared with the perfectly synchronized plunge by Paul D and his fellow chain-gang prisoners through the mud of their flooding cages. Sethe is pulled forward, despite a physically abused body and the absence of a guide, by the emotional bond to her children ("All I knew was I had to get my milk to my baby girl" [16]); Paul D, at least initially, by "the power of the chain" (110) that binds him for success or failure to the bod-ies of forty-five other men. Paul D reaches freedom alone, while Sethe joins her family and a welcoming community of free, freed, and fugitive Blacks. Each has been aided, Sethe by a "throw-away" (84) White woman on a jour-ney to Boston, Paul D and his companions by a Cherokee remnant who have refused to trek West. And each escape, though Sethe's is presented at greater length and in three separate sections, is among the most coherent narrations in the fragmented *recit*. Neither escape is, however, entirely successful. Such complete success, whether or not it ever occurs for these two characters, must wait for the living daughter Denver's later and no less heroic plunge from the family porch into a world dominated by White folks (244).

More to the structural point, though, the escape of Paul D's that chron-ologically parallels Sethe's is, for reasons never made entirely clear, a complete failure, except for the hope we may share with Sixo that his and Paul D's cap-ture provides opportunity for escape by the Thirty-Mile Woman and Sixo's unborn child. Apart from that hope, the escape attempt ends, Paul D thinks before we can know what he is thinking about, with "One crazy, one sold, one missing, one burnt, and me licking iron with my hands crossed behind me" (72). It is the failure of the slaves' plan that leaves Sethe on her own in her desperate effort to reach the children she has sent on ahead.

Schoolteacher heads up both the immediate capture of Paul D and Sixo and the party that arrives a month later at 124 Bluestone with a legal claim to self-stolen property. Sethe's reaction is represented more as a reflex than a considered decision:

> And if she thought anything, it was No. No. Nono. Nonono. Simple. She just flew. Collected every bit of life she had made, all the parts of her that were precious and fine and beautiful, and carried, pushed, dragged them through the veil, out, away, over there where no one could hurt them. (163)

Sethe knows even then, as she thinks of explaining to Beloved years later, where the impulse comes from. Not so much from the threat of physical abuse, though of this she bears evidence on her own back, or even from the threat of separation through sale, a new concern that gives urgency to the attempt at escape, her mind turns in explanation to the moment when she discovered that there was a demeaning and dehumanizing way of being seen that might become her children's way of seeing themselves. Like Faulkner's Sutpen, she backs away, physically and in the course her life takes, from something overheard that horrifies her:

> I heard [Schoolteacher] say, "No, no. That's not the way. I told you to put her human characteristics on the left; her animal ones on the right. And don't forget to line them up." I commenced to walk backward, didn't even look behind me to find out where I was headed. I just kept lifting my feet and pushing back. (193)[4]

Sethe's own negations ("No. No. Nono. Nonono.") echo Schoolteacher's when a month later she again does not look back and this time pushes her children ahead of her. The incident is given particular importance in her unspoken account to Beloved of her motives for murder, partly in the revelation that it had never before been disclosed to anyone, partly in Sethe's belief that "it might help explain something to you." "No notebook for my babies and no measuring string neither" (198), no return to those who could "Dirty you so bad you couldn't like yourself anymore" (251). It may be the book's only weakness that tact keeps Morrison from showing in other of the slaves or exslaves that Sethe's fears in fact are warranted. We take on faith a deprivation of humanity that the novel as a whole seems determined to deny.

What Sethe lives with is not just the deed itself of attempting to take her children to "safety" but a commitment to reject consolation or anything else that might suggest regret. Taken as pride by her neighbors, who feel rebuffed in their wish to wrap her in a consoling "cape of sound" (152), this commitment begins when she is taken away by the sheriff with "her head a bit too high? Her back a little too straight?" (152). It continues unabated into the story's present, with Paul D recognizing that "more important than what Sethe had done was what she claimed: It scared him" (164). To admit any doubt to herself about the murder of her daughter would be to admit more pain than she can tolerate. The closest she comes occurs early in the novel, in anger at Paul D's suggestion that she and Denver leave the ghost-infected house: "No more running—from nothing. . . . I took one journey and I paid for the ticket, but let me tell you something, Paul D Garner; it cost too much!" (15).

There is never an overt confession of doubt, but besides the need to explain ("although I know you don't need me to do it" [193]), such doubt is intimated early on when a question of Beloved's evokes "shameful" memories of Sethe's own mother. Asked why she was hanged, Sethe does not recall or admit or, perhaps, really know that flight was her mother's crime. Later, provoked by Beloved's accusations of abandonment, she clearly fears that her mother's behavior might be seen as a precedent for her own. Her denial that the mother she barely knew was hanged for attempting escape—"Because she was my ma'am and nobody's ma'am would run off and leave her daughter, would she?" (203)—fails to conceal the doubt that she must have harbored even earlier. But if flight from her daughter as well as from slavery is not the shameful thought about her mother that enters Sethe's mind in response to Beloved's question, then the thought that does, "something she had forgotten she knew" (61), is even more troubling. "As small girl Sethe, she was unimpressed" when told of her mother's having cared only for her among the children born to her. "As grown-up woman Sethe she was angry, but not certain at what" in the suddenly recalled story of all the others, with White fathers, that her mother "threw away" (62). There is no more likeness between these acts of infanticide and Sethe's than between either and Medea's deed, but there is, it appears, an inability to completely repress thoughts that her mother's abandonment of unwanted babies might reflect on her own effort to take her children to a safe place. Beloved would be less powerful in Sethe's life if the doubt and pain had not all along been demanding expression.

Though Sethe's professed lack of regret scares Paul D and leads him to question her humanity ("You got two feet, Sethe, not four"), it is not what scares him away. His remark, a thoughtless echo of Schoolteacher's racist anthropology, carries extra force because of that connection and because of Sethe's discomfort about the bearing of her mother's actions on her own. But it is his own shame rather than Sethe's, "his cold-house secret" with Beloved, not Sethe's "too thick love" (165), that Paul D cannot come to satisfactory terms with. Beloved would be less powerful in Paul D's life, too, if doubt and pain about his choice had not all along been present but hidden.

The seduction by Beloved in the cold-house culminates her effort to rid the household of Paul D and to assure the needy child's dominance in Sethe's life. From another perspective, its goal is to restore the past's control over any possible future. Paul D, too, emerges as if from the past, first appearing in the novel as the continuation of a paragraph in which we are told first of Sethe's efforts "to remember as close to nothing as was safe" and then shown "suddenly . . . Sweet Home rolling, rolling out before her eyes" (6). But Paul D comes, as if out from the memory of Sweet Home, to present Sethe with an alternative future. The dead daughter's human embodiment follows not only from Paul D's victorious battle against the haunting of the house, but also and more immediately, from one page to the next, from imagery of a possible future that soon enters Sethe's thoughts. Heading to a "Colored Thursday" at the carnival, "They were not holding hands, but their shadows were . . . all the time, no matter what they were doing . . . the shadows that shot out of their feet to the left held hands. Nobody noticed but Sethe and she stopped looking after she decided that it was a good sign. A life. Could be" (47). Though Paul D has just announced, with respect to the tension between Sethe's living daughter and him, "I'm not asking you to choose. Nobody would" (45), the dead daughter leaves no such room for compatibility or compromise.

"Moved," in both senses, by the strange young woman who calls herself Beloved, Paul D is made to feel like "a rag doll" (126), an image that eerily reappears when Denver later thinks about what her mother has become in submitting to Beloved's punishing demands (243). Doubts about his manhood, about whether Schoolteacher was indeed right in the matter of definitions, are provoked in Paul D when he finds himself "picked up and put back down anywhere any time by a girl" (126); and he thinks, "That was the wonder of Sixo, and even of Halle; it was always clear to Paul D that those two were men whether Garner said so or not. It troubled him that, concerning his own manhood, he could not satisfy himself on that point" (220). A review of the abortive escape years earlier reinforces his doubts when he contrasts himself returned to slavery to Sixo determined in making and affirming a choice, adamant in claiming a different fate.

Sixo's defiance, first in physical resistance and then in song, convinces Schoolteacher that, despite the economic loss, "This one will never be suitable" (226). A month later, Schoolteacher will find Sethe and the rest of his escaped property either dead or similarly unsuitable when he catches up with them in Ohio. But it is the two unsuitable slaves who at least partially get their way. As Paul D later thinks, of the response to Sixo's laughter, "They shoot him to shut him up. Have to" (226). They did not have to shoot Paul D, and Sixo stands, in Paul D's own terms, as a manly model of the alternative he did not take. Collared and chained back at Sweet Home, "He thinks he should have sung along. Loud, something loud and rolling to go with Sixo's tune" (227).

Instead he begins a process comparable to the emotional self-containment Sethe adopts in order to defend herself one month later in Ohio:

> It was some time before he could put Alfred, Georgia, Sixo, schoolteacher, Halle, his brothers, Sethe, Mister, the taste of iron, the sight of butter, the smell of hickory, notebook paper, one by one, into the tobacco tin lodged in his chest. By the time he got to 124 nothing in this world could pry it open. (113)

For Sethe as well, containment can sequester but cannot dispose of distressing feelings. Both characters will be pried open by something "in this world" but not of it.

The pain Paul D feels when Sethe speaks to him on the day of his capture joins doubt about manhood with "the shame of being collared like a beast" (273). Manhood and humanity are as much linked for him as are maternity and humanity for Sethe. The argument has been made that this is an ideological blunder on their part, a submission to "the narrations and master definitions constructed by White patriarchal culture and its various laws" (Schopp, 359). The claim has a certain theoretical logic, but it gains little support from the text itself, especially when joined with the claim that Morrison is on the side of the cultural studies angels in carrying her protagonists on a course of recovery from the "internalization of oppressors' values" (Ayer [Sitter], 191). James Berger provides a useful reminder—and possible corrective—in setting the composition of Beloved in the political context of the 1980s and that period's neoconservative appropriation of some of the data and conclusions offered two decades earlier by the Moynihan report, *The Negro Family: A Case for National Action* (1965). He suggests that the novel is sensitive to "perceived attacks on black manhood and womanhood" (412) as ineffectual on the one hand and emasculating on the other, a perspective present by implication in the Moynihan report and more concretely in the Reagan Administration's policies. Male independence and maternal bonding are, on the contrary, strongly affirmed in the novel. They are, moreover, despite Garner and his peculiar ways, on the record presented in *Beloved* among the gender roles slavery seeks to deny to slaves.

There is also an impulse to make a political point, though less elaborately developed, in the attention given to Beloved's departure at the height of her destructive power late in the novel. That scene involves the coincidental convergence at 124 Bluestone of thirty women intent on exorcism and, coming from the other direction, Edward Bodwin on his way to pick up Denver for her first day's work. Critics who comment at all are as likely as not to take the will for the deed and assume that it is the community (and perhaps Sethe herself) that forces Beloved to flee.[5] The community has a good deal to redeem itself for, having ostracized Sethe after the murder and, leading up to it, having failed to warn her of the approach of Schoolteacher and his companions. And perhaps its wish to aid now sufficiently redeems it. But its efforts are not what relieve Sethe. The error is instructive with regard to both Morrison's narrative technique and her thematic intentions.

At work here in the climactic moment in the present are, in miniature, some of the same proairetic elements that governed the deciphering of the climax in the past.[6] There, before the painstaking revelation of exactly what happened and why, we have been kept alert to these questions and have been led skillfully to anticipate answers. That is, we have been prompted to provide names for actions the narrative has not yet fully disclosed. Before we are able to make much, perhaps anything of the information, we learn that the baby whose "venom" (3) fills the house had had its "throat cut" and even more shockingly that its "baby blood had soaked [Sethe's] fingers" (5). To the fact of the baby's death, we may add the word "murder," along with its mother's proximity, and ask what could account for the infant's apparently violent death. Some hundred pages later, Denver's thoughts of the rupture in her year of schooling with Lady Jones add the word "murderer" to the reader's lexicon. Questions about Beloved's attack on Sethe's throat in the Clearing lead Denver to question her own loyalties and to memories of two questions posed by one of her fellow students: "Murder, Nelson Lord had said. 'Didn't your mother get locked away for murder? Wasn't you in there with her when she went?'" (104). Whether or not one recollects Sethe's earlier statement of, as if as a matter of choice, having gone "to jail instead" (42) of returning with Schoolteacher to Sweet Home, the questions Denver lingers over seem designed to raise suspicions about Sethe's role in the baby's death while raising equally troubling ones about why. Concurrently, Beloved's actions, till this point expressions of infantile need, come to seem tainted with a desire for revenge. But what could have led a woman so devoted to her children to brutally murder one of them? The facts, at least from Sethe's perspective, add the word "rescue" to the confirmation of "murder." Though the narrative of the past is variously fragmented, suspicions are fulfilled and the hermeneutic process is as fully resolved as in the best of well-made plots.

Having been trained in this manner to expect not only answers but answers that confirm suspicions, it is not surprising that so many readers assign the word "exorcism" or even, once again, "rescue" to the disappearance of Beloved at the end. Though it is a matter of intention rather than accomplishment, "It was Ella more than anyone who convinced the others that rescue was in order" (256). It is more surprising that Morrison, having so set us up for the satisfactions of effective communal action, chooses to deny us this doubly reassuring feel-good resolution. But this is the difference between the novel's horrific past and its uncertain present and future:

> Standing alone on the porch, Beloved is smiling. But now her hand is empty. Sethe is running away from her, running, and she feels the emptiness in the hand Sethe has been holding. Now she is running into the faces of the people out there, joining them and leaving Beloved behind. Alone. Again. (262)

These are Beloved's frightened thoughts, and we know, from Sethe's own, that it is not "away from her" but toward Mr. Bodwin that Sethe is running, not to join the others and "leav[e] Beloved behind," but to protect her. If Sethe is reliving, with a difference, an earlier event, Beloved is experiencing a devastating sameness, the recurrence of an earlier abandonment in which Sethe "never waved goodbye or even looked her way before running away from her" (242).

It is only by the most peculiarly indirect logic that it might be said either that the gathered women dispose of the dead daughter or that Sethe, having had enough of her, turns to the community for the comfort she rejected nineteen years earlier. The women's "wave of sound," silenced by Sethe's demeanor in the earlier incident, may be "wide enough to sound deep water and knock the pods off chestnut trees" and it may be that Sethe "trembled like the baptized in its wash" (261). But it is the power of misunderstanding that governs the action here, Sethe's of what is transpiring as Mr. Bodwin arrives in her yard and Beloved's of Sethe's flight into the crowd. (Later, to compound these errors, Sethe will misunderstand Beloved's motive for leaving.) Though the scene presents an extraordinary lesson in perception as a function of mental state (even for the undead), Morrison must knowingly be giving us less than we expect and less than would fully satisfy. She is also at this moment presenting Beloved not as the demon wrenched from its prey by a collective ur-prayer, but as the needy child at her most pathetic. We cannot simply cheer her departure.

To return to the question of gender roles, Sethe may at the end move somewhat from defining her humanity in terms of motherhood. At least to so move her seems to be Paul D's goal in his final words, "You your best thing, Sethe. You are," and may be Sethe's meaning in her response, "Me? Me?" (273), although the latter monosyllables may be read pretty much as the reader chooses. Paul D on the other hand, much more the subject of gender-critiquing commentary, is at the end much as he was at the beginning, unchanged in his view of manhood though more hopeful in his claim to it. And unchanged in the gentle responsiveness he is said to need to acquire. Almost the first thing we learn about him, though never recalled in this line of criticism, is that, "Not even trying he had become the kind of man who could walk into a house and make the women cry. Because with him, in his presence, they could. There was something blessed in his manner.... Strong women and wise saw him and told him things they only told each other ..." (17). And it is surely no lack of verbal resource that leads Morrison to have Sethe think the exact same thing in the same words in their final scene together. The earlier paragraph continues with his reaction to the sight of the "tree" on Sethe's back, also uncited in the midst of criticism of his insensitivity: "And when the top of her dress was around her hips and he saw the sculpture her back had become, like the decorative work of an ironsmith too passionate for display, he could think but not say, 'Aw, Lord, girl.' And he would tolerate no peace until he had touched every ridge and leaf of it with his mouth ..." (18). Instead attention is focused on his post-coital reaction to her scars and her breasts "that he could definitely live without" (21), more an effect of deflated fantasy than a rejection, in the aftermath, of the reality that supersedes it. Both characters soon overcome their disappointment.[7]

Even Paul D's unpremeditated expression of a desire for Sethe's pregnancy comes in an almost comic moment, a fallback from the impossibility of asking Sethe for help in combating the power of the girl who "moved" him, from saying to Sethe, "I am not a man": "Since he could not say what he planned to, he said something he didn't know was on his mind.... And suddenly it was a solution: a way to hold on to her, document his manhood and break out of the girl's spell—all in one" (128). Sethe comes to his aid, "solved everything with one blow" (130) by inviting him back to the bedroom "Where you belong" (131), and this is the last we hear of procreative wishes. It is not his penis whose power he needs reassurance of, but his man's will, the characteristic Garner had cultivated, that Sixo had demonstrated, and that Schoolteacher, as surely as in thinking of Sethe as a member of a hybrid species, had set out to undermine:

> But it was more than appetite that humiliated him and made him wonder if schoolteacher was right. It was being moved, placed where she wanted him, and there was nothing he was able to do about it. . . . And it was he, that man, who had walked from Georgia to Delaware, who could not go or stay put where he wanted to in 124—shame (126).

At the end, when he returns to 124, another beneficiary of Beloved's misunderstanding of her mother's motives, he sets out to comfort Sethe and in reassuring her recalls her unasked for reassurance of him nineteen years earlier:

> Her tenderness about his neck jewelry—its three wands, like attentive baby rattlers, curving two feet in the air. How she never mentioned or looked at it, so he did not have to feel the shame of being collared like a beast. Only this woman Sethe could have left him his manhood like that. He wants to put his story next to hers. (273)

Doubts about his manhood, provoked in the present by Beloved's power over him, have been with him since his choice of life and a return to slavery, just as Sethe's doubts about her maternal adequacy, and therefore humanity, also lanced by Beloved, have been with her since her choice of death as slavery's alternative. While these may not be the most enlightened gender identifications, arguing against them in this narrative seems peculiarly neglectful of the limitations slavery is shown to impose on the possibilities for self-definition. Moreover, these modes of definition—or any other claims to humanity—seem more an escape from the dominant culture's construction of the slave than an acquiescence to it.

In the novel's two main characters, Morrison starkly juxtaposes—or, as with so much else in *Beloved*, leaves it to her reader to juxtapose—the terrible choice between life as a slave and violent death that is almost the only choice slavery allows its victims. It is worth a moment to look a bit more carefully at the bases of these choices and to distinguish also between the choice of death by Sethe and Sixo, as different in their nature as either is from Paul D's choice of life. None of the three dies—or lives—for a cause or an abstract ideal, a characteristic Tzvetan Todorov uses to distinguish between what he calls the "heroic" and the "ordinary" virtues in his recent examination of behavior in the Warsaw ghetto and the Nazi concentration camps. Particular individuals may (or may not), in Todorov's terms, benefit from a heroic act, but the welfare of particular individuals is not the reason for that act. Sixo's death is closest to a heroic act, the one that term attaches to most readily, and indeed closest to the conventional model of manhood in that regard, but his death has much more to do with his own dignity, with slavery's power over him, than with an assault on the institution of slavery itself. This dignity is, in Todorov's formulation, "the first ordinary virtue, and it simply means the capacity of the individual to remain a subject with a will"; "that fact," he goes on to say in terms appropriate to the present discussion, "is enough to ensure membership in the human race" (16).

Sethe's choice of death for her children and herself, even if viewed as misguided, adds a second ordinary virtue. Her concern is not only for her own dignity but also for the dignity—membership in the human race—of her children. "I took and put my babies where they'd be safe" (164), she announces to Paul D. Her own death, like her own escape from Sweet Home, would be a matter of joining them rather than an effort intended for her own welfare. She sets out to kill them in their innocence as an expression of "caring," a kind of act Todorov is able to give examples of from the camps: "There are things we can do for others that we are incapable of doing solely for ourselves" (17).[8] Caring has figured in Sixo's sacrifice of freedom, in successfully diverting attention from the Thirty-Mile Woman, but, unlike Sethe's decision, his choice of death is an entirely separate act of defiance and free will.

Though Paul D affirms Sixo's choice and rejects Sethe's ("There could have been a way. Some other way" [165]), he misses in his own decision precisely the dignity that each of the others can claim to have secured, Sixo in acting in a way calculated to force the hand of his master, Sethe in more impulsively imposing her will on circumstances. Indeed, Paul D has at least given the appearance of having simply been passive, merely following Sixo in his diversionary tactic and then observing him. But just as Sethe is less confident than she claims with regard to her own behavior, there may be more to Paul D's choice than his sense of the requirements of manhood allows him to find in it. Staying alive damages Paul D's dignity, but is not accomplished at the expense of any other's dignity or well-being. Sixo's act makes a better story, but not, in its specificity, a better person. The test is in the aftermath, both in the persistence of escapes, the "other way" Paul D insists upon to Sethe, and in the quality of caring that survives his ordeal. His bad moment comes not in claiming life for himself, but, years later and under the pressure of Beloved's perceived presence, in demeaning Sethe's contrary decision.

The protagonists are not the only characters in the novel who make choices with regard to their status as slaves. The circumstances within which Halle and Stamp Paid choose life are different mainly in that one man goes mad in seeing his wife brutally abused and the other, abiding a less obviously brutal assault, doesn't. The difference isn't negligible, of course, and perhaps neither "choice" nor "life" perfectly describes Halle's portion, last seen by Paul D "squatting by the churn smearing the butter as well as its clabber all over his face because the milk they took is on his mind" (70). Stamp Paid's choice is to change his name and his life rather than follow his inclination to kill the master who temporarily took his wife or his wife once she is discarded. But both men accede where the alternative of resistance would likely have led to death.

In another implicit pairing of characters, two who risk death in choosing escape are Baby Suggs's "husband" and Sethe's mother, one perhaps successfully, the other, her body displayed as an example, evidently not. What they share is not only the risk of capture and death, but also the separation that flight entails. If we regard Suggs more sympathetically than we do Sethe's mother, it is probably because we sense a difference in the difficulty each has in separating from what is left behind. Sethe, as she finally acknowledges at the end, feels abandoned by her mother, and the text gives us no reason to take a different view.[9] Baby Suggs, on the other hand knows that her "husband" ran because doing so was a choice they had made together and for one another: "whichever got a chance to run would take it; together if possible, alone if not, and no looking back" (142).

This decision in Baby Suggs's past is disclosed when Mr. Garner, who has always known her as Jenny Whitlow, her bill-of-sale name, delivers her into freedom. Even this step, achieved through years of her son's labor, involves a wrenching, impossible decision in which the cost seems greater than the prize: "Of the two hard things—standing on her feet till she dropped or leaving her last and probably only living child—she chose the hard thing that made him happy, and never put to him the question she put to herself: What for?" (141). Her experience of "what for" with her first step on free ground— "there was nothing like it in this world" (141)—helps to explain Sethe's determination later not to allow her children to be returned to slavery.

A third stage in putting beside each other Sethe's and Paul D's stories—a follow-up to escape and, then, the response to recapture—comes in the present and with the arrival of Beloved. Acting single-mindedly toward her own goal of satisfying an insatiable hunger, she is for both protagonists "an outside thing that embraces while it accuses" (271), ironically, the former most dramatically and explicitly for Paul D, whom she sees as her enemy, the latter for Sethe, to whom she clings. Morrison guides us to a view of Beloved's role through Amy's harsh and consoling words while massaging Sethe's feet: "Anything dead coming back to life hurts" (35). This is true for Beloved herself after her journey from the other side, both in the pain she feels and in the pain she inflicts, as well as for Sethe and Paul D in their journey toward a fuller emotional life. This latter journey has already begun when Beloved appears on the scene, but with the implication that it cannot be completed, if it is to be completed at all, without facing up to something she evokes and represents. Almost simultaneously, "The closed portion of [Paul D's] head opened like a greased lock" (41) in his pleasure at being reunited with Sethe and Sethe begins to wonder, "Would it be all right to go ahead and feel" as "Emotions sped to the surface in his company" (38, 39). But it is also the case, as Paul D approaches an emotional limit, that:

> He would keep the rest where it belonged: in that tobacco tin buried in his chest where a red heart used to be. . . . He would not pry it loose now in front of this sweet sturdy woman, for if she got a whiff of the contents it would shame him. And it would hurt her to know that there was no red heart . . . beating in him. (72–73)

Sethe, at the same moment, thinks of "Working dough. Working, working dough. Nothing better than that to start the day's serious work of beating back the past" (73). Beloved "reminds me of something," Paul D comments for both of them late in the novel, "Something, look like, I'm supposed to remember" (234). If freedom is "to get to a place where you could love anything you chose" (162), emotional freedom, it appears, cannot be arrived at without fully admitting into one's present doubts about the past.

And so Beloved agitates memory, explicitly in Sethe, from whom she seeks, even while still a stranger, stories from Sethe's past. These forays into the past give Sethe "unexpected pleasure" (58), soon enough to turn into maddening pain when curious questions turn to insistent accusations of abandonment. The larger question is whether the pain was ever really absent or merely under a control that precluded healing. Healing is no part of Beloved's purpose, may leave a scar like the tree on Sethe's back if it occurs, may indeed never occur. Certainly it is not Sethe's goal at the end, absorbed as she is in her own feelings of abandonment. Opening old wounds creates, though, the condition of the possibility of healing.

Likewise for Paul D, Beloved's intervention opens old wounds, requires facing old decisions, and creates possibilities beyond her own self-interested intentions. Her goal is to "move" him out of Sethe's house and life; in shaming him into leaving, she also moves him beyond self-imposed and self-protective constraints on feeling that even love of Sethe had been unable to break through. He finds his "Red heart. Red heart. Red heart" (117) in coupling with her despite himself, and fully feels the pain of the past and the shame of his most significant choice. For Sethe, pain follows after pleasure in the process of coming back to life; for Paul D, there is something life-affirming within his humiliation. "Coupling with her wasn't even fun," he thinks after she has gone:

> It was more like a brainless urge to stay alive. Each time she came, pulled up her skirts, a life hunger overwhelmed him and he had no more control over it than over his lungs. And afterward, beached and gobbling air, in the midst of repulsion and personal shame, he was thankful too for having been escorted to some deep-ocean place he once belonged to. (264)

Morrison does not make it easy, or perhaps necessary or desirable or even possible, to completely analyze Paul D's feelings here. She does, though, provide language that tells us something, probably more than it tells Paul D, about why he acted as he did nineteen years earlier, made the choice that he made in not joining his lungs and voice to Sixo's song: then, too, a "brainless urge to stay alive" put him on a different course than his friend's.

Afterwards, with the others on the chain gang, he "killed the flirt whom folks called Life for leading them on"; later, with Beloved, in "her cock-teasing hug," he found himself "caring and looking forward, remembering and looking back" (109).

As repressed elements in the unconscious draw to them other unacceptable or traumatizing materials, Beloved, the dead daughter transformed and resurrected, includes within herself other figures of racial oppression, ranging from Sethe's antecedents during the Middle Passage to a young woman of Beloved's apparent age who had been "locked up in [a] house over by Deer Creek" (235).[10] But while she becomes more than Denver's sister—and especially becomes the past itself making a claim for attention—her motivations are always primarily and troublingly those of a young child who fears abandonment.[11] This fear is present as soon as she has discernible feelings and is, she believes, fulfilled when she sees Sethe merge months later into the crowd gathered outside the yard. The fear of abandonment motivates a murderous rage in the Clearing when Sethe's thoughts turn from her past with Halle to a future with Paul D and lies behind her cruelty to Sethe when she secures dominance over her. Fearing exclusion earlier, she now demands exclusive attention. But, though she is large and powerful and has achieved mastery of both Paul D and Sethe, she still has the vulnerability of the infant who every afternoon had "doubted anew the older woman's return" from work and in whose eyes Sethe had seen a longing that was "bottomless. Some plea barely in control" (57, 58). She weeps once, ostensibly in pain over an extracted tooth, but really, like Sethe at the end, over accumulated losses real and imagined. With Paul D's arrival, she is in danger of being disremembered even before her embodied return, and Morrison has contrived that there be unbearable sadness as well as relief in her passing. Even when she is at her most punishing, discussions of Beloved as a kind of succubus therefore leave too much out of account.[12]

It is possible to forget the sadness in the consolations of the final encounter between Paul D and Sethe, as I in fact did in my first reading of the novel, and simply not notice the existence of another two pages dealing with Beloved. But like the belief that each of the spores floating at the river's edge when Sethe delivers Denver "will become all of what is contained in [it]: will live out its days as planned, . . . [t]his moment of certainty lasts no longer than that . . ." (84). It is on a note of loss more than relief and of uncertainty more than either that the novel ends. With as much craft as earlier went into planting and concealing clues that would provide a reassuring as well as disturbing resolution to the mystery of the past, Morrison chooses to compound misunderstanding and unintended consequences with unanswered questions about the future. As Morrison said of her novels in an interview a few years before *Beloved* was published,

There is a resolution of a sort but there are always possibilities—choices, just knowing what those choices are or being able to make a commitment about those choices or knowing something that you would never have known had you not have had that experience—meaning the book. . . . it is Greek in the sense that the best you can hope for is some realization and that, you know, a certain amount of suffering is not just anxiety. It's also information. (Jones and Vinson, 177)

The choices in *Beloved* that slavery is shown to allow, even oblige, are inevitably and necessarily unthinkable choices between bad alternatives. This is especially true of the choice of life or of death made by Paul D and Sethe. There is no judgment to be made about these choices, any more than about Baby Suggs's heartbroken response to the one of them that touches her: "she could not approve or condemn Sethe's rough choice. One or the other might have saved her, but beaten up by the claim of both, she went to bed" (180).[13]

But while there is no judgment to be made about the choices these characters come to, Morrison does not allow them to view themselves as merely traumatized victims and does not encourage us to do so either. It is at least partly in accepting a burden of responsibility for their impossible choices that they, in the midst of their victimization, achieve and maintain the dignity that most defies what slavery would have them be. The humanity that invests, perhaps transcends, Sethe's and Paul D's specific gendered concerns with manhood and maternity comes through choosing to recognize themselves and their history in the choices history has implicated them in, forced upon them. This is perhaps the choice Morrison leaves us with in the novel's final pages, with their ambiguous assertion that the story we have been witness to is not one to pass *on* or not one to *pass* on. Memory, we are repeatedly reminded, is also a matter of choice in the novel, but that choice is present in how we remember, not in whether we do. Like Sweet Home (like Beloved), it "Comes back," as Sethe tells Denver, "whether we want it to or not" (14).

Notes

1. Reference to the possibility of linking the two characters' stories is made in passing by Furman, Levy, Powell, Samuels, and Schreiber. Aspects of the topic are dealt with more fully by Bowers, FitzGerald, Fulweiler, Moreland, Rushdy, and Schopp, none of whom assigns the importance I do here to Paul D's choice of life, in contrast to Sethe's choice of death, as the foundation for the comparison. The most complete linking of the two stories occurs in Barnett and Ayer (Sitter). Barnett proposes that it is rape, "the primacy of sexual assault over other experiences of brutality" (420), that brings together the stories of the novel's two protagonists (and

lesser characters) and that in this convergence is revealed Morrison's insight that sexual humiliation, regardless of gender, is the governing mode of dehumanization in slavery. Ayer (Sitter)'s focus, as discussed later in the essay, is on the characters' need to overcome oppressive gender definitions.

2. This absence of autonomy in slavery is the subject of Linehan's essay, where he argues that "without freedom of the will, actions can have no moral significance" (309). His position has the danger of denying Sethe and Paul D and others living under slavery precisely the humanity both Sethe and Morrison seem determined to affirm.

3. The best commentary on the difficulties of the novel's beginning is Morrison's own in her essay, "Unspeakable Things Unspoken: The Afro-American Presence in American Literature," where she writes of the "risk of confronting the reader with what must be immediately incomprehensible" (228). For the question of whether the narrative is "a story to pass on," seemingly denied in the text's final paragraphs, see, most interestingly, Phelan's analysis.

4. The passage I'm reminded of in *Absalom, Absalom!* occurs when Sutpen, in youthful "innocence" of how he and his people are regarded by wealthy Whites, is told "never to come to that front door again, but to go around to the back": "He didn't even remember leaving. All of a sudden he found himself running and already some distance from the house, and not toward home. He wasn't even mad. He just had to think. . . . He says he did not tell himself where to go: that his body, his feet just went there . . ." (188). Sutpen's awakening comes, already an irony, through the words of a slave. The West Indies serves as his escape from "home." The relation between the two novels is more fully discussed by Kodat.

5. In a survey of the criticism that makes no claim to exhaustiveness, among those discussions that give any attention to the circumstances involved in the flight of Beloved, at least the following attribute her behavior to the power of the women who have gathered to exorcise her: Berger (415), Bouson (157), Bowers (222–226), DeKoven (119), Furman (79), Harris (162–163 ["Beloved either leaves voluntarily or is driven out"]), Henderson (81), Levy (115), Rohrkemper (61), and Scarpa (97). Otten credits the departure to Sethe's love in seeking to protect her daughter (94), certainly not Beloved's own view of what is transpiring.

6. I take the term "proairetic" from Barthes's division of the readerly text into four codes in *S/Z:* "Thus to read (to perceive the readerly aspect of the text) is to proceed from name to name, from fold to fold; it is to fold the text according to one name and then to unfold it along the new folds of this name. This is proairetism: an artifice (or art) of reading that seeks out names, that tends toward them. . . ." (82–83). Sometimes, it appears, the name may come prematurely and refuse to be dislodged.

7. Ayer (Sitter) acknowledges as much in her analysis of this scene, in which she finds "sexual frustration . . . eventually transformed into sexual fulfillment" (201). It would better support her argument that Paul D undergoes a larger transformation in his ideas about gender if the fulfillment were delayed until that transformation was complete . . . or even begun.

8. The examples Todorov gives (19, 72) are mainly of infants or newborns. He does not linger over these "exceptional" cases, preferring to focus on less extreme instances of caring.

9. The disclosure occurs in a despairing moment in which Sethe conflates in her thoughts a number of the losses in her life and then utters to Paul D a statement that obscures, in its ambiguity, the boundaries between past and present:

> that she called but Howard and Buglar walked on down the railroad track and couldn't hear her; that Amy was scared to stay with her because her feet were ugly and her back looked so bad; that her ma'am had hurt her feelings and she couldn't find her hat anywhere and "Paul D?"
> "What, baby?"
> "She left me."
> "Aw, girl. Don't cry."
> "She was my best thing." (272)

Though Sethe is speaking of Beloved, she has just been thinking of her mother.

10. Rimmon-Kenan provides an admirable review of the various interpretations of Beloved's origin and identity (116–120). I agree with his conclusion that with regard to this matter the novel leaves us with an "insoluble ambiguity."

11. This element of Beloved's characterization is discussed in Wyatt (218–222) and, more fully, in Schapiro, who argues that the "consequences [of the absence of the mother] on the inner life of the child . . . constitute the underlying psychological drama of the novel" (194).

12. Barnett begins her essay by identifying Beloved as "the novel's dominant trope: the succubus figure" (418). This view of Beloved had been developed more fully by Harris (155–162).

13. When asked in an interview about her own view of Sethe's deed, Morrison said, "For me it was an impossible decision. Someone once gave me the line for it at one time which I have found useful. 'It was the right thing to do, but she had no right to do it'" (Moyers, 272).

Works Cited

Ayer (Sitter), Deborah. "The Making of a Man: Dialogic Meaning in Beloved." In Critical Essays on Toni Morrison's "Beloved," edited by Barbara H. Solomon, 189–204. New York: G. K. Hall, 1998.

Barnett, Pamela E. "Figurations of Rape and the Supernatural in Beloved." PMLA 112 (1997): 418–427.

Barthes, Roland. S/Z. New York: Hill and Wang, 1974.

Berger, James. "Ghosts of Liberalism: Morrison's Beloved and the Moynihan Report." PMLA 111 (1996): 408–420.

Bouson, J. Brooks. Quiet as It's Kept: Shame, Trauma, and Race in the Novels of Toni Morrison. Albany: State University of New York, 2000.

Bowers, Susan. "Beloved and the New Apocalypse." In Toni Morrison's Fiction: Contemporary Criticism, edited by David Middleton, 209–230. New York: Garland, 1997.

DeKoven, Marianne. "Postmodernism and Post-Utopian Desire in Toni Morrison and E. L. Doctorow." In Toni Morrison: Critical and Theoretical Approaches, edited by Nancy J. Peterson, 111–130. Baltimore: Johns Hopkins University Press, 1997.

Faulkner, William. Absalom, Absalom! New York: Vintage Books, 1990.

FitzGerald, Jennifer. "Selfhood and Community: Psychoanalysis and Discourse in *Beloved*." In *Toni Morrison: Contemporary Critical Essays*, edited by Linden Peach, 110–127. New York: St. Martin's Press, 1998.

Fulweiler, Howard W. "Belonging and Freedom in Morrison's *Beloved:* Slavery, Sentimentality, and the Evolution of Consciousness." *The Centennial Review* 40 (1996): 331–358.

Furman, Jan. *Toni Morrison's Fiction*. Columbia: University of South Carolina Press, 1996.

Harris, Trudier. *Fiction and Folklore: The Novels of Toni Morrison*. Knoxville: University of Tennessee Press, 1991.

Henderson, Mae. "Toni Morrison's *Beloved:* Re-Membering the Body as Historical Text." In *Comparative American Identities: Race, Sex, and Nationality in the Modern Text*, edited by Hortense J. Spillers, 62–86. New York: Routledge, 1991.

Jones, Bessie W., and Audrey Vinson. "An Interview with Toni Morrison." In *Conversations with Toni Morrison*, edited by Danille Taylor-Guthrie, 171–187. Jackson: University Press of Mississippi, 1994.

Kodat, Catherine Gunther. "A Postmodern *Absalom, Absalom!,* a Modern *Beloved:* The Dialectic of Form." In *Unflinching Gaze: Morrison and Faulkner Re-Envisioned*, edited by Carol A. Kolmerton, Stephen M. Ross, and Judith Bryant Wittenberg. Jackson: University Press of Mississippi, 1997.

Levy, Andrew. "Telling *Beloved*." *Texas Studies in Literature and Language* 33 (1991): 114–123.

Linehan, Thomas M. "Narrating the Self: Aspects of Moral Psychology in Toni Morrison's *Beloved*." *The Centennial Review* 41 (1997): 301–330.

Moreland, Richard C. "'He Wants to Put His Story Next to Hers': Putting Twain's Story Next to Hers in Morrison's *Beloved*." In *Toni Morrison: Critical and Theoretical Approaches*, edited by Nancy J. Peterson, 155–180. Baltimore: Johns Hopkins University Press, 1997.

Morrison, Toni. *Beloved*. New York: Plume, 1987.

———. "Unspeakable Things Unspoken: The Afro-American Presence in American Literature." In *Modern Critical Views: Toni Morrison*, edited by Harold Bloom, 201–230. Philadelphia: Chelsea House, 1990.

Moyers, Bill. "A Conversation with Toni Morrison." In *Conversations with Toni Morrison*, edited by Danille Taylor-Guthrie, 262–274. Jackson: University Press of Mississippi, 1994.

Otten, Terry. *The Crime of Innocence in the Fiction of Toni Morrison*. Columbia: University of Missouri Press, 1989.

Phelan, James. "Toward a Rhetorical Reader-Response Criticism: The Difficult, the Stubborn, and the Ending of *Beloved*." In *Toni Morrison: Critical and Theoretical Approaches*, edited by Nancy J. Peterson, 225–244. Baltimore: Johns Hopkins University Press, 1997.

Powell, Betty Jane. "'Will the Parts Hold': The Journey Toward a Coherent Self in *Beloved*." *Colby Quarterly* 31 (1995): 105–113.

Rimmon-Kenan, Shlomith. "Narration, Doubt, Retrieval: Toni Morrison's *Beloved*." *Narrative* 4 (1996) 109–123.

Rohrkemper, John. "'The Site of Memory': Narrative and Meaning in Toni Morrison's *Beloved*." *Midwestern Miscellany* 24 (1996): 51–62.

Rushdy, Ashraf H. A. "'Rememory': Primal Scenes and Constructions in Toni Morrison's Novels." In *Toni Morrison's Fiction: Contemporary Criticism*, edited by David Middleton, 135–164. New York: Garland, 1997.

Samuels, Wilfred D., and Clenora Hudson Weems. *Toni Morrison*. Boston: Twayne Publishers, 1990.

Scarpa, Giulia. "Narrative Possibilities at Play in Toni Morrison's *Beloved*." *MELUS* 17 (1991–1992): 91–103.

Schapiro, Barbara. "The Bonds of Love and the Boundaries of Self in Toni Morrison's *Beloved*." *Contemporary Literature* 32 (1991): 194–210.

Schopp, Andrew. "Narrative Control and Subjectivity: Dismantling Safety in Toni Morrison's *Beloved*." *The Centennial Review* 39 (1995): 355–379.

Schreiber, Evelyn Jaffe. "Reader, Text, and Subjectivity: Toni Morrison's *Beloved* as Lacan's Gaze Qua Object." *Style* 30 (1996): 445–461.

Todorov, Tzvetan. *Facing the Extreme: Moral Life in the Concentration Camps*. New York: Henry Holt, 1996.

Wyatt, Jean. "Giving Body to the Word: The Maternal Symbolic in Toni Morrison's *Beloved*." In *Critical Essays on Toni Morrison's "Beloved,"* edited by Barbara H. Solomon, 211–232. New York: G. K. Hall, 1998.

NANCY KANG

To Love and Be Loved:
Considering Black Masculinity and
the Misandric Impulse in Toni Morrison's Beloved

At the time of the incendiary Clarence Thomas-Anita Hill hearings on Capitol Hill, professor John H. Bracey made a startlingly ironic pronouncement: "Poor George Bush got the wrong Thomas! He went looking for 'Uncle' but came back with 'Bigger'" (qtd. in Thelwell 86). By juxtaposing the images of Harriet Beecher Stowe's servile but quintessentially agreeable "black Christ" figure, and Richard Wright's personification of twentieth-century racial hunger, it becomes apparent that modern black masculinity *as a notional category* has rarely been static or unproblematic. Other (stereo)types have particular emotional and cultural currency when addressing the construction of black masculinity in Toni Morrison's *Beloved* (1987). For instance, the bestial rapist limned in D. W. Griffiths's *The Birth of a Nation* (1915) schematizes white sexual terror—or in Fanonian parlance, offers proof that the phallic Negro is a "phobogenic object, a stimulus to anxiety" (Fanon 151). In contrast, there surges the "Herculean cultural heroism" of Michael Jordan in the popular imagination, a figure who has literally *flown* his way to stardom in a delightful reinscription of the mythic "flying African" utilized in Morrison's *Song of Solomon* (1977). Jordan has become a cultural lodestar through the Ur-athleticism of the black male body (Dyson 408). Between the representational zenith and nadir, an opportunity exists for meditations upon a more expansive

Callaloo, Volume 26, Number 3 (Summer 2003): pp. 836–854. Copyright © 2003 The Johns Hopkins University Press.

25

spectrum of assumptions and schemas that alternately diminish or aggrandize Afro-American male personae.

A relative dearth of critical material explores the matrifocal *Beloved* as a masculinist text, or conversely, one informed by highly misandric (or androphobic) impulses. As Deborah Horvitz summarizes, the novel is about "matrilineal ancestry and the relationships among enslaved, freed, alive, and dead mothers and daughters" (Horvitz 93). Bernard W. Bell seconds this reading, declaring that the novel is "Toni Morrison's most extraordinary and spellbinding *womanist* remembrance of things past" (emphasis added; 166). This discussion seeks to interrogate the possibility of a misandric impulse that accompanies the novel's well-documented engagement with specifically woman-centered issues like motherhood. It is important not to mistake the purported anti-male sentiments as those of Morrison herself, an author whose similarly haunted *Song of Solomon* could be construed as a celebratory exploration of Afro-American masculinity in transition. Also vital is the recognition that a *thematics* of misandry does not necessarily imply a bald figuration of hatred directed against males. Morrison's writing style in *Beloved,* a historiographical structure simultaneously fixed and fragmented, oneiric and yet firmly grounded in material realities of black life during the Reconstruction, does not easily allow for the slide into Manichean agitprop, comfortable overgeneralization, or dilation into radical feminist rant. Rather, like Eve Kosofsky Sedgwick's conceptualization of the homosocial continuum, a range of relationships encompassing the filiastic to the antagonistic between individuals of the same sex, misandry is a sliding signifier. In one sense, the discussion of masculinity is a *peripheral* discourse; the desire that demands and subsumes the protagonist Sethe is part of the hermeneutically dense presence of Beloved (part-ghost, part-flesh, individual and collective memory separately and simultaneously). This force-field of desire is clearly feminine and filial, at least at its most visible level. The discourse of masculinity is often overshadowed by a stronger female presence and by extension, essence. As expected, however, the text is an open invitation to interpret. Just as Morrison's *Playing in the Dark: Whiteness and the Literary Imagination* (1992) suggests that the natures of literary blackness and literary whiteness are consubstantial, the notional categories of black masculinity and black femininity are similarly entwined. It is within this matrix of sexed positions that merge into, converge with, and diverge from one another that the possibility of sustained emotional and sexual partnership exists. Given this, cross-pressures inevitably arose at the post-Emancipation moment. Due to political instabilities, pent-up frustrations on the part of the white majority (a reaction against the sea change in their social supremacy), and the desire to reify, sublimate, or elicit a cathexis of conflictual drives, what resulted was the formation of a new double consciousness: fear and hatred of the ex-slaves, or else an avoidance of their issues, alongside a simultaneously necessary investment in their lives. For blacks, self-formation and individuation were still a Scylla and Charybdis under white supremacy's yoke of material and psychological servitude that continued long after the Emancipation Proclamation of 1864.

In twentieth-century gender theory, much discussion has centered upon the constructed nature of gender as "a reiterative or ritual practice," how the modalities of sexuality are made manifest through the "repeated and violent circumscription of cultural intelligibility," and how sexed positions are—like history—not devoid of lacunae (Butler 8, vii–xii). As Judith Butler infers, it is within these hermeneutically-rich gaps that the locus of "a potentially productive crisis" emerges (8). To highlight this idea using a popular linguistic analogy, gender relates to the social subject in the same way that a predicate completes a grammatical subject. In both cases, there is no guarantee of coherence despite the expectations nourished by convention and coercive strategies of social inculcation. Moreover, as with Wlad Godzich's definition of *theoria*, to conceptualize gender through the vagaries of history and literary representation is to understand "'the passage from the seen to the told' . . . a form of cognition modeled upon (public) utterance rather than upon (private) perception" (xiv–xv). Slave narratives capture this double mode—both private and public—with striking accuracy, and it is for this reason that such critics as Bell tend to categorize *Beloved* as a "neo-slave narrative."

In Frederick Douglass's pivotal narrative of 1845, the acquisition of a full-fledged masculine persona is predicated upon the ability to become an economic agent through the "hiring-out" of one's time and earning a wage, albeit meagre. In his accelerated, self-fashioning drive from the ontological stasis of "being" a slave to the flux of "becoming" a man, Douglass not only re-appropriates some of his power as an alienated worker, he demonstrates a new-found *psychological* resilience that emerges in the wake of a physical confrontation with his master, Mr. Covey. Indeed, Douglass suggests, manliness is an anxiety-provoking issue for the black individual since he is perpetually undermined by the infantilizing and deprecating nomenclature of white supremacy. The predominant manifestation of this racialized misandry is, as James Baldwin has observed in a national context, constant recourse to the black man's sexuality as his number one (dis)qualifier: "It is still true, alas, that to be an American Negro male is also to be a kind of walking phallic symbol: which means that one pays, in one's own personality, for the sexual insecurity of others" (290).[1] While speaking a century after Douglass, Maya Angelou's observation in *I Know Why the Caged Bird Sings* (1969) reflects the stress placed on the resources of the black self when the integrity of his (or her) name, the typical signifier of a discrete individuality, is placed in jeopardy: "Every person I knew had a hellish horror of being 'called out of his name.' It was a danger to call a Negro anything that could be loosely construed as insulting because of the centuries of having been called niggers, jigs, dinges, blackbirds, crows, boots and spooks" (106). "Spook" has particular currency in *Beloved* because it is not the black man who is the demonic force (to add such examples as "haint" or "bogeyman" to the roster of names) but rather the female who appropriates the "dark, abiding, [and] signing" Africanist presence (Morrison, *Playing* 5).

Parallel anxieties in a lattice-work of controls—control of self *by* self and control by others: this scenario roughly describes the collocation of black males and females in Morrison's text. Stephen Greenblatt has made the astute observation that while culture is comprised of "a structure of limits," the selfsame structure also functions "as the regulator and guarantor of movement" (228). In effect, this is an articulation of the familiar poststructural understanding evinced by Foucault that currents of power are immanently unstable and often contain within them the mechanisms of their own subversion. For instance, Douglass's literary precedent, the author of *The Interesting Narrative of the Life of Olaudah Equiano, or Gustavus Vassa the African* (1792), includes as part of the frontispiece a medal inscribed, "Am I not a man and a brother." The image is one of a chained slave, his kneeling posture a cross between a downtrodden, servile chattel begging for approbation and inclusion, and its obverse, the emergent individual with his face raised to the Du Boisian dawn of "self-consciousness, self-realization, [and] self-respect" (49).[2] This is the perfect image to accompany a strain of humanist rhetoric insisting that one may be chained in body while his or her soul ranges freely. And so, the supplicating slave is in fact about to rise up from his knees to what Fanon would identify as "the human level" (9).[3] Readers who notice that there is no question mark concluding or stopping the sentence will realize that it may be construed in a diptych fashion, either as a question (and thus signify weakness and hope on the part of the speaker), or as a more assured statement of what is undoubtedly believed by him to be axiomatic.

Just as the medal invites various interpretations, appearing easy but proving hard, I aim to resist creating a monolithic narrative of loss and redemption for the black male characters (centered upon Paul D), or one of oppression and homogenous self-righteousness for their white counterparts. Critic bell hooks has been vocal among critics who speak out against the creation of ideological monoliths about black masculinity, although she does concede that "there has never been a time in the history of the United States when black folks, particularly black men, have not been enraged by the dominant culture's stereotypical, fantastical representations of black masculinity"(89). Given this tendency, it must also be remembered that round characterization of black individuals can and *does* exist without the immediate contingency of white characters. *Beloved* is arguably less a study in cross-racial discourse at the moment of narration and more a coming to terms with the sins and psychological ruptures of a racially haunted past. This is not to say that the nurturing of a "historical sense," defined by T. S. Eliot in the context of the European literary tradition as an awareness of the "pastness of the past" and its simultaneous presence, is to be ignored (38). Morrison's narrative is set in 1873 during the Reconstruction, obviously in the wake of a period of historical upheaval within national borders. It would be myopic for readers to assume that the lack of openly racist attack on 124 Bluestone Road (that is, after the shed incident years earlier in 1855), as well as the absence of a white protagonist or other major white character signifies any complacency in the psyches of white Ohioans, or white Americans for that matter. Just as Beloved seems to coalesce fully-formed from a natural setting that not only *allows* abiogenesis but also seems to *encourage* it in a kind of eerily numinous *Lebenswelt* (or "life world"), there exists within the novel a series of "underground presences" (to borrow Saidian phrasing), or nuances which work alongside and within the context of race. A thematics of misandry stands as an example of such a volatile hermeneutic reservoir, one that invites interpretive plunges as much as it resists them.

I. Le Rouge et le Noir: Tropologies of Blood and Nationhood

To recognize misandry is to sense that masculinity—black masculinity in particular—is threatened, under stress, or remains a dynamic force that has been constrained to the extent that it has nowhere to go. This limbo is arguably an outgrowth of a larger dis-ease: the state of emotional suspension in the post-war psyche that signifies a concurrent crisis of national and personal definition. Wariness and paranoia prevent Paul D from turning out the "room-and-board witch" Beloved (whom critics like Trudier Harris call a variation on "the traditional succubus, the female spirit who drains the male's life force" [131]) into territory "infected" by the Klan. Morrison continues with this description rich in interpretive potential: "Desperately thirsty for black blood, without which it could not live, the dragon swam the Ohio at will" (66). The metaphor of infection and contamination becomes especially germane within the spectrum of Beloved's parasitic relationship with Sethe[4] and her disruption of Paul's plans for "a life" (66). A "life" means the semblance of a stable family, one that most importantly includes him, and would ideally adopt him as its nucleus. The vampiric imagery used to describe the Klan (an etymological hybrid of the Greek *kukloj* for "circle" and *clann* from Gaelic for "race, family") returns rather paradoxically to the signifying space of Beloved. The Klan experienced a series of deaths and resurrections in popularity that simultaneously drew blood and sought to ethnically cleanse a "fallen," postbellum America. According to the rhetoric of pastoralism, it was an age of iron, an attempt at reconstitution and reinvention of the American self as a robust and weathered survivor.

This was the frontiersman archetype, a man who has "had losses" but in a Wordsworthian and elegaic sense, "finds strength in what remains behind."[5] Tasting iron for Paul is about more than a metal bit in the mouth that draws equally ferrous blood; it has to do with a meditation upon, and participation in a profoundly contradictory and melancholic national discourse. Blood inevitably blackens when it dries and coagulates; black blood (and the blood of blacks) symbolizes the stain of subjugation that has been used, among others, by Hawthorne to symbolize the cruxes between psychic and physiological coloration among his ancestors, the founding fathers: "His son, too, inherited the persecuting spirit, and made himself so conspicuous in the martyrdom of the witches that their blood may fairly be said to have left a stain upon him" (9). In this instance, the coeval nature of evil and violence, staining both the victim and the perpetrator, restates the devastating effects of slavery on the entire national populace.

Paul D, as part of this tropology of blood and bloodlines, is a touchstone figure for America's false consciousness. By this I refer to the technicolor promise of the "new dawn" that such early authors as Thoreau in *Walden*[6] and even Du Bois[7] use as a sign of the promise and perfectibility of the American self. Placing in stark relief the racial exclusions implicit in this ideal, Cornel West complains, "American discourses on innocence, deliverance or freedom overlook the atrocities of violence, subjugation or slavery in our past or present" (xvii). The essence of the republic is the sum of "blood drenched battles on a tear-soaked terrain in which our lives and deaths are at stake" (xv). To speak of blood is to speak of a nation's circulation—of ideas, of people, of goods—as well as its cycles of renewal, its violent scleroses, its internal fluctuations, and its insistent historical stains on the collective consciousness. Divided into 28 sections to mirror the female menstrual cycle, *Beloved* signifies a shedding of blood and contemplates the meaning of bloodshed in a shed, but this purview largely excludes black males. At the moment of crisis, Stamp Paid becomes a "crazy old nigger" who stands by with an axe that he cannot (or does not) use, and mewls with "low, cat noises" (149). When Paul D hears about the murder, he breaks with Sethe and resumes his unmoored lifestyle until the text's conclusion. Given these unflattering portrayals, masculinity must be drawn back into the semiotic field of iron and blood. To speak of iron is to recall a classical ideal of manhood, intimately linked to the notion of a master race. In *The Aeneid*, the warrior Numanus brags, "We are by our birth a hard race . . . . [a]nd our young men work and endure and are trained to privation; constantly they harrow and master the land; or set towns quaking in warfare. *At every age we are bruised by iron*" (emphasis added; 244). This is an image of a master(ful) group, the ideal of patriarchal masculinity made manifest by conquering either human or physical environments (or both) through transformative work or epic violence. While these images of tribulation may arguably characterize either the black *or* the white race in the wake of the Civil War, the greater irony lies in the portrayal of black men as lazy good-for-nothings despite their labors under slavery. Hooks argues that white supremacist attitudes have attempted to obscure the fact that black men, larger in number than black females, formed the "backbone of slave economy" through "ongoing brute physical labour" (90). Thus, when prominent Western writers of the nineteenth century like Briton Thomas Carlyle conjure up an idle, pumpkinglutted Negro named Quashee,[8] or American Harriet Beecher Stowe takes a comedic plunge with her macaroni mimic-man Adolphe (a slave who adopts the name, address, and sartorial style of his master),[9] readers are directed away from the reality of hardship and drudgery faced to the brunt by male slaves. Seduced by an obscurantist, racist vision, they gradually become oblivious to the gravity of black males' contributions to, and exploitation under, the economic and political machinery of modern, capitalist America.

II. Reine of Terror: Paul's Misandric Subjugation under Beloved

One of the ways in which *Beloved* details a misandric impulse against the black male is by broaching the aesthetic conundrums of representing desire and articulating pain. These tasks are not exclusively male concerns, but they become centralized in the context of sexual abuse. In particular, the novel includes the rape *of*—not *by*—the black male. Critic Pamela Barnett stresses how Paul is the victim of sexual assault by both Beloved and by the prison guards in Alfred, Georgia.[10] Beloved's status as an infant is no guarantee of neutrality, benignity, or innocence. Furthermore, the matching of a male name (Alfred) with a female name (Georgia) renders ironical the ritual acts of sexual violence perpetrated against the blacks in the homosocial arena of the chain gang. For readers who recall Alfred in *The Color Purple* by Alice Walker (who is, incidentally, a Georgian), he is a character that attempts to rape Celie's sister Nettie, carries on a shameless affair, and subjects his wife to years of psychological torture and manipulation. Underlying his actions is a marked disrespect for women. Thus, rape as an act of torture can also be an act of hatred, and when directed against men *by* men, it also constitutes a form of self-reflexive misandry. Also in the novel, a similar instance of ironical gender juxtaposition arises when we learn that Sethe bears a man's name (62), and that her namesake is a black man with whom her mother had consensual, not forced sexual relations. These inversions and pairings point up a tacit desire for heterosexual partnership, the laying of stories as well as bodies against one another ("Only this woman Sethe could have left him his manhood like that. He wants to put his story next to hers" [273]). However, for Paul, each memory of his subservience to the sexual "whim of a guard, or two, or three" [107]) excoriates and prematurely forecloses that possibility of sustained heterosexual partnership which he very much desires

("'[M]e and you, we got more yesterday than anybody. We need some kind of tomorrow'" [273]).

Beloved is the prime mover in a misandric project that parallels, as Barnett suggests, "institutionalized rape under slavery" of both men and women (74). This incarnate force acts as a strange catalyst, forcing Paul to face his memories of abuse by homeopathically *amplifying* it. With the intent to deny him both companionship and ready sexual access to Sethe, Beloved moves him out of Sethe's room and places him in the emasculating maternal space of the rocking chair. Then, she stealthily propels him into the geriatric expanse of Baby Suggs's bed, degrades him to the use-less aridity of the storeroom, and finally evicts him from the domestic arena of 124 into the dormant cold house outdoors (114). He attempts to resist, but cannot because he has been stripped of his agency, just as he was by the prison guards ("She came, and he wanted to knock her down" [116]). Her sexual violence, unlike theirs, is subtle in that it forces him to confront the unwarranted guilt of having slept with the equivalent of a (step)daughter: "he had come to be a rag doll—picked up and put back down anywhere any time by a girl young enough to be his daughter" (128). This is a twist, perhaps, on incest-rape scenarios that surface in Morrison's *The Bluest Eye* with Mr. Breedlove, and Mr. Trueblood in Ralph Ellison's *Invisible Man*. Although the resurrected Beloved instinctively hates Paul for being a threat to her hermetic feminine monopoly of Sethe, Denver also issues forth a version of her sister's "threads of malice" (131). Hers is a rational dislike based on family loyalty and a resistance to change: "And carnival or no carnival, Denver preferred the venomous baby to him any day" (104). She "cusses [him] out" twice, but considers him more an irritation than a threat (44). Her greeting, "Good morning, Mr. D" (266) near the end of the novel affirms his status as a substantial person, especially in Sethe's life. At first, however, considerable irony resides in this shared aversion for Paul because of these three individuals' coeval importance as signifiers of stifled potential and unresolved longing.

Sexual violence, like other forms of violence, is often construed as a breakdown in language, but currents in contemporary trauma theory have put forth the idea that it is a *continuation* as opposed to an erasure of language. For Paul, we must ask how it is possible to express desire (desire for self, sexual desire, desire for belonging in a community) when one's body has already been so overdetermined by history. The act of claiming a self-fashioning individuality is immanently disabled by a history of being claimed as property, as expenditure, as someone else's status-symbol, as fetish-object, as Lacanian symptom (s/he who gives another's being its fundamental ontological consistency), and as outlet for sexual aggression and insecurity. A vicious circle of stereotyped representations ("Ain't no nigger men," argues a farmer to the adamant Mr. Garner [10]) has also contributed to the peripheral status of the black male subject. Moreover, as it is possible to lose without knowing exactly *what* has been lost, we must ask what are the means by which such loss surfaces as language *in* language. Paul confesses to Sethe that he has attempted to break his silence but does not know whether he has done so in a manner that befits the gravity of his experience. "I don't know," he reflects, "I never have talked about it. Not to a soul. Sang it sometimes, but I never *told* a soul" (71; emphasis added). Singing is an example of an alternative register, but it is not an explicitly gendered one. Sethe speaks of how the language of female bonding excludes Paul as a man ("Hearing the three of them laughing at something he wasn't in on. The code they used among themselves that he could not break" [132]). To acknowledge his exclusion and the negativity surrounding his presence as a male in a "womanspace" ("Beloved went on probing her mouth with her finger. 'Make him go away,' she said" [133]) is to understand the incongruencies in the male and female experiences of pain.

Earlier in the novel, Sethe recalls a vivid, quasi-pastoral imago that includes boys and trees. The boys are perhaps a tangential reference to her two sons, but could be construed as a mutedly affectionate reference to the Sweet Home men. The preference is clear: "It shamed her—remembering the wonderful soughing trees rather than the boys. Try as she might to make it otherwise, the sycamores beat out the children every time" (6). The trees point to a contemplation of her own experience, the experience of the chokecherry tree beat into her while she was pregnant, her womanist communion with the "whitegirl" Amy, and the milk that was stolen by the nephews in an act that is an affront and mockery of motherhood. She feels guilty about not privileging the boys because she still assumes that the role of mother is superior to the role of self-nurturer. It is also the beginning of Sethe's temporary turning away from the men-folk in her life as a conduit to happiness and a means of future sustenance. Shutting out men, including Stamp Paid, is a loaded act that signifies the fracture of patriarchal supremacy as an ideology, although it was already distorted in light of slavery's dissolution of the black family. The revelation about Halle passively watching her assault and his subsequent madness, the abandonment by Paul who "counted her feet and didn't even say goodbye" (189), the firing by her employer of sixteen years for one late morning—all these incidents contribute to a radical turn away from dependence on heterosexual reciprocity. In sum, they serve the interests of a gynocratic, post-genital, female-centered self-sufficiency. While such a vision is not openly misandric, it is certainly exclusionary, and taken to extremes, defines Beloved's misandric attitude towards Paul.[11]

In Paul's view, the tree on Sethe's backside is a "revolting clump of scars" (21). It is the hermeneutic disparity centered around the tree that foreshadows an alternating pattern of advance and retreat before Paul's eventual disconnection from Sethe's life. For him, peace and male companionship reside in the sylvan image of Brother from Sweet Home: "trees were inviting; things you could trust and be near; talk to if you wanted to" (21). It is also a memento of masculine community, however provisional ("[he] sat under it, alone sometimes, sometimes with Halle or the other Pauls, but more often with Sixo" [21]). Later, Paul impresses the image of a tree onto the feeling of tentative hope he had under Garner, although he realizes that it was a naïve vision of possibility: "His little love was a tree, of course, but not like Brother—old, wide, and beckoning" (221). Apart from this short-lived tranquility with brothers under Brother, the closest equivalent to a communal male activity would be the raping of the calves. Here again, however, the calves are a substitute for an absent female presence. The males in *Beloved* do not rape one another, surprisingly; the reason for this is a moot point: either there is a diminished need to assert dominance within their general position of subordination, or the true tenor of their comradeship is constrained by the exigencies of work and a belief in the "self-same," or that one's own hardships are contiguous with another's. This understanding results in a stance of fraternity rather than aggression, dominance, and competition. Within Morrison's re-inscription of the Sedgwickian triangle, from two males dueling over a female into a male and a female dueling over a female, there is little sense of a fair contest. Speaking transhistorically, hooks argues that this has been the status quo for a great number of Afro-American males. The meaning of black male pain coincides with the ineffability of pain itself and the lack of discursive space available for the expression of such discontent:

> Black males are unable to fully articulate and acknowledge the pain in their lives. They do not have the public discourse or audience within racist society that enables them to give their pain a hearing. Sadly, black men often evoke racist rhetoric that identifies the black male as animal, speaking of themselves as "endangered species," as "primitive," in their bid to gain recognition of their suffering. (34)

In light of this tendency toward diminution by self and by society, Paul D's first name (like that of Garner's other Pauls) quite fittingly comes from the Latin for "little" or "small" (*paulus*). For Morrison to choose such a name is appropriate considering Paul's subservience to, as Deborah Ayer-Sitter suggests, "an ideal of manhood that distorts his images of self and others" (191). His struggle to accept himself involves a recognition that "his expectations for himself [are] high, too high" (131). At the same time that Morrison expresses the narrowness of Paul's self-concept, as well as the heroic imperative to enlarge that vision, she critiques tangentially the parochialism of a society that can allow any individual to feel diminished without offering any balm or support.

While absent in the text as character, the heroic (white) ideal is present in Paul's mind as a fantastic and impossibly desirable Other. It is for this reason, suggests Ayer-Sitter, that the driving out of the spirit from 124 and the tepid lovemaking that follows prove to be more a whimper than a bang: "Romantic illusion is followed by romantic disillusion, and both are subjected to reality testing" (193). This is not to say that Paul suffers from a racial inferiority complex, the prime manifestations of which would be the desire to be white and the repudiation of blackness. Inculcation of the inferiority of his place and race (in other words, Schoolteacher's legacy) has left Paul in a troubling condition of doubt. He wishes to experience the accompanying *status* of whiteness that supremacist ideology has constructed as a totalizing hermeneutic of power and a privileged domain of difference. Racism, after all, is the conglomerative effect of preexisting social constructions. As a result, Paul suffers from an Ovidian split awareness, a *psychomachia* of sorts, wherein his sense of integrity as a worthwhile individual—a survivor—clashes with his lowly position. He feels that he has earned his manhood through what Nietzsche would term ennoblement (that is, elevation through suffering), but it is a tenuous self-image that requires sustained buttressing like most projects of self-aggregation after cerebral crisis. Neither Sethe, nor Stamp, nor a desire to fight back against his abusers by living well offer him the psychological apparatus by which to strengthen his attenuated sense of maleness:

> He who had eaten raw meat barely dead, who under plum trees bursting with blossoms had crunched through a dove's breast before its heart stopped beating. Because he was a man and a man could do what he would: be still for six hours in a dry well while night dropped; fight raccoon with his hands and win; watch another man, whom he loved better than his brothers, roast without a tear just so the roasters would know what a man was like. (126)

From the time that her presence prompts him to be "soaked so thoroughly in a wave of grief" that he almost cries (9), Beloved works incessantly to corrode Paul's self-concept and emasculate him. As Harris observes, "The picture of him sitting on the church steps, liquor bottle in hand, stripped of the very maleness that enables him to caress and love the wounded Sethe, is one that shows Beloved's power" (132). The figure of an indigent Paul lingering on the porch and in the cellar of the church suggests his inability to find places of rest, even in the traditionally "safe" domain of the church. Throughout his years "on the road," he has found tentative peace at the "base of certain trees, here and there; a wharf, a bench, a rowboat once, a haystack usually" (114). And yet this image of a restless church-dweller is not solely a negative one. As the lowest level of the church, the cellar as a kind of basement room is somewhat suggestive of Paul's subordinate position in the social hierarchy ("base/men"). In larger churches, basements are places usually used for communion and celebration (wedding dinners and Sunday school classes, for example), both of which have not existed in Paul's life. As the church used to be a dry-goods store, it symbolizes the possibilities of shifting from an economy of price and value (the black man's milieu during slavery) into a redeeming mode of the spiritual and non-material. The church is also a generative site for masculine patriarchal power as distilled into the figure of the preacher, a latter-day remnant of an enduring patristic heritage. This is suggested in the church's plan to adjust the platform, allowing them to "raise the preacher a few inches above his congregation" (220). This does not mean that the church is a masculinist space that oppresses women and apotheosizes men, of course; Paul fleeing to the church to collect himself is a prefiguration of the exorcism that will eventually drive Beloved away. Such an act foreshadows conjugal relations between Paul and Sethe within the sphere of heteronormativity, and anticipates their reintegration into the community.

Similar subversive potential exists when Beloved strips Paul both of his emotional and physical life force (that is, his sperm) in characteristic succubus fashion. In Spanish idiom, the metaphor *"mala leche"* ("bad milk") denotes the recipient of milk from a mother who has questionable health, morals, or lifestyle. It also tropes upon a man's semen, but negatively embellishes it with connotations of illness, bad humor, and general moral and physical lethargy.[12] Thus, the signifier slides on a referential continuum from being undoubtedly female to undeniably male. The metaphor is ultimately a transgendered one (with the kinetic prefix "trans" suggesting "movement across" or "beyond"), for it reminds readers of Sethe's stolen milk, the gag-inducing semen symbolically "nursed" from fellating the prison guards, the bloodied milk that Denver imbibes after the murder, and the semen that Beloved rapes from Paul that also plants seeds of discontent in his mind. This critical intermingling of gendered images—milk, blood, semen, breasts, phalluses—constitutes a form of "embodied" language that uses a series of re-turns (that is, tropes and flashbacks) to suggest the inextricable link between black, white, male, and female bodies. For indeed, to understand the slavery experience is to recognize and situate in the body not only its exploitative potential, but also its position as a redemptive tool, a mutable symbol for greater and more revolutionary social and cultural maneuvers.

III. Cock-sure: Masculine Personae and Variations on the American Dream

The construction and negotiation of masculinity, like femininity, is contingent upon a variety of forces beyond the individual's control. Beloved's textual/sexual "man"ipulation of Paul mimics the actions of myth-building and stereotyping in a larger social context. Butler, for instance, observes that insofar as sex is the "sedimented effect of a reiterative or ritual practice" through which it adopts the guise of "nature," there are "gaps and fissures . . . opened up as the constitutive instabilities in such constructions" (8). By this token, it is ironical that Paul resembles a figure in the popular imagination that is not usually an African(ist) persona, does not associate with many women (a substratum of gynophobia exists in the accompanying genre, although contestable), and remains highly prized as an avatar of masculinist self-sufficiency: the Western hero. The essence of the Western hero is his independence (Paul has been wandering alone for eighteen years), his renegade status (he is an escapee from the chain gang), his cooperative but wary relationships with other men (the men of Sweet Home, and later the chain gang constitute a reluctantly united "posse"), and his ambulatory nature. He may drift towards a woman, but he never settles with her permanently, opportunistically pleading the "call of the wild," a euphemism for his ultimate preference for freedom over conjugal responsibilities ("Move. Walk. Run. Hide. Steal and move on. Only once had it been possible for him to stay in one spot—with a woman, or a family—for longer than a few months" [66]). The Western hero, a silhouette riding perpetually into the dawn either by himself or with a trusty male companion, personifies self-perfectibility as well as self-absorption. There are issues that he has to deal with, and movement is a metaphor for the wandering restlessness of his mind, and his inability to find peace: "Afterward, after the Cherokee pointed and sent him running toward blossoms, he wanted simply to move, go, pick up one day and be somewhere else the next" (221). Familial ties are difficult to maintain, if not impossible: "Resigned to life without aunts, cousins, children. Even a woman, until Sethe" (221). He is closely related on a continuum of American manhood to the more urbanized phenomenon of the "self-made" man, the *genius loci* of the American Dream. But Paul D is no young Jay Gatsby; Fitzgerald's penultimate image is of a green light, not the sorrow-full red Paul sees upon entering 124. The assumption of an "orgiastic" future which is paired with a vague totality of people who "beat on, boats against the current, borne back ceaselessly into the past" (172) betrays a nostalgia absent from the Morrisonian ex-slave's daily work of "beating back the past" (73).

The blurring of Paul as an abject figure (the church basement tramp) and figurative apex of masculine self-sufficiency (the Western hero) helps to enunciate the desire to claim and reify America as a "romantic project, in which a paradise, a land of dreams, is fanned and fueled with a religion of vast possibility" (West xvi). Such a desire surely resides in Paul's so-called Africanist psyche as much as in its theoretical white counterpart's. Fantasy, however, is not always a safe place. The acknowledgement of this truism is reminiscent of how the novelist Angelou has reflected upon her own displacement as a southern black female. She images the awareness as "rust on the razor that threatens the throat" (6). It is such acute self-awareness that causes Paul to plunge into reticence and the solitary life, suppressing his memories in what he calls the rusted tobacco tin of his heart (113), and masking the sexual repression at the core of his necessary asceticism. As he wanders in the wilderness, following the trail of tree flowers ("a dark ragged figure guided by the blossoming plums" [113]), he conjures up more unconventional images: the *homo silvarum* ("man of the woods," reminiscent of Thoreau in *Walden*), the carefree hobo, and the desert saint. He is, of course, none of these. It is the juxtaposition of asceticism and fruition that proves striking, reminding readers that amid the pastoralism of cherry, magnolia, chinaberry, pecan, walnut and prickly pear (112), there is also displacement and decimation of an indigenous populace, a denial of the disruptive nature of human desire, and a masking of trauma that accompanies not being allowed to have an autonomous, sentient body. The solitary figure's freedom is indeed the image of an isolated, incommunicable self in multiform combinations. Paul's desire is nostalgic since he longs for a home, but there is a difference between a position of vagrancy (which carries no real prefiguration of home) and migrancy (which involves a provisional, if not ghostly prolepsis of home, work, and a future). This last connection, in conjunction with Paul's name, recalls St. Paul's letter to the Corinthians describing the abject, and yet ultimately liberating, position of the Outsider:

> 9 : For I think that God hath set forth us the apostles last, as it were appointed to death: for we are made a spectacle unto the world, and to angels, and to men.
> 10 : We are fools for Christ's sake, but ye are wise in Christ; we are weak, but ye are strong; ye are honourable, but we are despised.
> 11 : Even unto this present hour we both hunger, and thirst, and are naked, and are buffeted, and have no certain dwelling-place;
> 12 : And labour, working with our own hands: being reviled, we bless; being persecuted, we suffer it. (1 Corinthians 4: 9–12)

This lexicon—"spectacle," "hunger and thirst," "naked[ness]," "buffeted," "no certain dwelling place," "labor," "suffer," "working with our own hands," "being persecuted,"—describes Paul's experience of slavery with shocking precision. The rhetoric, however, is as idealistic as it is apocalyptic; Paul's suffering is not for suffering's sake, or for glory either, and his tendency is towards concealment rather than revelation. Often in victims of traumatic experience, *anhedonia,* or the inability to feel pleasure, coalesces with a more extensive dissociation and reconfiguration of sensibility. What results is a bifurcation of the *soma* from the *psyche,* or the eerie sensation of looking at oneself from the outside, as if the body were an/Other's. After the ritualistic abuse of the chain gang, Paul's body appears to swing between two interconnected modes of "embodied" discourse: the protopathic, which involves "crude" sensations like heat, pain, and cold, meaning those sensory faculties that residually remain once the finer neural distinctions have been dulled into submission; and the epicritic, or the contrastive and hypersensitive faculty that results in such delusions as the smiling rooster, Mister, and the paranoid vulnerability of being watched ("Walking past the roosters looking at them look at me" [71]). These are primarily somatic equivalents to the problem of distilling pain into an articulate language, which is Morrison's office throughout the text.

When Paul D imagines the mocking smile of Mister, the imperious and significantly colored rooster who has the leisure time to sunbathe while Paul labours, he directs a misandric impulse towards his own compromised position as a black male slave, subordinate even to an animal. Mister's story anthropomorphizes the American dream, but with a gangland flavor. The Napoleonic leader of almost fifty hens, this diminutive creature morphs into a grotesquely endowed fighter able to "whup everything in the yard" (71–72). Originally having been assumed a dud egg (or, as Paul's highly figurative parlance suggests, a "blank"), Mister begins his rise from the domain of the abject. A "blank" is potentially a gendered or racialized trope—that is, it could be a useless bullet from a phallic gun, a euphemism for nonviable sperm, or chromatically speaking, either whiteness or a complete absence of color. The figure of Mister is nineteenth-century slavery's version of Chaucer's aristocratic "gentil cok" Chaunticleer.[13] His small but mighty stature also gestures to the significant colloquial slurring of God and cock in the Elizabethan epithet, "By Cock!"[14] Either way, the paradox of power residing in such a meager individual persists if we consider how the rooster has already appeared numerous times in a semiotics of black male masculinity. Such works as Richard Wright's *Black Boy* (1945) describe how the protagonist feels like he is being pitted against another boy in a human cockfight for no reason other than his white employers' bloodlust. The Battle Royale scene in *Invisible Man* also resurrects cockfighting symbolism in more ways than one; black males must spar against one another after being titillated by a fleshly, feminine, and unattainable version of American beauty. Given American society's inflated symbolic investment in the black penis, the significance of "cock" is evident even in late twentieth, early twenty-first century urban slang as a synonym for the phallus. Finally, Mister's name, like his species, is loaded because it is a title denied to the man who "delivered" him, midwife-like, from the constraining and symbolically potent white shell of his birth. Mister has sexual license and space for its expression, whereas "yearning fashion[s] every note" at Sweet Home (40).

IV. "Flail the Conquering Hero": *Beloved* and the Spectacular Failure of Closure

Although more conventional a catalyst than Beloved, Paul prompts a shift in the sterile dynamics of daily life at 124 Bluestone Road: "Emotions sped to the surface in his company. Things became what they were: drabness looked drab; heat was hot. Windows suddenly had view" (39). It is his singing, too, that humanizes him, revealing a deceptively cheerful, conciliatory demeanor as he mends the furniture destroyed during his bout with the baby-ghost. The violent act of emptying the exclusively female domain of the house by "beat[ing] it to pieces" (21) not only asserts his status as a physically capable individual, able to effect change outside the realm of a master's command, it also allows him to don the masculine persona of a conquering hero. He becomes a masterful (and now *de facto* master-less) alpha male penetrating an exclusionary, misandric sphere. For indeed, Howard and Buglar, Sethe's young sons, have already taken their leave because of the baby's relentless venom. The family dog, also a male, avoids the house altogether due to the mutilating violence inflicted by the vengeful spirit ("[she] picked up Here Boy and slammed him into the wall hard enough to break two of his legs and dislocate his eye, so hard he went into convulsions and chewed up his tongue" [12]). Domestic violence lives up to its etymological roots (*domus*, the feminine noun for "home" in Latin), reversing the traditional schema of the abusive male inflicting harm upon the woman, children, and household pets, and situating power in the unlikely locus of the female infant.

Like wild animals, recalcitrant slaves had to be "broken" by a combination of physical aggression and psychological harassment, their tongues depressed by bits, bitten into submissive silence, and silenced by colonizing languages (although Sixo is one, however, who repudiates English [25]). Paul reflects bitterly that Schoolteacher "broke into children what Garner had raised into men" (220). He echoes Douglass who comments that the treatment of slaves brings them down to the Hobbesian, pre-civilized model of humanity—indeed, by extension, to the animal level:

> I first went there, but a few months of this discipline tamed me. Mr. Covey succeeded in breaking me. I was broken in body, soul, and spirit. My natural elasticity was crushed, my intellect languished, the disposition to read departed, the cheerful spark that lingered

about my eye died; the dark night of slavery closed in upon me; and behold a man transformed into a brute! (293)

By this token, "Here Boy," albeit a name, gestures tangentially to the treatment of the Afro-American male inside and outside the home, both locally and in the wider national context which Baldwin calls "the sunlit prison of the American dream" (19). Not only was dog-like obedience demanded of men like Paul by the master, they were perpetually commanded in the same abrupt, dehumanizing, and emasculating[15] manner—"Here, Boy!"—to approach, submit, and perform. Even Sethe momentarily calls Paul "dog" when she realizes that during their precipitous lovemaking, he did not bother to remove his shirt (22).[16] Baby Suggs's dismissal of men ("maybe a man was nothing but a man" [22]) resonates, a derisive echo from her daughter-in-law's lips, suggesting that under the cross-pressures of slavery, many Afro-American women lost patience with the powerlessness and apparent irresponsibility of the black men they desired to be their partners and protectors. Paul D's attenuated and doubt-ridden self-concept (Sethe: "'Is that you?'" Paul D: "'What's left'" [6]), struggling alongside the absent presence of Halle, undoubtedly contributes to the hegemonic power of the infant ghost. Sethe becomes more inclined on an unconscious level to dismiss "the last of the Sweet Home men" (9) whose unspectacular sexual performance ("It was over before they could get their clothes off" [20]) is synecdochally linked to the assumption of greater inefficacies. His comforting but bland presence belies a romantically-tinged ontology: that of being the "last" among a generation, race, or group. It is a position that he returns to in the presence of the Cherokee, another population decimated by American expansionism and the double-edged meaning of "frontier" as a margin as well as an unclaimed, unexplored expanse of land: "Alone, the last man with buffalo hair among the ailing Cherokee, Paul D finally woke up and, admitting his ignorance, asked how he might get North. Free North. Magical North" (112). The proverbial "last" is the individual in whom a tacit legacy and often unrealistic expectation rests ("Trust things and remember things because the last of the Sweet Home men was there to catch her if she sank" [19]). His life adopts a concentrated symbolic significance. Outsiders invest more in his presence than he expects. Denver's jealous retort, "How come everybody run off from Sweet Home can't stop talking about it? Look like if it was so sweet you would have stayed" (13) reveals how she views him as the personification of her exclusion. In essence, his sudden, ragged presence, as a metaphor for the memory of the other Sweet Home men, proves to be far from romantic: "One crazy, one sold, one missing, one burnt and me licking iron with my hands crossed behind me" (73). To Denver, however, his person speaks of a historical moment and an intimacy—the desire of a daughter for her absent father—that is inaccessible to her ("Only those who knew him [Halle] . . . could claim his absence for themselves" [13]). Because Paul knew Halle, and because he supplants Halle's position as Sethe's lover, Denver senses the betrayal of her ghostly and idealized father; by sentimental extrapolation, she hates Paul. He inadvertently walks into the simultaneously over- and underdetermined position of the mimic man, the adulterated "almost," and ultimately, the wrong *revenant*.

Here Boy's travails and his inability as a "dumb" animal to express his experience in language signify upon the experience of black slaves, especially that of black men. Similar violence has rendered Paul hyper-conscious of his own body and its latent fragilities: "his hands shook so bad he couldn't smoke or even scratch properly" (18). If we recall how Amy Denver tells the prostrate and pregnant Sethe that "Anything dead coming back to life hurts" (35), we will recognize how this statement applies to Paul's resurrection from the degrading "soul-death" of the chain gang experience. His circumscription in a trench overflowing with mud is reminiscent of a war experience, both in its traumatic physical conditions and in the sense of helplessness and disconnection with the body: "Paul D thought he was screaming; his mouth was open and there was this loud throat-splitting sound—but it may have been someone else. Then he thought he was crying" (110). As Cathy Caruth observes, "trauma" etymologically denotes "wound" in Greek, but the theoretical emphasis has shifted from the literal wound on the body to the psychological aberration which reflects an "oscillation between the *crisis of death* and its correlative *crisis of life* [;] between the story of the unbearable nature of an event and the story of the unbearable nature of its survival" (3–4, 7). The essence of Paul's trauma is that it is both fluid and fungible, able to apply to an individual and to a collective, in the past and in the present. It is a dynamic used throughout *Beloved*. For instance, during the fight between Paul and the spirit, Morrison accomplishes one of the most pivotal reversals. This is a duel between the resident feminine evil (or to Sethe, "sad[ness]," although judging from the torment it inflicts, "Sade-ness" might be more appropriate) and the shouting, smashing male ex-slave. Fought between man and superwoman, this duel illustrates a troubling k/not within the fabric of American history when the metanarrative is construed as a pattern of Manichean oppositions. According to West, "American discourses on innocence, deliverance or freedom overlook the atrocities of violence, subjugation or slavery in our past or present" (xvii). Morrison, in *Playing*, impresses West's solicitude onto a template of literary representations of race from early American literature. She juxtaposes the white tradition's construction of America as a land of infinite potential, freedom, and innocence alongside "the image of reined-in, bound, suppressed, and repressed darkness" (35, 39). White literary heroes have depended on these "Africanist" personae for a base upon which to fashion themselves differentially and, according to the Lacanian theory of the symptom, develop a fundamental ontological structure in the context of inchoate and often decentered surroundings. I argue that the division, however, is not exclusively along the color line; it can also be a series of fault-lines *within* the unself-certain subject.

Beloved and Paul, one "hazelnut" brown and the other "thunderblack," occupy separate points upon a gendered and chromatic continuum. Together, they represent the clash and eventual pairing of the contrastive values which writers like Morrison and West delineate under the singular aegis of the Afro-American slave experience. As suggested earlier, the contingency of whiteness is not of seminal importance here. For instance, the baby's itinerary from birth to death is a gradation from innocence to corruption. But like the eternally circular reasoning of the "chicken-and-egg" riddle, the direction of the gradation is unclear. Delivered from the womb to what appears to be a place of refuge, she achieves another version of freedom—the metaphysical freedom of death—through Sethe's pyrrhic victory against the slaveholders. Her story allegorically is that of the foreclosure of innocence and of post-war idealism, and of residual *destruction* within the period paradoxically called the Re*construction*. Her return to the earthly, fleshly plane as Beloved suggests that closure has been incomplete, and that the hermeneutic circle which West describes as the essence of modernity ("In short, the hermeneutic circle in which we find ourselves, as historical beings in search of meaning for ourselves, is virtuous, not vicious, because we never transcend or complete the circle" [xvi]) can indeed be vicious.

Between the status of a lowly dog and a household god ("There was something blessed in his manner. Women saw him and wanted to weep—to tell him that their chest hurt and their knees did too" [17]), Paul lashes out at the ghost in residual frustration from having both his self-esteem and person "[l]ocked up and chained down" (18). In this sense, Beloved enters the antagonist position that the white slave owners previously held. Paul, especially by dint of his recursive appearances at 124, represents the force that works against psychological disconnection, venomous desire for revenge, and destructive obsession with the past. As the pattern of the numbers 1, 2, and 4 suggests, these forces are exponential, doubling and proliferating to the extent that they take over one's life, just as Beloved subsumes Sethe's. By "screaming back at the screaming house" (18), Paul dispels any assumption that a baby-ghost must necessarily be an angel in the house, and that a wandering ex-slave must fit the mold of a typically white masculine sublime—as Ayer-Sitter proposes, a "demon-slaying hero returned to claim his prize" (193).[17] Paul's symbolic office exceeds the calcifications of stereotype and encourages the reader to seek a metaphysics of identity that shifts, adapts, challenges, but ultimately champions the integrity of the self, sufficient in itself.

The exact *why* of the misandric impulse in *Beloved* is an open question. One reason may be that misandry, like misogyny, is a corollary and symptom of, or even precursor to that apex of human hatreds, misanthropy. Slavery, racism, war, and other forms of social violence testify to a profound lack of appreciation for human commonality and meliorist potential. By this token, *Beloved* also functions in the postcolonial and feminist mode by highlighting how certain forms of exploitation and abuse are contiguous with others; as a vector quality (that which has a variable magnitude and direction), abuse travels more easily from female to male than we usually assume. To place such "unconventional" but nonetheless extant themes and patterns of behavior into stark(er) relief gestures to a critical imperative: we must avoid ghettoizing a complex work like *Beloved* as a solely feminist text. Instead, we must allow for a dialogic and dynamic relationship to unfold with each textual experience. In so far as *Beloved* is a text simultaneously embedded in history and a series of interpenetrating histories embedded in text, we as *readers* must enter its discourse as a community beyond *Bildung*. Our immersion mirrors the endemic nature of slavery in the black consciousness, how its traumas and degradations surface in language(s) and act(s), and how the struggle against self-estrangement demands an understanding of how our representations shape us, and how we shape our representations.

NOTES

1. See also "The Negro and Psychopathology" in Fanon's *Black Skin, White Masks,* chapter six, for a discussion of the hyper-sexualization of the black male body ("In relation to the Negro, everything takes place on the genital level" [157]).

2. George Elliott Clarke suggests that the posture on the medal (which is one of the House of Wedgwood's creations) is also that of almost any Christian saint or martyr in popular iconic representations. Clarke, memo to the article author, 8 May 2002.

3. Cf. "The black man wants to be white. The white man slaves to reach a human level" (9). I intentionally invert Fanon's phrasing.

4. For an incisive commentary on the vampiric and monstrous aspects of Beloved, see Trudier Harris, *Fiction and Folklore: The Novels of Toni Morrison* (Knoxville: University of Tennessee Press, 1991) 151–164. Reprinted as *"Beloved:* 'Woman, Thy Name is Demon,'" *Critical Essays on Toni Morrison's* Beloved, ed. Barbara H. Solomon (New York: G. K. Hall, 1998), 127–137.

5. This line comes from Wordsworth's "Ode: Intimations of Immortality from Recollections of Early Childhood": "Though nothing can bring back the hour/ Of splendor in the grass, of glory in the flower/ We will grieve not, rather find/ Strength in what remains behind" (10. 178–181).

6. For a discussion of such authors as Poe and Hemingway, see Toni Morrison, *Playing in the Dark: Whiteness and the Literary Imagination* (New York: Vintage, 1992).

7. Du Bois names his second chapter in *The Souls of Black Folk* "Of the Dawn of Freedom." It is also worth noting instances of dawn and sunshine imagery in Harriet Jacobs' *Incidents in the Life of a Slave Girl*. See Chapter 30: "The next morning I was on deck as soon as the day dawned. I called Fanny to see the sun rise, for the first time in our lives, on free soil; for such I *then* believed it to be. We watched the reddening sky, and saw the great orb come up slowly out of the water, as it seemed. Soon the waves began to sparkle, and every thing caught the beautiful glow" (477); in Chapter 33: "The old feeling of insecurity, especially with regard to my children, often threw its dark shadow across my sunshine" (485); and in Chapter 39: "The next morning, she [Ellen, Jacobs' daughter] and her uncle started on their journey to the village in New York, where she was to be placed at school. It seemed as if all the sunshine had gone away" (502). See Harriet Jacobs, "Incidents in the Life of a Slave Girl," *The Classic Slave Narratives*, ed. Henry Louis Gates, Jr. (New York: Penguin, 1987) 341–513.

8. See Thomas Carlyle, "Occasional Discourse on the Nigger Question," *The Latter-Day Pamphlets* 1853 (Manchester, NH: Ayer Company, 1977).

9. See especially Chapter 18 in Harriet Beecher Stowe, *Uncle Tom's Cabin, or Life Among the Lowly*, ed. Ann Douglas (New York: Penguin, 1981).

10. See Pamela Barnett, "Figurations of Rape and the Supernatural in *Beloved*," *Columbia Critical Guides: Toni Morrison's* Beloved, ed. Carl Plasa (New York: Columbia University Press, 1998), 73-85. Reprinted from *PMLA* 112 (1997): 418–427.

11. See Ntozake Shange, *For Colored Girls Who Have Considered Suicide/when the Rainbow is Enuf* (New York: Simon and Schuster, 1997) for an examination of a similar thematics of gender extremes.

12. See Edward F. Stanton, *Hemingway and Spain* (Washington: University of Washington Press, 1989) 155–159.

13. See Geoffrey Chaucer, "The Nun's Priest's Prologue and Tale," *The Canterbury Tales*, ed. V. A. Kolve and Glending Olson (New York: W. W. Norton, 1989) 214–231; 217.

14. See, for instance, *Hamlet*, IV.v. 60–61 in Ophelia's song, "Young men will do't if they come to't,/By Cock they are to blame." *The Riverside Shakespeare*, ed. G. Blakemore Evans et al. (Boston: Houghton Mifflin, 1997) 1221.

15. By using the term "emasculating," I do not imply any necessary or accompanying feminization, although often the identification tends to go in that binarized direction.

16. This canine symbolism, however, has been appropriated by contemporary hip-hop artists such as Snoop Dogg and L'il Bow Wow as a sign of virility and trickster-like versatility. See also, Jim Jarmusch's 2000 film *Ghost Dog: The Way of the Samurai* (starring Forest Whitaker) as another embrace of the symbolism. For more on the significance of the trickster figure in Afro-American culture, see Lawrence W. Levine, *Black Culture and Black Consciousness—Afro-American Folk Thought from Slavery to Freedom* (Oxford: Oxford University Press, 1977, 1989).

17. For a particularly lucid and in-depth study of American chivalric constructions, see John Fraser, *America and the Patterns of Chivalry* (New Rochelle, NY: Cambridge University Press, 1982).

Works Cited

Angelou, Maya. *I Know Why the Caged Bird Sings*. New York: Random House, 1969.

Ayer-Sitter, Deborah. "The Making of a Man: Dialogic Meaning in *Beloved*." *Critical Essays on Toni Morrison's* Beloved. Ed. Barbara H. Solomon. New York: G. K. Hall, 1998. 189–205.

Baldwin, James. "Everybody's Protest Novel." *Notes of a Native Son*. Boston: Beacon Press, 1955. 13–23.

———. "The Black Boy Who Looks Like a White Boy." *The Price of the Ticket: Collected Non-Fiction 1948–1985*. New York: St. Martin's, 1985. 289–303.

Barnett, Pamela. "Figurations of Rape and the Supernatural in *Beloved*." *Columbia Critical Guides: Toni Morrison's* Beloved. Ed. Carl Plasa. New York: Columbia University Press, 1998. 73–85.

Beecher Stowe, Harriet. *Uncle Tom's Cabin, or Life Among the Lowly*. New York: Penguin, 1981.

Bell, Bernard W. "*Beloved:* A Womanist Neo-Slave Narrative; or Multivocal Remembrances of Things Past." Solomon 266–276.

Butler, Judith. *Bodies That Matter: On the Discursive Limits of 'Sex'*. New York: Routledge, 1993.

Carlyle, Thomas. "Occasional Discourse on the Nigger Question." *The Latter-Day Pamphlets*. 1853. Manchester, NH: Ayer Company, 1977.

Caruth, Cathy. Introduction. *Unclaimed Experience: Trauma, Narrative, and History*. By Caruth. Baltimore: Johns Hopkins University Press, 1996.

Chaucer, Geoffrey. "The Nun's Priest's Prologue and Tale." *The Canterbury Tales*. Ed. V. A. Kolve and Glending Olson. New York: W. W. Norton, 1989. 214–231.

Douglass, Frederick. *The Narrative of the Life of Frederick Douglass, An American Slave. Classic Slave Narratives*. Ed. Henry Louis Gates, Jr. New York: Mentor-Penguin, 1987. 245–331.

Du Bois, W. E. B. *The Souls of Black Folk*. New York: Signet, 1995.

Dyson, Michael Eric. "Be Like Mike? Michael Jordan and the Pedagogy of Desire." *Signifyin(g), Sanctifyin,' and Slam Dunking—A Reader in African American Expressive Culture*. Ed. Gena Dagel Caponi. Amherst: University of Massachusetts Press, 407–416.

Eliot, T. S. "Tradition and the Individual Talent." *Selected Prose of T. S. Eliot*. Ed. Frank Kermode. London: Faber and Faber, 1975. 37–44.

Fanon, Frantz. *Black Skin, White Masks*. Trans. Charles Lam Markmann. New York: Grove Press, 1967.

Fitzgerald, F. Scott. *The Great Gatsby*. New York: Simon and Schuster, 1995.

Godwich, Wlad. Foreword. *The Resistance to Theory*. By Paul de Man. Minneapolis: Minnesota University Press, 1986. xiv–xv.

Greenblatt, Stephen. "Culture." *Critical Terms for Literary Study*. Ed. Frank Lentricchia and Thomas McLaughlin. Chicago: University of Chicago Press, 1990. 226–232.

Harris, Trudier. "*Beloved:* 'Woman, Thy Name is Demon." Solomon 127–137.

Hawthorne, Nathaniel. "The Custom House— Introductory to *The Scarlet Letter*." *The Scarlet Letter—An Authoritative Text and Essays in Criticism and Scholarship*. Ed. Seymour Glass et al. New York: W. W. Norton, 1988. 4–34.

hooks, bell. *Black Looks: Race and Representation*. Boston: South End Press, 1992.

Horvitz, Deborah. "Nameless Ghosts: Possession and Dispossession in *Beloved*." Solomon 93–103.

Jacobs, Harriet. *Incidents in the Life of a Slave Girl. The Classic Slave Narratives.* Ed. Henry Louis Gates, Jr. New York: Penguin, 1987. 341–513.

Morrison, Toni. *Beloved.* New York: Vintage, 1987.

———. *Playing in the Dark—Whiteness and the Literary Imagination.* New York: Vintage, 1992.

Sedgwick, Eve Kosofsky. *Between Men: English Literature and Male Homosocial Desire.* New York: Columbia University Press, 1993.

Shakespeare, William. *Hamlet. The Riverside Shakespeare.* Ed. G. Blakemore Evans et al. Boston: Houghton-Mifflin, 1997.

Stanton, Edward F. *Hemingway and Spain.* Washington: University of Washington Press, 1989.

Thelwell, Michael. "False, Fleeting, Perjured Clarence: Yale's Brightest and Blackest Go to Washington." *Race-in Justice, En-gendering Power: Essays on Anita Hill, Clarence Thomas, and the Construction of Social Reality.* Ed. Toni Morrison. New York: Pantheon, 1992. 86–126.

Virgil. *The Aeneid.* Trans. W. K. Jackson Knight. London: Penguin, 1958.

West, Cornel. Introduction. "To be Modern, Human and American." *The Cornel West Reader.* New York: Basic Civitas, 1999. xv–xx.

TERESA N. WASHINGTON

The Mother-Daughter Àjẹ́ Relationship in Toni Morrison's Beloved

Introduction

Toni Morrison has often expressed disappointment with critical analyses of her art. In an interview with Thomas LeClair she said, "I have yet to read criticism that understands my work or is prepared to understand it. I don't care if the critic likes or dislikes it. I would just like to feel less isolated. It's like having a linguist who doesn't understand your language tell you what you're saying" (128). To my reasoning, Morrison is calling for an analysis that complements the art, one that is grounded in the artist's culture, language, worldview, and milieu. My goal with this essay is to attempt to address Morrison's critical challenge by using an Africana theoretical perspective centered on a force called *Àjẹ́* to interpret the intricacies of the mother-daughter relationship in *Beloved*.

Àjẹ́ is a Yoruba word and concept that describes a spiritual force that is thought to be inherent in Africana women; additionally, spiritually empowered humans are called *Àjẹ́*. The stately and reserved women of *Àjẹ́* are feared and revered in Yoruba society. Commonly and erroneously defined as witches, *Àjẹ́* are astrally-inclined human beings who enforce earthly and cosmic laws, and they keep society balanced by ensuring that human beings follow those laws or are punished for their transgressions. These women, honored as "our

African American Review, Volume 39, Numbers 1–2 (Spring–Summer 2005): pp. 171–188.

mothers" (àwọn ìyá wa), "my mother" (ìyá mi), and the elders of the night, are recognized as the owners and controllers of everything on Earth (Drewal and Drewal 7). Àjẹ́'s suzerainty comes from the fact that it is considered the origin of all earthly existence, and women of Àjẹ́ are euphemistically called "Earth" (ayé).

Odùduwà, the tutelary Òrìṣà (Select Head) of Àjẹ́, is heralded as the "Womb of Creation" (Fatunmbi 85) and is symbolized by the life-giving pot of origins and also the "wicked bag" or earthen tomb in which all life forms find eternal rest and also regeneration. Àjẹ́, the "daughters" of Odùduwà, are said to oversee creation and destruction, divination, healing, and the power of the word. Given its female ownership and administration, it is fitting that Àjẹ́'s terrestrial source of birth, actualization, and manifestation is the womb. Owners of Àjẹ́ are said to control reproductive organs, and they are bonded through the cosmic power and the life-giving force of menstrual blood. Importantly, Àjẹ́ can be genetically passed from mother to child.

Àjẹ́ "sister systems" are found throughout Africa, and Àjẹ́ also survived the Middle Passage to exert marked influence on neo-African communities. However, while a Yoruba proverb asserts, "Kàkà kó sàn lára àjẹ́ ó nbi ọmọ obìnrin jọ́ ẹye wá nyí lu ẹyẹ" ["Instead of the Àjẹ́ changing for the better, she continues to have more daughters, producing more and more 'birds'"] (Lawal 34), Africana literature is not overly reflective of the mother-daughter Àjẹ́ relationship. Most writers depict Àjẹ́ as a controlling matriarch who uses her power, forcefully or gently, to guide her family and often the community. Another depiction is that of the young Àjẹ́ who is misunderstood by a mother who denies or is incognizant of her daughter's force. In this case, it is often a surrogate mother Àjẹ́ who guides the young woman towards self-actualization. This surrogacy is apparent in Indigo and Aunt Haydee's relationship in Ntozake Shange's novel Sassafrass, Cypress, & Indigo; in Peaches's connection to Maggie in Toni Cade Bambara's short story "Maggie of the Green Bottles"; and to a more intricate extent, in Shug Avery's mentoring of the adult Celie in Alice Walker's The Color Purple.

Narrative/protagonist control also affects concurrent mother-daughter Àjẹ́ interactions. To forestall full conflict between the mother and daughter, many works depict a mother Àjẹ́ who is nearing death or has a waning force while the daughter's Àjẹ́ is latent, as is the case with Janie and Nanny in Their Eyes Were Watching God. If both women are simultaneously active, they usually find separate spheres of existence and expression, as is apparent in Amos Tutuola's My Life in the Bush of Ghosts, in which an uninitiated Àjẹ́ daughter flees her initiated Àjẹ́ parents and lives alone honing her force (114–118). Also in Toni Morrison's Sula, emergent Àjẹ́ Sula Peace returns to Medallion to place her grandmother and community matriarch Àjẹ́ into the Sunnydale nursing home (94). Sula initiates a changing of the guard of Àjẹ́;

by removing Eva from the sphere of influence and interaction, Sula is free to realize and savor her personal and textual climaxes. Like most Africana textual communities, Medallion, the setting of *Sula,* is not large enough for two concurrently active *Àjé,* but there are texts that deal with this powerful confluence of forces.

Mother-Daughter *Àjé*'s Literary Lineage

To craft fiction in which there are two simultaneously active *Àjé* is to create a work humming with the layering and unveiling of indivisible paradoxical complexities. When *Àjé* is passed genetically and amalgamates spiritually and physically, the result is mothers and daughters enmeshed in a web of creation and destruction, love and hate, silence and signification. Although this study's focus is Morrison's *Beloved,* to clarify the intricacies of the mother-daughter *Àjé* relationship, I will frame my analysis within a brief discussion of two other works of lineage *Àjé:* Audre Lorde's "biomythography" *Zami: A New Spelling of My Name* and Jamaica Kincaid's short story, "My Mother." These three works are linked in their interpretation of the role of the father in the mother-daughter *Àjé* relationship and in their exploration of sacred space.

Àjé is a woman-owned and woman-administered force but, reflecting the structure of Yoruba cosmology, *Àjé* is a force of balance based on complementary pairs. The male aspect is essential to *Àjé;* and many males have this power and exercise it. However, in *Zami,* "My Mother," and *Beloved,* the fathers and father figures are dead, not mentioned, or exiled from the sphere of spiritual interaction. In "My Mother," no father is mentioned, and in *Beloved,* Halle, Sethe's husband and the father of her children, is largely irrelevant to the primary action. Even if a father figure is present, as with Paul D in *Beloved,* he is pushed out of the sphere of interaction so that the lineage *Àjé* can define themselves for and against themselves. While the removal of the male aspect from the space of interactions may be a commentary on the horrific struggles Africana men faced in lands riddled with slavery, neo-slavery, and colonization, these three texts intimate that a larger cosmic agenda is at work. Within the family unit the father occupies a position of indisputable relevance—even in his absence. However, in the mother-daughter *Àjé* relationship, the father is necessarily relegated to the outside.

Zami gives the clearest articulation of the role of the father in the mother-daughter *Àjé* relationship. In Lorde's text we find the male force essential to creation but irrelevant, and possibly an impediment, to full spiritual expansion. Lineage *Àjé* finds its apex in a matrilineal trinity: "I have felt the age-old triangle of mother father and child, with the 'I' at its eternal core, elongate and flatten out into the elegantly strong triad of grandmother mother and daughter, with the 'I' moving back and forth flowing in either or both directions as needed" (Lorde 7). As Lorde describes a movement from a one-dimensional transference to a unified multidimensional spiritual trinity of *Àjẹ́,* the triangle of origins, in which the father is indispensable, becomes a seamless matrix of Mother Power that imparts articulation, recognition of shared identity, and the ability to experience the individual wealth of *Àjẹ́* concurrent to that of the group.

In addition to patriarchal absence, these women of *Àjẹ́* navigate through a charged space that alternately symbolizes death and destruction, on the one hand, and creative and spiritual development, on the other hand. In *Zami,* the narrator describes the way her mother Linda, "a very powerful woman" and a "commander," uses her *Àjẹ́* to redefine destructive concepts—and to infuse them with power—for the sake of her and her progeny's survival: "My mother's words teaching me all manner of wily and diversionary defenses learned from the white man's tongue, from out of the mouth of her father. She had to use these defenses, and had survived by them, and had also died by them a little. . . . All the colors change and become each other, merge and separate, flow into rainbows and nooses" (Lorde 58).

While Linda's struggles give Audre the skills to survive, the source of Linda and Audre's power lies not in the master's tools but in the Mother's Text. Lorde writes, "I grew Black as my need for life, for affirmation, for love, for sharing—copying from my mother what was in her, unfulfilled. I grew Black as *Seboulisa,* who I was to find in the cool mud halls of Abomey several lifetimes later—and, as alone" (58). Linda's seemingly blank pages bear the faded ink of the Book of Destiny *(Fa),* as penned by Seboulisa, Creator Mother and "Great determiner of destiny" (Gaba 79).[1]

Lorde, as black as ink and filled with signifying properties, uses *Zami* to consecrate a curvilinear space of juba, born of spirit, flesh, and text: *"Ma-Liz, DeLois, Louise Briscoe, Aunt Anni, Linda, and Genevieve; MawuLisa, thunder, sky, sun, the great mother of us all; and Afrekete, her youngest daughter, the mischievous linguist, trickster, best-beloved, whom we must all become"* (255, emphasis in the original). At the conclusion of *Zami,* as foreshadowed in the preface, Lorde's matrix of *Àjẹ́* is boundless and ever-welcoming of evolved friends, ancestors, and kin. At the center of the matrix is the deity Afrekete, the cosmic, textual, and physical mother, who, laughing at the nooses and crying through the rainbows, emerges from the ink as an original reflection of the Africana woman's Self.

The unnamed characters of Kincaid's "My Mother" navigate through a charged space that morphs from brackish pond to impenetrable darkness to ocean. The mother initiates her daughter into the force of *Àjẹ́* by proving that space to be not a void but the expansiveness of Odùduwà (the *Òrìsà* of creative and biological origins). The mother extracts educational and transformational tools from Odùduwà's bottomless pot, and she shares her finds with her progeny. For example, when the daughter sits on her mother's bed "trying to get a good look" at herself in a completely dark room, the mother lights candles, and, by doing so, teaches her daughter about their multi-tiered powers of signification: "We sat mesmerized because our shadows had made a place between themselves, as if they were making room for someone else. Nothing filled up the space between them, and the shadow of my mother sighed" (Kincaid 54). Rather than illuminating the singular self, a mirrored unity is revealed, and the mother and daughter witness the singularity of their indivisible selves and their material and spiritual forms.

The profundity of and possibilities within blackness move the mother first to sigh and later to juba. The daughter's shadow joins the mother's in texturing free space with rhythm, vibration, and expression. The women sing praisesongs and pay one another homage: "The shadow of my mother danced around the room to a tune that my own shadow sang, and then they stopped" (Kincaid 54). Just as light made their shadow-spirits visible, their shadows reciprocate and impart existence through the space, in the light, and between the shadows. The mother reveals the space between her self and her daughter to be not a void, but a spiritual playground and classroom. The mother even enters into the cosmic space herself and emerges as a daughter of the Vodun serpent deity Damballah-Hwedo (Kincaid 55). However, the mother's tutorials on spiritual expansion, that are also promises of shared power, provide brief respite for the daughter who vacillates between rapturous awe of her mother and pathological desire to destroy her.

Realizing her daughter's paradoxical impasse, the mother conjures an ocean from a brackish pond, and sends her daughter on a boat ride to the Self. Having crossed the void she created only to find the architect of her existence reflecting her Self as always, the daughter finally enters into a "complete union" with her mother. Their union is metaphysical: "I could not see where she left off and I began, or where I left off and she began." It is also physical: "I fit perfectly in the crook of my mother's arm, on the curve of her back, in the hollow of her stomach" (Kincaid 60). The daughter anticipates reaching the same spiritual apex of amalgamated *Àjé* that Lorde achieves: "As we walk through the rooms, we merge and separate, merge and separate; *soon we shall enter the final stage of our evolution*" (60–61, emphasis added).

A Beloved Re-Embodiment of *Àjé*

"My Mother" is a text woven on a largely ahistorical tapestry, and liberated in that free space, the protagonists themselves constitute their only barriers to expansion. *Beloved* also revolves around a mother and daughter's desire to enjoy a perfect unity. However, as the narrator poignantly reveals, enslaved Africans in America were struggling for existence in lands in which they could list relatives, especially children, who had been less loved than "run off or been hanged, got rented out, loaned out, bought up, brought back, stored

up, mortgaged, won, stolen or seized" (23). Rather than subject their progeny
to the financially motivated, sexually depraved, and morally bankrupt
whims of their oppressors, some mothers of *Àjé* returned the creations of
their wombs to the tomb-like "wicked bag" that holds destruction, creation,
and re-creation. Although many discussions of lineage *Àjé* describe the
mother killing (mentally, spiritually, or physically) her daughter, Morrison's
work forces us to re-evaluate this simplistic assessment. Tormented mothers
of *Àjé* are not destroying their progeny. To quote Sethe, they are putting
them "where they'd be safe."

Having a safe, sacred space has always been of paramount importance
to displaced African peoples, and under circumstances only she could have
imagined, Odùduwà's enslaved progeny attempted to recreate her sacred space
of creation. Such spaces have been called the Arbor Church, the Conjuring
Lodge, the crossroads, and the praying ground. What occurs in these spaces
has been called many things, but it is all juba. In *Zami,* the space of juba is
manifest in the linguistic tools and silences of Linda that are transformed by
the daughter Audre. In "My Mother," the space of spiritual interaction is the
ever-present, ever-malleable brackish pond. In *Beloved,* various forms of juba
are discussed in relation to the sacred spaces and times that facilitated them.[2]
Fittingly, the juba that is created by Sethe and Beloved, twice in the novel, is
the exemplar melding of the spiritual and material under *Àjé*, and this *Àjé*-
juba occurs both times at 124.

The primary setting of *Beloved* is a home at 124 Bluestone Road in
Cincinnati, Ohio. From the opening of the work, it is apparent that 124
is a space of freedom, juba, and *Àjé* so complex that it can be considered a
character. Morrison emphasizes 124's humanity at the beginning of each
of the novel's three sections, which respectively describe 124 as "spiteful,"
"loud," and "quiet." Sethe's daughter Denver regards 124 as "a person rather
than a structure. A person that wept, sighed, trembled and fell into fits"
(23).[3] While these descriptions of 124's vitality are due to Beloved's spiritual presence, the domicile had long been an arena for cosmic and material interrelations, and this development may be the result of its spiritual
and numerological stationing. Perhaps Morrison named Bluestone Road
after the healing bluestone that, when applied to a cut, "burns like hell"
but heals instantly (Grant-Boyd). The number 124 is the numerological
equivalent of seven, the number of Òrìsà Ògún, owner of iron, technology,
and weaponry. Ògún's role in protecting and empowering enslaved Africans and complementing Sethe's Àjé is profoundly important. Additionally,
Ousseynou Traore contends that readers unconsciously register the unseen
number three in *1-2-4*. The number three often indicates spiritual unity,
and it is also the number of the alternately silent and signifying Yoruba

trickster Èṣù, who, similar to the *concept* of Beloved (discussed below), is omnipresent and omniscient.

Located on the "free side" of the Ohio River, 124 is where runaways and the officially free went to find succor, connect with lost relatives, and rebalance their shattered equilibrium. However, Baby Suggs transforms it into a space of spiritual healing. When the elder woman realizes and actualizes her Òrò (power of the word), 124 becomes a healing gateway for the transformational juba of the Clearing. Located just outside 124, the Clearing is the African American equivalent of the sacred spiritual groves where West and Central African initiations and rituals, including sacrifice, take place. Similar to the Grandmother deity of Anlo people, Baby Suggs, holy consecrates the Clearing as the "Ground of all being," and uses the Clearing and 124 to help her community determine its destiny (Gaba 79).

Communal mother and mother-in-law to Sethe, Baby Suggs uses the complementary spiritual forces of 124 and the Clearing for a two-tiered communal initiation process. After she has mended, as well as she can, the torn lives of the newly freed and still seeking, she calls them to the Clearing to mend their spirits.

> They knew she was ready when she put her stick down. Then she shouted, "Let the children come!" and they ran from the trees toward her. . . .
> "Let your mothers hear you laugh. . . ."
> Then "Let the grown men come," she shouted. . . .
> "Let your wives and your children see you dance. . . ."
> Finally she called the women to her. "Cry," she told them. "For the living and the dead. Just cry. . . ."
> It started that way: laughing children, dancing men, crying women and then it got mixed up. Women stopped crying and danced, men sat down and cried; children danced, women laughed, children cried until, exhausted and riven, all and each lay about the Clearing damp and gasping for breath. (87–88)

Fully indicative of juba—the confluence of song, dance, prayer, lamentation, and exultation—calls in the Clearing invite the resolution of all conflicts and the unification of everything bifurcated. Initially, Suggs specifies roles for gender and age groups. As these roles become transformed through her *Àjé*, they are bonded and melded to the point that such divisions are rendered meaningless because of their interdependence. The *Àjé* of Africana women, the *Oṣó* (male spiritual power) of Africana men and the *àṣe* (power to make things happen) of both, as manifest in the promise of their children, are united in the Clearing through Baby Suggs, holy.

The orature that accompanies the juba is not a religious sermon or catechism but a spiritual charge that transforms into a unified whole the few things that the Clearing participants dare lay claim—their bodies and spirits, and most fragile, their love:

> Here . . . in this here place, we flesh; flesh that weeps, laughs, flesh that dances on bare feet in grass. Love it. Love it hard. Yonder they do not love your flesh. They despise it. They don't love your eyes; they'd just as soon pick em out. No more do they love the skin on your back. Yonder they flay it. And O my people they do not love your hands. Those they only use, tie, bind, chop off and leave empty. Love your hands! Love them. Raise them up and kiss them. Touch others with them . . . stroke them on your face 'cause they don't love that either. *You* got to love it, *you*! (88)

Suggs's Clearing calls invite all dichotomies to return to their original unified state. The power of her word transforms gender roles and individual and anatomical character until everything is merged and shared holistically. Revising the concept of human sacrifice, Baby Suggs, holy leads each communal member to submit every element of themselves—section by section, entity by entity—in order to reestablish connection with the communal Self and the "Ground of All Being."

Baby Suggs is the *Ìyánlá* (Great Mother) of the textual community. She is the quintessential *Àjé*: a benevolent force of determination who galvanizes the powers of the Earth with her staff of *àse*. As the governing heart of her community, Suggs is not merely the initiator of action, but she is also subject to communal critique and correction for improper actions. Twenty-eight days, one monthly moon after the arrival of Sethe and the newborn Denver, Suggs celebrates the arrival and life of her progeny by turning two buckets of blackberries and a few chickens into a feast to feed the entire community. The 28 days' celebration of unity is a false one that calls Suggs's application of *Àjé* into question. Interpreting Suggs's feast of joy as a personal flaunting of wealth and a show of pride, the community removes its complementary protection from her. The Ohio community's critique is subtle, methodical, and devastating. Rather than sending a warning about the riders who have entered town to steal her progeny, the community stands in perfect silence. Suggs's trespass and the resulting communal correction spark the first pattern of mother-daughter *Àjé* interactions.

Àjé are associated with birds that act as spiritual media. The Spirit Bird, *Eye Òrò*, is capable of aesthetic creativity, astral *cum* physical destruction, and sublime protection. A Yoruba praisesong describes the force of the Spirit Bird and the women who wield it.

Mo lẹye nílé (I have a bird in the house)
Mo lẹye níta (I have a bird outside)
Ti mo bá lọ sode (When I go on outings)
E fọwò mi wò mí o—(Give me my proper respect)
　　(T. Washington 55)

The "bird in the house" is a figurative reference to Odùduwà's primal womb of power, which is replicated in all Africana women; the "bird in the house" is also a literal reference to the sacred calabash, in which the Spirit Bird is housed (Ojo 135). When this spiritually-charged Bird emerges and goes on outings, its power and potential are awesome.

Àjé's birds of power take to wing often in Morrison's fiction. In *Paradise*, buzzards circle over and signify at a wedding (272–273); in *Sula*, sparrows signal the changing of the guard (89). In *Jazz*, Violet is introduced as living with and later releasing her flock of birds, and Wild, Violet's seeming mother-in-law and re-embodiment of Beloved, is signified by "blue-black birds with the bolt of red on their wings" (176).[4] The Spirit Bird both recurs as a symbolic totem and regularly assists Morrison's women of *Àjé* with their confounding actions. In *Sula*, matriarch Eva Peace is described in terms of *Àjé*. Swooping like a "giant heron," Eva extends her arm in the manner of "the great wing of an eagle," as she douses her son in kerosene before setting him ablaze (46–47). This mother creator-destroyer-protector, who "held [her son] real close" before killing him, also takes wing later in the novel and jumps out of her window in an attempt to save her daughter, who inadvertently has set herself on fire (75–76). Following Eva's path, when Sethe sees schoolteacher's hat, she sees a life that cannot be tolerated. She snatches up her children like Eyẹ Òrò, "like a hawk on the wing . . . face beaked . . . hands work[ing] like claws," to put them in a safe place.

> She was squatting in the garden and when she saw them coming and recognized schoolteacher's hat, *she heard wings. Little hummingbirds stuck their needle beaks right through her headcloth into her hair and beat their wings.* And if she thought anything it was No. No. Nono. Nonono. Simple. *She just flew.* Collected every bit of life she had made, all the parts of her that were precious and fine and beautiful, and carried, pushed, dragged them through the veil, out, away, over there where no one could hurt them. Over there. Outside this place, where they would be safe. *And the hummingbird wings beat on.* (163, emphasis added)

Guided by an invisible collective of *Àjé* hummingbirds, Sethe hides her children in the woodshed of 124. Melding her *Àjé* with the existent power of the Clearing and 124, Sethe creates in the woodshed an *ojúbọ*, or praisehouse, where Òrìṣà are kept and worshipped with libation and sacrifice. Sethe takes her children, whom she defines as minor Òrìṣà—her "precious," "fine," and "beautiful" creations or re-embodiments of herself—inside the *ojúbọ*/wood-shed. There, the terrestrial mother *Àjẹ́* begins the work of transformation—placing her children back into Odùduwà's pot of existence and creativity. Under the institution of slavery, this return may well be the most profound expression of devotion. Using a handsaw, one of the iron implements of Ògún, as a tool of facilitation, Sethe returns the living deities of her self to the Mother, aware that *Àjẹ́* and *Ìyánlá*, the Great Mother, are the only forces that can ensure her children's safety.

It is well-known that *Beloved* is a re-membering and re-ordering of the life, actions, and *Àjẹ́* of a woman named Margaret Garner. In "The Negro Woman," Herbert Aptheker recalls Garner's act of *Àjẹ́*, which occurred in 1856: "One may better understand now a Margaret Garner, fugitive slave, who, when trapped near Cincinnati, killed her own daughter and tried to kill herself. She rejoiced that the girl was dead—'now she would never know what a woman suffers as a slave'—and pleaded to be tried for murder. 'I shall go singing to the gallows rather than be returned to slavery'" (qtd. in Davis 21). Garner ordered her existence, and that of her progeny, with the only means available to her—her *Àjẹ́*. And Sethe uses the same maternal, retributive, protective *Àjẹ́* as the historical Garner. However, due to the brutality of the institution of slavery, the actions of Sethe and Garner are not rare or unique.

The Unwritten History of Slavery identifies another child-saving *Àjẹ́* in Fannie of Eden, Tennessee. Fannie's daughter Cornelia recalled that her mother was "the smartest black woman in Eden" and a woman with an *Àjẹ́*-esque duality. Fannie "could do anything": "She was as quick as a flash of lightening, and whatever she did could not be done better." But she was also "a demon." As her daughter recalled, "Ma fussed, fought, and kicked all the time. . . . She said that she wouldn't be whipped. She was loud and boisterous . . . . She was too high-spirited and independent" to be a slave. "I tell you, she was a captain" (Rawick, *Unwritten History* 283). An enslaved captain, Fannie ingrained *Àjẹ́* survival tactics into Cornelia from childhood, telling her, "*I'll kill you, gal, if you don't stand up for yourself. . . . fight, and if you can't fight, kick; if you can't kick, then bite*" (Rawick, *Unwritten History* 284).

As a living example of *Àjẹ́*-resistance, when the plantation mistress struck her, Fannie beat her, chased her into the street, and ripped off her clothes.[5] Fannie declared, "Why, I'll kill her dead if she ever strikes me again." Fannie is clearly historical mother to Sixo, the ever-self-possessed enslaved African in *Beloved* who grabbed his captor's gun to provoke a stand-off. Cornelia recounted her mother's reaction to the county whippers who had been employed to chastise her for beating Mrs. Jennings:

She knew what they were coming for, and she intended to meet them halfway. She swooped upon them like a hawk on chickens. I believe they were afraid of her or thought she was crazy. One man had a long beard which she grabbed with one hand, and the lash with the other. . . . She was a good match for them. Mr. Jennings came and pulled her away. I don't know what would have happened if he hadn't come at that moment, for one man had already pulled his gun out. Ma did not see the gun until Mr. Jennings came up. On catching sight of it, she said, "Use your gun, use it and blow my brains out if you will." (Rawick, *Unwritten History* 287)

When Fannie declared, as would Brer Rabbit, "I'll go to hell or anywhere else, but I won't be whipped," Jennings decided to send his unbeatable slave out of his Eden, but he told Fannie she could not take her infant, his "property," with her. Truly Garner's (and literarily, Sethe's) sister of struggle, on the day she was to leave, Fannie took her infant, held it by its feet, and, weeping, "vowed to smash its brains out before she'd leave it." Cornelia concludes, "Ma took her baby with her" (Rawick, *Unwritten History* 288). And yet Fannie was not exiled. She and her husband returned from Memphis to Eden and their children with "new clothes and a pair of beautiful earrings" (Rawick, *Unwritten History* 289). Fannie lived the rest of her life in as much peace as her *Àjẹ́* and an oppressive society could afford her. Indicative of biological acquisition of *Àjẹ́*, Cornelia grew to be just as *Àjẹ́*-influenced as her mother.

Cornelia's oral testimony about her mother is included in George P. Rawick's *The Unwritten History of Slavery*. Morrison corrects the ostensible oversight implied in Rawick's title when she writes the history and sprinkles the spirit of Fannie—from swooping vengeance to whip-grabbing standoff to beautiful earrings—throughout *Beloved*. Using the methodology of the traditional Yoruba *Eye Òrò*, Sethe's actions in her sacred space blend the lives of both historical Ìyá, Garner and Fannie. Sethe, as did Margaret Garner, succeeds in killing her third child, the oldest girl. When schoolteacher and his men enter the woodshed, Sethe holds Denver by her feet fully prepared to bash her newly born head open on the rafters. It is apparently important to Sethe, Margaret, and Fannie that the girl-children be made safe, first and foremost. They are the ones who can grow to have their milk stolen, their wombs defiled, their womanhood mocked.

When *Beloved* opens, nearly 18 years after Beloved's death, the home that was a sanctuary for Sethe and countless other displaced Africans is the desolate stomping ground for a wrathful "baby ghost," who is the daughter successfully sent to the other side. Sethe and Denver live alone with the "ghost," exiled from the community not because of fear, but because the community finds Sethe's show of love, similar to that of Suggs, too prideful and selfish. From the outset, a condemnation of the grounds of pride seems a stretch in Sethe's case. She is remembered as holding her head too high and carrying her neck too stiffly as the police led her away. It seems either the community is too judgmental or that Morrison is plying narrative control; however, from a Yoruba perspective, Sethe and Baby Suggs have trespassed a law of *Àjé* that "one must not display wealth" (Opeola). The community, acting very much as a society of traditional African elders would, punishes Baby Suggs with silence after she celebrates her spiritual and material wealth with the magnificent feast. As a runaway slave, Sethe does not even own herself, let alone her children, by American standards. However, she dares to love and protect them with the only means at her disposal. By doing what no other communal member would conceive of doing to protect his or her wealth, Sethe's private work of protection becomes a grandiose display. Her knowledge of her wealth and power is made obvious in her refusal to weep or beg forgiveness for her deed. Showing no remorse and exuding an air of "serenity and tranquility" after her actions, she loses communal respect and consideration.

Sethe's crime of displaying wealth is an ironic one that speaks volumes about the complexities of the Africana community. In an interview with Elsie B. Washington, Morrison elaborated on the centrality of self worth to enslaved Africans in America: "Those people could not live without value. They had prices, but no value in the white world, so they made their own, and they decided what was valuable. It was usually eleemosynary, usually something they were doing for somebody else" (235). Sethe clearly values her children, as is evident in her descriptions of them, and she does for them what no person can do. But her trespass is better understood in the light of Morrison's next statement: "Nobody in the novel, no adult Black person, survives by self-regard, narcissism, selfishness." One could argue that the community doesn't punish Sethe for saving her daughter; they punish the non-communal narcissism surrounding that act.

Sethe clearly understands what has the ultimate value in life and also the role racist oppression plays in devaluing what Nikki Giovanni calls "Black wealth":

> That anybody white could take your whole self for anything that comes to mind. Not just work, kill, or maim you, but dirty you. Dirty you so bad you couldn't like yourself anymore. Dirty you so bad you forgot who you were and could think it up. And though she and others lived through and got over it, she could never let it happen to her own. The best thing she was, was her children. Whites might dirty *her* alright, but not her best thing, her beautiful, magical best thing. (*Beloved* 251)

Although the divine part of Sethe becomes maimed, dirtied, and twisted nearly beyond repair, her children emerge from her womb as whole, perfect, and shining as she once was. The statement, "The best thing she was, was her children," makes it clear that Sethe's act is not just an attempt to save the deified progeny that she has created, but an attempt also to claim the "magical," priceless, and most exquisite aspect of her divine original Self.

Abandoned by every living person except the daughter who nearly became the second recipient of her "thick" love, Sethe and her spiritual and terrestrial daughters exist in a perfect trinity of Mother, Daughter, and Spirit, that is broken only when Sethe goes out to work. 124's isolation from the larger Africana community emphasizes Morrison's point about Sethe's choosing individuality over communality, and it also facilitates the lineage *Àjẹ́*'s unification. Sethe's desire to help her "best thing" understand her actions and Denver's loneliness and frustration move the two women to summon their spiritual third. In invoking Beloved—"come on, come on, you may as well just come on"—Denver and Sethe use power of the word *(Òrò)* to impart unification of spiritual, physical, and geographic planes of existence at 124. In other words, they invite the hidden number three, the unifying spiritual member, to share their material space. Beloved, having received a ritual invitation, begins crossing all boundaries to enter the sacred realm prepared by her mother. However, the existence of enslaved Africans in America imparts a new dimension to invocative transformational juba: Beloved was sent to a safe place through the violent protective *Àjẹ́* of a handsaw. In cosmic reciprocity, it is violence that precipitates her reembodiment.

In Chinua Achebe's *Things Fall Apart*, after a child named Onwumbiko dies, Okagbue, the healer and diviner, gives the corpse special treatment. Because Onwumbiko is an *ogbanje* (*àbíkù* in Yoruba), a spirit child who torments parents by dying soon after birth, Okagbue slashes the corpse, and, holding it by one foot, drags it into the forest for burial.[6] In a revision of Okagbue's treatment of Onwumbiko, Paul D takes a chair and beats Beloved's spirit without mercy as soon as he enters 124 (19). The healer and Paul D seem to have the same thing on their minds: "After such treatment it [the spirit child] would think twice before coming again" (Achebe 54). However, to quote Okagbue, Beloved is "one of the stubborn ones who returned, carrying the stamp of their mutilation—a missing finger or perhaps a dark line where the medicine-man's razor had cut them." Paul D's seemingly successful exorcism actually forces Beloved from the spiritual to the material realm. She arrives, and Sethe takes her in as she would any other young, orphaned African American woman.

Great scholarly debate continues to surge over who Beloved is and what she represents. The common theory that Beloved is a ghost is dubious because she eats, defecates, makes vicious love, dribbles and urinates, and washes and folds clothes on request. Beloved could be defined as ghost prior to Paul D's arrival, but the woman who reveals his Red Heart is no ghost. Morrison describes Beloved as a multifaceted entity: Beloved is "a spirit on one hand, literally she is what Sethe thinks she is, her child returned to her from the dead. And she must function like that in the text. She is also another kind of dead that is not spiritual but flesh, which is, a survivor from the true, factual slave ship. She speaks the language, a traumatized language of her own experience" (Darling 247). Beloved is each of these three things, and being a confluence of all, she is infinitely more.

Beloved reflects and represents all manner of *Àjẹ́*'s "ravage and renewal," for a people locked in the forgetfulness of the atrocities that have befallen them. As a spiritual force of sufficient tangibility to impregnate, Beloved is a ravished girl newly escaped from a defiler's prison: because she is too weak to walk, she glides over the earth or two-steps. Beloved is the "marked" child in African American culture who is affected, *in vitro*, by the horrors the mother witnessed.[7] She is also the *àbíkù* child of the Yoruba—the one born-to-die—who is slashed and scarred to prevent return, but re-enters, from the spirit realm, the traumatized womb for rebirth and perhaps a chance at terrestrial longevity. A child of countless sacrifices and as many Mothers, Beloved bears on her neck the scar of the one for whom she vows to bite away a choking, silencing "iron circle." Beloved, as *Àjẹ́*, is *aláàwọ̀ méjì* (one of two colors). As a spirit, she kneels beside Sethe in white, the hue of ancestral transmigration, and arrives physically at 124 Bluestone Road clothed in black. Seated on the stump of cultural, ethnic, and ancestral cognition, the blackness of Beloved is the life-soil enriching the forgotten roots and the far-flung branches of the African family tree. Describing her journey through the Middle Passage, Beloved is the walking recollection of atrocities too horrible to remember, and she is the Mother who saved her descendants so that they would have the luxury to forget. The Mother whom enslaved Africans first thanked for their safe landings, no matter how vile the journey or the arrival, was Yemoja: the Mother of Waters, the Mother of Fishes. John Mason finds that Yemoja symbolizes the "universal principle of the survival of the species" (308). Beloved is Yemoja's strolling promise. Indeed, when Beloved stalks into the forest at the end of her textual existence, it is not surprising that she bears the Great Mother's fish on her Select/ed Head. Occupying various identities and positions—including those of protagonist, author, and intended Africana audience—Beloved defies any and encompasses all definitions.

As it relates to the textual mother-daughter *Àjẹ́* relationship, in the initial stages of her arrival, Sethe is too close to the truth of Beloved's life, death, and return to recognize her as her daughter. However, Denver, who took mother's milk and sister's blood in one swallow, realizes what one will not reveal and the other cannot see. It is through the slow process of *rememory* that Sethe understands who Beloved is. Carole Boyce Davies defines rememory as "the re-membering or the bringing back together of the disparate members of the family in painful recall," involving "crossing the boundaries of space, time, history, place, language, corporeality and restricted consciousness in order to make reconnections and mark or name gaps and absences" (17). Beloved travels through the cosmic 16 crossroads, where *Àjẹ́* meet (T. Washington 27, 53), to return home to 124. Upon arrival she opens Sethe's "restricted consciousness" and demands the naming and claiming of her dismembered self therein.

As Morrison develops it in *Beloved*, rememory is an unalterable, unforeseeable, and frightening process that is related to material and spiritual spaces and also to books.[8] Beloved initiates the process by which she will be remembered gently. As she sits and watches Sethe comb Denver's hair, she asks, "your woman she never fix up your hair?" and takes Sethe psychically back to the plantation where she grew up and to the mother with whom she had almost no encounters. Sethe verbally rememories that her mother showed her the brand burned into her breast and that her mother was so horribly lynched that "by the time they cut her down nobody could tell whether she had a circle and a cross or not" (61). Before the force of rememory can overwhelm her, the telling of the narrative is transferred. It is Sethe's "restricted consciousness" that rememories being taught an African language by both her mother and her caregiver, Nan. Sethe's rememory enlightens the reader to the fact that her *Àjẹ́* and its methodology are as biologically derived as Fannie's and Cornelia's. Memories of Nan telling Sethe that her mother named her after a man whom she had loved, one whom she had "put her arms around," and that she had killed the products of rape she gave birth to, well up in Sethe's consciousness but do not cross her lips. While Sethe's verbal rememory clearly helps Beloved cement her transitory spiritual self in the material world, the unspoken orature provides a doorway for other dismembered selves to enter.

The subconscious rememories, recounted in third person by an omniscient narrator, are "spaces" that the author and historical and extra-textual communal members must fill (Wilentz 85). For example, Beloved's inquiries about Sethe's "diamonds," her request that Sethe "tell me your earrings," places at the mother's knee the historical Cornelia, who had been briefly abandoned in "Eden"; the fragmented Sethe, who had chosen to forget a gift from "Sweet Home"; the authorial Morrison; and all other seeking survivors. Additionally, in the passage where Sethe's concept of value is defined, as a result of free indirect discourse, the "you" that can be dirtied, shamed, used egregiously, and fouled is at once Sethe, potentially her children, Margaret Garner and her children, and also the reading audience. While it initially appears that the passage is comprised of Sethe's ruminations as directed to

Denver, it is the narrator of *Beloved* who articulates Sethe's logical epiphany on value and opens the discourse and pronouns to include textual and extra-textual audience members. For another example, the question "How did she know?" follows Beloved's first spate of inquires (63). Although the reader assumes Sethe is thinking to herself, the space within the unspecified pronoun is quite wide. "She" can refer as easily to Beloved as to Morrison; furthermore, the query seems subtly directed at readers—as a question *we* must answer, a space *we* are obligated to fill.

As author-narrator, Toni Morrison is clearly the medium of rememory. When the coalescence of history and tragedy are too much for her characters to bear, it is Morrison who writes the "unwritten" and her constructed narrator who verbalizes the "unspoken." It is not Paul D who recounts a flooded wooden cage, the Hi-Man, and a breakfast of horror. He had placed these painful humiliations "one by one, into the tobacco tin lodged in his chest [and] nothing in this world could pry it open" (113). It is Morrison, as other-worldly "Beloved" Self, who, at the three-road junction of history, the spirit realm, and the present, can share Paul D's rememory comprehensively. Expanding Lorde's Afrekete-centered matrix of *Àjẹ́*, the holistic aesthetic of Morrison, the mediating *Ìyá-Ìwé* (Mother of the Text), makes the act of reading *Beloved* an initiation into the Beloved Self, the Beloved Spirit, and the ever-present past for spiritual, historical, and contemporary audiences. As the novel's biblical epigraph makes clear, Beloved is a divine Pan-African paradox: she is human and spirit; recognized and dis-remembered; other and self; novel, character, and reality; *"Sixty Million and more."* The very existence of *Beloved*, let alone our reading the work, becomes a cosmic application of a necessarily stinging bluestone for every Africana person who bears but has ignored the genetic scars of slavery in order to survive but must remember every fragmented affliction in order to heal and evolve fully.

Although Sethe, as most Africana people, cannot safely re-member without sliding into an abyss of pain, she can and does articulate the painful uncontrollable process of rememory to Denver, and explains why she had to open her pot of creativity and place her best, most exquisite and magical creations safely inside it—away from the ever-threatening force of rememory and the more terrifying threat of repetition:

> Someday you be walking down the road and you hear something or see something going on. So clear. And you think it's you thinking it up. A thought picture. But no. It's when you bump into a rememory that belongs to somebody else. Where I was before I came here, that place is real. It's never going away. Even if the whole farm—every tree and grass blade of it dies. The picture is still there and what's more, if you go there—you who never was there—if you go there

and stand in the place where it was, it will happen again; it will be there for you, waiting for you. So Denver, you can't never go there. Never. Because even though it's all over—over and done with—it's going to always be there waiting for you. That's how come I had to get all my children out. No matter what. (36)

Sethe, like so many continental and dislocated Africans, attempts to escape a past that cannot be outrun, a past that follows, taints, and tickles. By using *Àjẹ́* to save her daughter and exorcise the force of Sweet Home from her and her progeny's existence, Sethe consecrates an infinitely more powerful space of rememory. And when Sethe and Denver summon her, Beloved returns with an *Àjẹ́* antithetically equal to the love, intensity, and killing-pain of her mother-self.

Morrison has explained the doubling at work between Sethe and Beloved as what occurs when a "good woman" displaces "the self, her self." Morrison describes that dislocated "self" as the Igbo describe the *chi*, the personal spirit who guides one to one's destiny and as the Yoruba describe the *ẹnìkejì*, the heavenly twin soul with whom one makes agreements before birth. With *Beloved* and also *Jazz*, Morrison has said that she tried to "put a space between [the] words ['your' and 'self'], as though the self were really a *twin* or a thirst or something that sits right next to you and watches you" (Naylor 208). Most relevant to *Beloved*, Babatunde Lawal and Ikenga Metuh make it clear that the *ẹnìkejì* and *chi* can become offended and angered by their earthly representative's actions. Just as the spirit twin can protect its human complement from harm, "offending one's spirit double or heavenly comrade may cause it to withdraw its spiritual protection," leaving one susceptible to death (Lawal 261, Metuh 69–70, respectively). Beloved is more than a daughter; she is Sethe's "self," her "best thing." Like the *chi*, she is a deity to Sethe. However, Sethe's "best thing" revises African cosmology; she withdraws her dubious spiritual protection only to go directly to her mother, at her request no less, for full re-membering.

Beloved, her life, death, and return, represents the juncture between the rememory/reality of Sweet Home, the bonding and bloody jubas of 124, and the cycles of tragically dislocated Africana peoples—who are doomed to repeat past lessons if we fail to remember and evolve from them. As the women at 124 navigate this immense matrix of love and pain, shades of the daughter *Àjẹ́*'s desire to kill her mother, also prevalent in Kincaid's work, emerge in *Beloved*. However, Beloved does not want to destroy Sethe. Instead, she wants the two of them to "join" and return fully unified to the "other side."

In addition to complete re-memberment, Beloved desires free, uninterrupted discourse with the fascinating entity who put her in a safe place of loneliness and confusion. To achieve her aim, Beloved uses her *Àjẹ́* to force Paul D, with his distracting "love" for Sethe, out of 124, and Paul D facilitates the process. Having found out about Sethe's saving action, he demands that Sethe explain what to her is elementary. Rather than answer him directly, Sethe circles—the kitchen, the topic, the answer. She circles as would a buzzard, that spiritual messenger; she moves in the manner of the spirit-hummingbirds that hover over her head. Sethe's circles constitute issue avoidance, and for many reasons: (1) explaining her actions to Paul D would be tantamount to explicating the esoteric to the layman; (2) her actions are beyond the justification that his silent query seeks; (3) Morrison makes it clear that no human being, including the "last of the Sweet Home men," can judge Sethe (Darling 248). The questions Paul D asks belong only to Beloved. But from another perspective, Sethe's circular response to Paul D is also no more than useless perambulation. Until we address the Continental terror that forced millions out of Africa and onto alien lands, concerning bones bleaching in the Atlantic and ancestor-warriors chained on auction blocks, Africana people will run without aim, circle about, and seek out safe havens, but will always bump into that silently waiting and watching self.

Aside from Sethe's reaction, Paul D's inquiry about the newspaper and his counting Sethe's feet make it clear that he is simply not ready, and he does not become prepared until the novel's end, to be the complement that Sethe needs. Paul D is the primary male force in the novel, and it is in his Westernized masculinity—his acts of violence, his audacious attempts to query and judge, his revision of his tender Sethe song, and his refusal to accept Sethe's "thick" love—that his unpreparedness is apparent. Consequently, he is moved out of the sphere and cannot move anything in it.

With the male aspect exorcised, Sethe and Denver harness all their power to re-member Beloved, and with the latter's physical-spiritual reality, the three women become a trinity of Mother, Daughter, and Daughter-Divinity similar to the cosmic matriarchal trinity that Audre Lorde describes in *Zami*. But rather than the shared signifying "I," a possessive "mine" flows among the women: "Beloved, she my daughter. She mine"; "Beloved is my sister"; "I am Beloved and she [Sethe] is mine" (200, 205, 211). Rather than the customary narrative style, to accommodate the space and the unspoken language of love of this trinity of *Àjé*, Morrison uses open-ended lyric free verse:

You are my face; I am you. Why did you leave me who am you?
I will never leave you again
Don't ever leave me again
You will never leave me again
You went in the water
I drank your blood
I brought your milk

You forgot to smile
I loved you
You hurt me
You came back to me
You left me
I waited for you
You are mine
You are mine
You are mine (216–217)

More clearly here, Morrison expands English syntax to accommodate Beloved and to provide space for lost-found souls and intended audience members to enter.[9] With the first line of the passage, *Beloved* becomes a mirror. The fathomless depths of the black ink encompass, absorb, and reflect every communal member, the pages provide reflection and refraction, the margins seem to radiate with unseen but impending revelations. But the glimpse of eternity Morrison offers her reader glints with a different light for Sethe.

Within the rhythms, de-riddling, and reunion of Beloved, Sethe, and Denver are accusations, gatherings-up of pain, demands of ownership, and reminders of debts impossible to pay. Sethe's *ęnìkejì* would ordinarily texture her existence and consciousness from the sacred realm. But in having equated her best self with her children, making the decision to save that precious self, and summoning the self for a discussion, Sethe comes face to face with her spirit, her embodied conscience, and her own (and all her people's) past. As any good mother would, Sethe is resolved to nourish her own and our own "best thing," but she doesn't have the balance, discretion, or distance of the elder in "My Mother," and she may not need it.

Sethe has recognized and become enamored by the living presence of her exquisite self, and she seeks to feed that self:

The bigger Beloved got, the smaller Sethe became; the brighter Beloved's eyes, the more those eyes that used never to look away became slits of sleeplessness. Sethe no longer combed her hair or splashed her face with water. She sat in the chair licking her lips like a chastised child while *Beloved ate up her life, took it, swelled up with it, grew taller on it. And the older woman yielded it up without a murmur.* (250, emphasis added)

Eventually, Beloved forces Denver out of 124, and Beloved and Sethe, like Kincaid's protagonists, revel in the voracious singularity of their duality. The Beloved-Sethe-Self has returned for what she was denied: maternal bonding, verbal milk, and complete reunification. With no other means to appease her physical *ẹnìkejì* (spiritual guide), Sethe gives herself to her Self.

Although the community women understand Beloved to be the slain daughter, she also represents Sethe's best self, that of each of the communal women, and through Morrison's efforts, the best self of all Africana people. Given the all-encompassing totality of Beloved, Sethe's initial saving act is not as selfish as it seems because she saves Beloved, who returns to remind, confound, and heal both textual and extra-textual Africana communities. However, by community standards, Beloved, as an all-in-one Deity, is too complicated, too brilliant, and far too painful for existence. Embracing the most superficial and the least painful aspect of Beloved's multitudinous Self, the communal women gather to destroy the "devil child" who is also their individual and collective "best thing."

The overwhelming and paradoxical truth of Beloved and the grief undergirding their collective consciousness move the women to take "a step back to the beginning." In the beginning, there were no whippings, no bits to suck, no lynching, no sanctioned lessons in racist brutality that tutored Hitler and the Boers. There was only *Òrò*. Rowland Abiodun, in the essay "Verbal and Visual Metaphors: Mythical Allusions in Yoruba Ritualistic Art of *Orí*," reveals the cosmic dimensions of the word *Òrò*. Stating that "words" is a lay translation, *Òrò* is also "a matter, that is something that is the subject of discussion, concern, or action," and it is the "power of the word" (Abiodun 252). An important "matter" and serious subject of concern, Beloved embodies and attracts *Òrò*. And just as *Òrò*, the power of the word, opened the path for wisdom *(ogbón)*, knowledge *(ìmò)*, and understanding *(òye)* to enter the world at the beginning of creation (Abiodun 253–255), so too does the communal women's *Òrò* catalyze their creative, destructive, and interpretive abilities.

The communal mothers converge on 124, and they harmonize the vibrations of *Òrò Àjé*, the vibrations Odùduwà made when she pulled existence out of her Pot. They interrupt Sethe and Beloved's joining and invite them into the Clearing brought to their front lawn. Sethe's carefully nurtured "best thing" emerges as an *àbíkù* soon to give birth:

> The singing women recognized Sethe at once and surprised themselves by their absence of fear when they saw what stood next to her. The devil-child was clever, they thought. And beautiful. It had taken the shape of a pregnant woman, naked and smiling in the heat of the afternoon sun. Thunderblack and glistening, she stood on long straight legs, her belly big and tight. Vines of hair twisted all over her head. Jesus. Her smile was dazzling. (261)

The women's response to the beauty of Sethe's Beloved-Self helps readers better understand the mother's rapture, devotion, and vanity. What is
more, although condemning her in Western terms, the women have no fear
of Beloved, for they know her well. Beloved is, like Denver, "everybody's
child." These women do not bond to exorcise Beloved because she is "evil"
or the "devil." I believe the women gather to destroy her because her presence and their acknowledgment of her reality, which is the answer and the
rememory of each question and event pushed deeply into the subconscious,
would quite simply break their hearts.

Sethe, for all her alleged vanity and pride, appears to be the text's most
progressive figure. Having conferred with Odùduwà, she knows what "value"
is and is not, and she knows how to protect what is priceless, not just for her
personal satisfaction but for the evolution of the community. Sethe also turns
the community's gifts of sustenance for her into sacrifices that nourish Beloved's pregnancy. And it is possible that Beloved's unborn child symbolizes
the perfect and complete healing and evolution of Africana peoples. Additionally, and despite a case of mistaken identity, Sethe's personal development
is apparent in her decision to kill Bodwin, the Euro-American abolitionist
owner of 124.

In this community, still reeling from the horrors of slavery and outraged
by neo-enslavement, it is the external factor, that of Euro-America, that gives
the priceless dollar values, that dirties the best thing, and that textually, moves
stasis to action. Just as with schoolteacher, the arrival of Bodwin, new employer of Denver and owner of a Sambo figurine, expedites the convergence
of the twin circles of *Àjé*. Bodwin is ignorant of two orbs of *Àjé* and his role
in uniting them, but when Sethe sees him approaching, she thinks the defiler has returned, again, to enslave, sully, and steal her "best thing," and she
releases her Spirit Bird: "She hears wings. Little hummingbirds stick their
needle beaks right through her headcloth into her hair and beat their wings.
And if she thinks anything, it is no. No. Nonono. She flies. The ice pick is
not in her hand; it is her hand" (263). When Sethe mounts on wings of *Àjé*
to attack Bodwin, the communal women thwart her, and, again, through violence there is partial unification. The women save Bodwin and re-integrate
Sethe. Her mother's violent community reunion leaves Beloved abandoned,
but smiling. Her ultimate desire for holistic unification aborted, Beloved ex-
plodes, leaving "precious" and "fine" vestiges of her unspeakable self to take
root in the soil, float on the waters, make darker and more defined the ink of
the text, and burrow into the recesses and tickle the consciousness of all too
forgetful minds.

This is healing ink. As blood, it stains memory and mind. Chemical oil
scent laced with indigo, this ink is difficult to wash from the fingertips. It tat-
toos the soul. This ink demystifies sweet homes, discombobulates linear time.

This ink, so Black it is rainbowed, so pure it signifies despite the Ethiopic's salty waters, so rich even its clarity complicates, could only have come from Odùduwà's cosmic womb. Bound by ink-blood oaths, buried solutions, and a proclivity for evolution, Lorde, Kincaid, and Morrison confab with the cosmic and re-fashion the forgotten. Dipping deep into the ink of *Àjé*, their words dance the jubas of mothers and daughters forsaken, lost, and found, and leave lessons to help us re-determine our Destiny.

Notes

1. MawuLisa and Mawu Sebou Lisa are synonymous terms for the West African Mother-Father Deity created by Great Mother Nana Bùrúkù to give the Earth its form, rotation, and revolution, and to provide human beings with knowledge of their destiny through the Book of Fa. The worship of MawuLisa/ Mawu Sebou Lisa, Nana Bùrúkù and other deities in this spiritual system is indigenous to the Fon, Anlo, Ewe, and many other West African peoples. The Vodun deities and the Fa divination system of the Fon are similar to the Òrìsà and the Ifá divination system of the Yoruba. See Gaba 79; M. J. Herskovits 124, 155, 176; and M. J. Herskovits and F. S. Herskovits 135.

2. Sethe witnessed shape-shifting juba as a child (31). The other form of juba represented in *Beloved* is in relation to the character Sixo who, when he was caught fleeing, first grabbed the gun of one of the captors for a stand-off and then began singing as he was burned alive. The narrator describes the words of the song and its rhythm as having a "hatred so loose it was juba" (225–226).

3. Cf. Hayes.

4. Morrison has discussed *Beloved, Jazz,* and *Paradise* as being a quasi-trilogy with the character Beloved being re-embodied in each text. See Cutter, "The Story Must Go On and On."

5. For one woman to "naked" (strip) another in a battle is a common tactic of humiliation I have witnessed several times in West Africa. See Alkali 84–85.

6. See Christopher N. Okonkwo's "A Critical Divination: Reading *Sula* as Ogbanje-Abiku" in *African American Review* 38 (2004): 651–668.

7. See Rawick, *Kansas* 91 and Rawick, *Georgia* 338.

8. In her review of J. Brooks Bouson's *Quiet As It's Kept,* Martha Cutter states, "Repeatedly, my students report that Morrison's novels unsettle and perhaps even traumatize them as readers" (672).

9. Handley discusses Morrison's "incantory powers [to] summon not only ghosts but also readers" (691). Also see Sale 42.

Works Cited

Abiodun, Rowland. "Verbal and Visual Metaphors: Mythical Allusions in Yoruba Ritualistic Art of *Orí." Word and Image Journal of Verbal-visual Inquiry* 3.3 (1987): 252–270.

Achebe, Chinua. *Things Fall Apart.* London: Heinemann, 1958.

Alkali, Zaynab. *The Stillborn.* Essex: Longman, 1988.

Butler, Octavia E. *Wildseed.* New York: Warner, 1980.

Cutter, Martha J. Rev. of *Quiet As It's Kept: Shame, Trauma, and Race in the Novels of Toni Morrison* by J. Brooks Bouson. *African American Review* 35 (2001): 671–672.

———. "The Story Must Go On and On: The Fantastic, Narration, and Intertextuality in Toni Morrison's *Beloved* and *Jazz*." *African American Review* 34 (2000): 61–75.

Darling, Marsha. "In the Realm of Responsibility: A Conversation with Toni Morrison." Taylor-Guthrie 246–254.

Davies, Carole Boyce. *Black Women, Writing and Identity: Migrations of the Subject*. New York: Routledge, 1994.

Davis, Angela. *Women, Race and Class*. New York: Vintage, 1983.

Drewal, Henry John, and Margaret Thompson Drewal. *Gelede: Art and Female Power Among the Yoruba*. 1983. Bloomington: Indiana University Press, 1990.

Fatunmbi, Awo Fa'lokun. *Ìwà-pèlé: Ifá Quest: The Search for Santería and Lucumí*. Bronx: Original, 1991.

Gaba, Christian R. *Scriptures of an African People: Ritual Utterances of the Anlo*. New York: Nok, 1973.

Grant-Boyd, Joan H. Personal communication. 9 Nov. 2000.

Handley, William R. "The House a Ghost Built" *Contemporary Literature* 36.4 (1995): 677–701.

Hayes, Elizabeth T. "The Named and the Nameless: Morrison's 124 and Naytor's 'the Other Place' as Semiotic *Chorae*." *African American Review* 38 (2004): 669–681.

Herskovits, Melville J. *Dahomey, an Ancient West African Kingdom*. Vol. 2. Evanston: Northwestern University Press, 1967.

———, and Frances S. Herskovits, eds. *Dahomean Narrative: A Cross Cultural Analysis*. Evanston: Northwestern University Press, 1958.

Kincaid, Jamaica. "My Mother." *At the Bottom of the River*. New York: Adventura, 1983. 53–61.

Lawal, Babatunde. *The Gèlèdé Spectacle*. Seattle: University of Washington Press, 1996.

LeClair, Thomas. "The Language Must Not Sweat: A Conversation with Toni Morrison." Taylor-Guthrie 119–128.

Lorde, Audre. *Zami: A New Spelling of My Name*. Freedom, NY: Crossing Press, 1982.

Mason, John. *Orin Òrìṣà: Songs for Selected Heads*. Rev. 2nd ed. Brooklyn: Yoruba Theological Archministry, 1992.

Metuh, Emefie Ikenga. *God and Man in African Religion*. London: Geoffrey Chapman, 1981.

Morrison Toni. *Beloved*. New York: Plume, 1987.

———. *Jazz*. New York: Knopf, 1992.

———. *Paradise*. New York: Plume, 1997.

———. *Sula*. New York: Plume, 1973.

Naylor, Gloria. "A Conversation: Gloria Naylor and Toni Morrison." Taylor-Guthrie 188–217.

Ojo, J. R. O. "The Position of Women in Yoruba Traditional Society." *Department of History: University of Ifè Seminar Papers, 1978–1979*. Ile-Ife: Kosalabaro, 1980. 132–157.

Opeola, Samuel Modupeola. Personal communication. Obafemi Awolowo University, Ile-Ife, Nigeria, 1998.

Rawick, George P. *Georgia Narratives Part 3 and 4*. Vol. 13. *The American Slave a Composite Autobiography*. Westport, CT: Greenwood Press, 1972.

———. *Kansas, Kentucky, Maryland, Ohio, Virginia and Tennessee Narratives*. Vol. 16. *The American Slave a Composite Autobiography*. Westport, CT: Greenwood Press, 1972.

————. *The Unwritten History of Slavery*. Vol. 18. *The American Slave: A Composite Autobiography*. Westport, CT. Greenwood Press, 1972.

Sale, Maggie. "Call and Response as Critical Method: African-American Oral Traditions and *Beloved*." *African American Review* 26 (1992): 41–50.

Taylor-Guthrie, Danille, ed. *Conversations with Toni Morrison*. Jackson: University Press of Mississippi, 1994.

Traore, Ousseynou B. "Figuring Beloved/*Beloved:* Re/membering the Body African and Yoruba Mythography." Black Expressive Culture Association Conference. University of Maryland Eastern Shore, Princess Anne. 11 Nov. 2000.

Tutuola, Amos. *The Palm-Wine Drinkard* (1954) and *My Life in the Bush of Ghosts* (1954). New York: Grove, 1994. 17–174.

Washington, Elsie B. "Talk with Toni Morrison." Taylor-Guthrie 234–245.

Washington, Teresa N. "Manifestations of Àjé in Africana Literature." Diss. Obafemi Awolowo University, Ife, Nigeria, 2000.

Wilentz, Gay. *Binding Cultures*. Bloomington: Indiana University Press, 1992.

JEFFREY ANDREW WEINSTOCK

Ten Minutes for Seven Letters:
Reading Beloved's *Epitaph*

You haven't really read something until you've read it as an epitaph, said a friend of a friend of mine to whom I told this title. Tell them that.

Cynthia Chase

"Tell them that." The last reported words from an anonymous "friend of a friend." Taken by itself, the command raises ambiguity to its highest level—the imperative for someone to tell something to others. Read contextually, the implied "you" of the imperative "Tell" is Cynthia Chase. The "them" is the audience at the 1993 New York University conference "Deconstruction is/in America" listening to Chase's "Reading Epitaphs" presentation. The "that" is "You haven't really read something until you've read it as an epitaph." Yet the "that" of Chase's related comment raises even more questions: what is an epitaph? How does one read it? How and why does this reading differ from normal reading—or rather, how does reading something as an epitaph constitute reading in its essence such that texts read otherwise aren't "really read"? And how can something that is not an epitaph be read as an epitaph?

One can begin to approach the dilemmas posed by the idea of reading epitaphs by observing that to read something as an epitaph, as written on a gravestone, is, first of all, to make the relationship between language and

Arizona Quarterly, Volume 61, Number 3 (Autumn 2005): pp. 129–152. Copyright © 2005 Jeffrey Andrew Weinstock.

death explicit—epitaphs are always curious types of dead letters that mediate the relationship between the living and the dead. Reading something as an epitaph forces one to consider the strange materiality of language, the way in which the sign can persist in the absence of both its producer and addressee. The epitaph marks a site of memory, a powerful zone of contact between the living and the dead. It performs the complicated function of calling to mind the departed as departed, that is, of foregrounding the present absence of the beloved. To read the epitaph is to remember its referent, to conjure the dead, while at the same time to be struck by the ephemerality of living. The materiality, the weightiness, the persistence of words literally etched in stone contrast with the fleetingness and fragility of life.

However, can one ever really "read" an epitaph? If the epitaph functions to refer beyond itself, to call to mind the departed, then to read the text of the epitaph as *text*, divorced from its referential function, is not to read it as epitaph. To read an epitaph as a poem, for instance, to celebrate the beauty of its composition rather than to reflect on the absence of the deceased, is not to read it as an epitaph. Contrarily, to read the epitaph as epitaph, as that which commemorates the deceased and insistently gestures towards the present absence of its referent, is not to read the epitaph as text. The question of reading the epitaph therefore introduces an ethical dimension to reading. Is it ethical to consider an epitaph as "literature" and to perform the same critical analyses and manipulations one might apply to, say, a "normal" poem? Can an epitaph be aestheticized and still be an epitaph? The reverse of this question also applies, especially in light of my *epigraph:* can one consider the "normal" poem as *epitaph*? At bottom here is the vexed question of the relationship of language to that which exists outside language. If, as Hegel suggests, the word is the death of the thing, then is not every word, in some sense, an epitaph? The imperative to read as epitaph suggests that somehow reading is connected to absence, that to read is always to recognize or undergo an experience of loss.

In order to approach the subject of spectrality in Toni Morrison's *Beloved* and its relation to language and to the possibility of justice for the living and the dead, one must start with the complex mediation performed by the epitaph, because, from start to finish, *Beloved* is a story about an epitaph, the name "Beloved," "the one word that mattered" etched into "dawn-colored stone" (5). Everything in *Beloved*, from title to last word, circles around the name, the ways in which the word "beloved" connotes both the most intense intimacy and communal gatherings, the celebration of new life together and the sundering of bonds by death. To read Beloved's epitaph, to read *Beloved* as epitaph, is to confront the haunting limitations of language and to engage in a process of mourning that inevitably will fail to capture or reconstitute the other. However, the frightening recognition of loss that the epitaph compels serves as the precondition for learning to live and for the opening of the future as something other than a repetition of the present.

Ten Minutes for Seven Letters

What Derrida says in *Given Time* of Baudelaire's short story "Counterfeit Money," that "it is as if the text did nothing but play with its title" (97), can also be said of Morrison's *Beloved*. From start to finish, as Deborah Horvitz has observed, Morrison's text is "enveloped" by the presence of a problematic *name*—the epitaph "Beloved" carved onto the gravestone of Sethe's "crawling already?" baby, named only in death (157). Prostituting her body to the engraver, "her knees wide open as any grave," Sethe exchanges "ten minutes for seven letters" (5), ten minutes of sex for the inscription of the word "Beloved" on the tombstone of her murdered child. This complicated transaction functions as a nexus of sex, time, and writing, love, lust, hatred, and death. It thus figures in microcosm many of the key terms of the text as a whole.[1] Sethe, in this relationship of exchange, is the lover, her dead child, the beloved, and the engraver the third party who will mediate this relationship between living and dead through language. The relationship between Sethe and her departed child is contrasted with the relationship between Sethe and the engraver, which is not one of tenderness but of tender, of capital. What this contrast foregrounds is the insistent theme of Morrison's text that there is no beloved of a transaction. One of the most dramatic movements of Morrison's text is its insistence that love relationships must exist outside of the economy of exchange and possession.

The irony of the phrase "ten minutes for seven letters" lies in the disparate valuations of the epitaph to the engraver, to Sethe, and to the reader. The seven letters that she chooses mean nothing more to the engraver than the opportunity to vent his lust, while they, as epitaph, as "the one word that mattered" from the preacher's eulogy, as an expression of love, mean significantly more to Sethe—a value not reducible to a cost per letter. And, beyond Sethe's desire to remember her daughter, these same seven letters govern the entire momentum of the text for the reader, serving as its title, the text's last word, and designating one of its central characters. The overwhelming irony of the reduction of "Beloved" to ten minutes is most evident when one observes that Beloved herself is symbolic of the "sixty million and more" Africans who died during the Middle Passage of slavery. The whole structure of Morrison's text works to counter this tragic reduction that seeks to measure lives in terms of minutes (in this respect, it is significant that Beloved's tombstone bears no dates), or to calculate the value of lives in terms of units of material exchange.

The overdetermination of the epitaph "beloved" functions on several levels to foreground the mediation of language between self and other and living and dead. As Caroline Rody observes, the term "expresses at once the greatest anonymity and the dearest specificity" (104). It is the private name each person gives to his or her most intimate relations and personal treasures. However, in addition to serving as "an address conferred by the lover on the object of affection," the term "beloved" also names everyone in the impersonal rhetoric of the Church and, as noted by May G. Henderson, is "used in matrimonial and eulogistic discourse, both commemorative, linguistic events: the former prefiguring the future, the latter refiguring the past" (67). In the "Dearly Beloved" of the marriage ceremony and the funeral eulogy, the term "beloved" unites the celebrants or mourners in a present moment of anticipation or commemoration. In its public contexts, it functions simultaneously in two capacities, marking both the specific relationship of the affianced to each other or the bereaved to the deceased, and the general relation of the Church to all. In its various uses, the term thus connects public with private, the intimacy of the individual love relationship with communal gatherings of both celebration and grief. The term also structures a tension between the timeless present of one's most intimate encounters and the communal marking of time through the rememoration of significant events in the lives of individuals—particularly the joining of marriage and the passing of death. The use of the term, at least in its public contexts, thereby marks a vacillation, a wavering in time, the fullness of a present marked by a past—and an openness to a future beyond the event.

The name "Beloved" thus acts on several levels, as Valerie Smith remarks, as "a site where a number of oppositions are interrogated" (350). As an epitaph on a tombstone, the "public inscription of a private memorial" (Henderson 67), as well as an element of Church rhetoric and a term that everyone deploys to identify her or his own most intimate relations, it serves to link public to private. In its use in public contexts, it serves to foreground the presentness of both the past and the future. However, as Smith observes, the word "beloved" itself is a site of opposition and ambiguity. "Simultaneously adjective and noun, the world [sic] problematizes the distinction between the characteristics of a thing and the thing itself" (350).

This instability of the word, a word that deprived of context can be either noun or adjective, that vacillates in time, that figures both intimate moments and public gathering, arises from the fact that, as Morrison's text is well aware, "beloved," by itself, is nothing. For there to be a beloved, or for someone to be beloved, there must be a lover. Conversely, if there is a lover, there must be a beloved. Herein lies the ambiguity and imperative of Morrison's title: the starkness of this overdetermined epitaph demands some sort of context. Beloved of whom? Morrison's text does a neat spin on this question by making both it and its inverse, "who is Beloved?" two of the most important questions of the text. The answers to both these questions replicate the tendency of the term "beloved" itself to vacillate between private and public, to slip beyond the borders of any singular context.

The term "beloved" thereby functions metonymically, always gesturing beyond itself toward some other term. Separated from the rest of the preacher's funeral eulogy, "Beloved" points backward to "Dearly" and forward to the rest of the oration. Sethe wonders, "With another ten could she have gotten 'Dearly' too?" (5). What Sethe is able to purchase with her body is a link from a longer chain of language addressed to the community in general. Her extraction of the term "beloved" from the rest of the funeral eulogy, her mistaking the "Dearly Beloved" as an address to her dead child rather than to the assembled crowd (Rody 104), and, finally, the decontextualized "Beloved" of the epitaph, function as failures of language—failures that figure the complex relationship of public to private in the novel and implicate the community in the circumstances of her daughter's demise and subsequent return—that complicate but do not efface Sethe's own accountability for her actions.

The text of *Beloved* enacts a movement from public to private as Sethe withdraws from the world following Beloved's return, and then shifts from private back to public as Denver steps out into the yard to seek assistance from the community—the same community initially connected to the events leading up to primal scene of Beloved's murder. What is important about this is that Beloved is thus both Sethe's personal ghost and a communal problem. Indeed, Beloved's return and expulsion ultimately result in the reintegration of Denver, and, to a certain extent, Sethe, into the community. The return of the dead thus acts on a personal level for Sethe as the disruption of social bonds and simultaneously acts on a communal level as an imperative toward cooperation and healing.

Beloved, as a ghost story, turns on the various significations and resonances of its title. To read *Beloved*, one therefore must engage in the vexing task of reading epitaphs—which is to allow oneself to be haunted by the absence toward which the epitaph gestures. This situation is made even more complicated by Morrison's use of the term "beloved" to designate both one and many. Caroline Rody observes that, although the name "Beloved" refers to everyone in the rhetoric of the Church and names everyone who is intimately loved, it "does not name the forgotten" (104). She continues, "Morrison has the name perform precisely this last function; the novel's defining conceit is to call the unnamed 'beloved.' Part of Beloved's strangeness derives, then, from the emotional burden she carries as a symbolic compression of innumerable forgotten people in one miraculously resurrected personality, the remembering of the 'sixty million' in one youthful body" (104).

What Rody refers to as Beloved's "strangeness," the fact that she simultaneously incarnates the return of Sethe's murdered child and symbolizes the African holocaust of the Middle Passage, the "Sixty Million and more" of

Morrison's dedication, one might also consider as the complexity of the novel itself "its allegorical overlay. Beloved, inseparable from her name, is both one and many, and Beloved the ghost, like "beloved" the epitaph, mediates between private and public, self and other, and living and dead. The haunting she performs pushes Sethe, her community, and the reader toward the momentous recognition of the possibility of loss and, as a result, introduces the necessity of mourning—mourning that fails to domesticate the strangeness of absence and thereby introduces a "chance for the future."

The Social Structuration of Haunting

Avery Gordon, in her *Ghostly Matters: Haunting and the Sociological Imagination,* insists that "haunting is a constitutive feature of social life" (23). A haunting describes "how that which appears to be not there is often a seething presence" (8). Gordon explains, "A disappearance is real only when it is apparitional because the ghost or the apparition is the principal form by which something lost or invisible or seemingly not there makes itself known or apparent to us" (63): The ghost, in other words, functions as the trace of an absent presence, the "evidence of things not seen" (195). And, as Gordon points out, only that which has not been completely forgotten can return as a ghost. Ghosts are inducts of uneasy minds—of problematic knowing—not complete ignorance.

In the case of the specific story of Sethe's murder of her daughter, Beloved can be read as the return of Sethe's murdered "crawling already?" baby. However, to read Beloved's return as solely the "return of the repressed" of Sethe is mistaken. As Sally Keenan observes, "Sethe has not forgotten either her daughter or the fact that she killed her ... suggesting that remembering or acknowledgment is not the problem, but, rather, how to forget, how to lay the past to rest, is" (71).[2] Importantly, this past is not purely Sethe's past, nor can she "lay it to rest" on her own. Indeed, the moral dilemma intrinsic in the attempt to judge Sethe's actions—a difficulty evident in the ways in which the huge mass of critical literature carefully evades even the question of Sethe's accountability for her crime—lies in the complex web of social forces that result in the act.[3] Sethe's "tough response to the Fugitive Slave Bill" (171), her decision to kill her children rather than allow them to he remanded back into slavery, is the culmination of her personal experience as a black woman living in the social context of the existence of black slavery. She is placed in an impossible situation—the only way to keep her children is to lose them, the only place where they will be safe is in death (164). Additionally, her actions also result from the failure of the black community to warn the residents of 124 of the approaching horsemen. Jan Furman observes that the black community in *Beloved* "fails its obligation" to Sethe when it "betrays Baby Suggs and her family by failing to warn of what they instinctively know is trouble"

(72). This failure of communication is then continued when Sethe extracts the one word "beloved" from the funeral eulogy and uses it, at least in part, as a *weapon* against the community, as an answer to "one more preacher, one more abolitionist, and a town full of disgust" (5).

Sethe's actions, therefore, cannot be excised from the social context in which they occur, and the return of Beloved, the presence of the ghost, the "fearful claim of the past on the present" (Rody 104), is not an isolated event affecting Sethe, but a social phenomenon implicating the community and the culture at large that facilitated Sethe's action. Beloved's return affects the community since it, through "spite, jealousy, and meanness" (Furman 72), allowed the conditions for Sethe's act to develop. Ultimately, it is the community that must come together at the end of the novel to expel Beloved, which points to the social constitution of haunting and the collective nature of memory itself.

That haunting is a social phenomenon is most readily apparent in *Beloved* when one considers Beloved as the symbol for the millions who died during the Middle Passage. As Gordon observes, *Beloved* "is about the lingering inheritance of racial slavery, the unfinished project of Reconstruction, and the compulsions and forces that all of us inevitably experience in the face of slavery's having even once existed in our nation. Slavery has ended, but something of it continues to live on. . . . Such endings that are not over is what haunting is about" (139). Beyond the particular story of the return of Sethe's murdered child, beyond even the implication of Sethe's community in her crime and its results, *Beloved*, as a contemporary ghost story, as an effort at "reclamation" (Morrison, "A Conversation" 199), is the attempt to address a contemporary haunting, the social trauma of slavery that lives on in American culture. Implicit in Morrison's project of reclamation of black history is the objective of healing. Keenan remarks that "If Beloved's spectral return into the slave family represents within the narrative the eruption of that which has lived on as memory but has remained unspoken, the text, *Beloved*, signals a current discursive renegotiation with their history by African Americans which amounts to a contestation of the ways that past has been erased or subsumed within the historical discourse of hegemonic culture" (48). Reclaiming or revisioning this history in the present is thus proposed as part of a healing process directed at the wounds of a traumatic past. However, as I will argue below, the most dramatic recognition prompted by Beloved's uncanny irruption is that the forgotten, and, by extension, the past itself, cannot he recovered or recover. The opening of a future-yet-to-come, a future different from that which can be envisioned today, is contingent upon learning to read epitaphs, on learning to preserve the alterity of the other by mourning the lostness of the lost.

The Oppressed Past

Caroline Rody writes that "*Beloved* is manifestly about the filling of historical gaps" (93) and suggests that one consider fiction such as *Beloved* as "structures of historiographic desire," that is, as "attempts to span a vast gap of time, loss, and ignorance to achieve an intimate bond, a bridge of restitution or healing, between the authorial present and the ancestral past" (97). Morrison herself speaks of this process as one of "assuming responsibility" ("In the Realm" 247) for the forgotten and the dispossessed. This responsibility, is one of "artistically burying" the unburied ("A Conversation" 209), that, Morrison acknowledges as "just one step" in the process of the reclamation of black history ("Interview With Toni Morrison" 413). However, the pressing questions here are how does one remember the forgotten? How can one bear witness to what one has not experienced? And to what extent can a work of *fiction*, a ghost story, participate in these endeavors?

In an interview with Christina Davis, Morrison explains that:

> The reclamation of the history of black people in this country is paramount in its importance because while you can't really blame the conqueror for writing history his own way, you can certainly debate it. There's a great deal of obfuscation and distortion and erasure, so that the presence and the heartbeat of black people has been systematically annihilated in many, many ways and the job of recovery is ours. It's a serious responsibility and one single human being can only do a very very tiny part of that, but it seems to me to be both secular and non-secular work for a writer. ("Interview with Toni Morrison" 413)

Morrison is thus participating in, to quote Walter Benjamin, the "fight for the oppressed past" ("Theses" 263). She recognizes, with Hortense Spillers, that "[Events] *do* occur, to be sure, but in part according to the conventions dictating how we receive, imagine, and pass them on" (176). This is to say that there ire multiple perspectives on any given event and one perspective assumes prominence only at the expense of other, competing interpretations. In the rewriting of the event, the revisioning of history that the ghost prompts, Gordon observes that, "a different story or history is made possible" (163). For Gordon, the encounter with the ghost is the moment at which one no longer can stand divorced from history and objectively survey its field. Rather, in experiencing a haunting, the wheels of history stop and one is faced with uncertainty, with the disturbing realization that something is missing, that the story is incomplete.

The ghost, as the trace of an absent presence, thus has ethical ramifications for Gordon; it is both "the symptom of something missing" and a "loss," but also "a future possibility, a hope" (64). It can "lead you toward what has been missing" (58) and "mak[e] you see things you did not see before" (98). Ultimately, it "forces a reckoning" (130). The ghost as such is a "living force" (179) that pushes those who encounter it toward a "something to be done" (203). Yet how can a work of fiction, a ghost story, participate in the task of historical reclamation and prompt this something to be done? How can *Beloved* fight for the oppressed past?

In her essay, "The Site of Memory," Morrison comments explicitly on the line between history and fiction in her writing, a negotiation that she describes as "literary archeology." She writes, "on the basis of some information and a little bit of guesswork you journey to a site to see what remains were left behind and to reconstruct the world that these remains imply. What makes it fiction is the nature of the imaginative act: my reliance on the image—on the remains—in addition to recollection, to yield up a kind of truth" (112). Morrison thus attempts to reconstitute a life from an epitaph—in a sense, to summon spirits—to imagine what is missing based on the remains.

Intriguingly, in this process of imaginative reconstruction, Morrison does not oppose truth and fiction. Rather, she writes, "the crucial distinction for me is not the difference between fact and fiction, but the distinction between fact and truth. Because facts can exist without human intelligence, but truth cannot" (113). To gain access to the interior life of historical subjects, to "rip the veil drawn over 'proceedings too terrible to relate'" (110), to get at the *truth* of historical silences and forgettings, "Only the act of the imagination can help" (111). Attempting to get at the truth, to do justice to the dispossessed, and, in the process, to live more justly oneself, therefore depends precisely upon the act of imagining. What Morrison indicates is that sometimes fiction paradoxically can be more "truthful" than facts. Or rather, the imagination "animates the remains," brings "dead" facts to life in such a way so as to turn "inhuman" facts into a living narrative. The imagination thereby provides a framework for learning, for comprehending undigestable facts. And yet to read a story as epitaph is to remember not only that any story is never the whole story, that the real, the other, always exceeds, escapes language, but also that the imaginative animation of the remains cannot help but to foreground what is missing. The task of recovery, of reclamation, therefore also entails a letting go, a recognition of loss, and healing, learning to live for the future, requires a mourning of and for the past. Reading epitaphs is both about remembering the dead and remembering to live before one joins them. Reading epitaphs is about summoning spirits and coming to terms with ghosts, not about exorcising them.

Learning to Live

In this respect, philosopher Jacques Derrida's comments in the "Exordium" to his *Specters of Marx* are particularly striking. Derrida begins by writing, "someone, you or me, comes forward and says: *I would like to learn to live finally*" (xvii)—a remarkably strange turn of phrase, as Derrida himself notes. Why does anyone need to learn this? And how? And from whom? And why "finally"? The phrase implies that one can be alive without living, that, paradoxically, living needs to be learned, and that this learning is a task. The weight that Derrida places on this task is suggested by the finality of the "finally": at the end of it all, after having lived without living—or having forgotten how to live—to be left with living. The finality of "finally" implies that one can only learn to live by encountering the end, the limit of life, by and through death, through "com[ing] to terms with death" (xviii). Derrida writes, "If it—learning to live—remains to be done, it can happen only between life and death. Neither in life nor death *alone*" (xviii). Life, by itself, is meaningless. Without the fact of mortality, learning to live is impossible, for life would not be a gift, and living would lack all urgency. For Derrida, this task of learning to live is "ethics itself" (xviii) and "has no sense and cannot be *just* unless it comes to terms with death" (xviii).

Learning to live and coming to terms with death can only happen in the between, in an uncanny space between life and death—which is the space and time of the ghost. Derrida continues, "What happens between two, and between all the 'two's' one likes, such as between life and death, can only *maintain itself* with some ghost, can only *talk with or about* some ghost [s'entretenir *de quelque fantôme*]. So it would he necessary to learn spirits" (xviii). Learning to live thus means to "learn spirits," to learn to live *with* spirits, which is to learn to live with a restless past and one's own being-towards-death. And this "being-with specters," this acceptance of spirits, which also amounts to a "*politics* of memory, of inheritance, and of generations" (xix), allows one to live "otherwise" and "more justly" (xviii)—because justice entails a responsibility both to the dead and the still to be born: "No justice . . . seems possible or thinkable without some *responsibility*, beyond all living present . . . before the ghosts of those who are not yet born or who are already dead" (xix).

Derrida goes on to identify the classes of these already dead to which one owes some debt, toward which one bears some responsibility: "victims of wars, political or other kinds of violence, nationalist, racist, colonialist, sexist, or other kinds of exterminations, victims of the oppressions of capitalist imperialism or any of the forms of totalitarianism" (xix). The ghosts that come back to haunt, "these unburied, or at least unceremoniously buried" dead (Morrison, "A Conversation" 209), victims of the most extreme acts of violence, raise the question of the possibility of justice in its starkest form—how can justice be served? How can one discharge a debt to the dead? How can hurt be undone? These are not happy spirits or friendly ghosts that return. The question that Derrida raises here—and that *Beloved* forcefully engages—is the question of how to live with these spirits, victims of brutal violence, victims of the Middle Passage. How does one live with a history or an inheritance that is too painful or shameful to be remembered—one that an individual or a community or an entire culture desperately wishes to forget—and yet which is too important to be forgotten? How can one do justice to the dead and, if this is the task that is required to live justly, or to learn to live at all, is learning to live even possible?

For Derrida, the opening of the future as something other than a repetition of the present is dependent precisely upon the work of mourning, and, importantly, on mourning that never succeeds fully in working through or domesticating the trauma of loss, mourning that fails in "introjecting" the absent loved one. The absence of the other remains and this absence, this loss, can never be filled with words, can never itself be articulated completely. The epitaph gestures toward the absence that remains.[4] Against this absence of the other, narcissism reaches a limit as "we realize that, will what we might, we cannot rewrite the other back into life, remaking history so that she is still with us. She is gone. In her very absence we feel the pull of otherness" (Cornell 73). One can remember, but not recall to life. For Derrida, one cannot eliminate the absence of the other that propels one to mourn.

However, as Drucilla Cornell notes, "Ironically, it is only through this failure to fully recollect the Other that we 'succeed' in mourning the Other as Other" (73). To mourn the "Other as Other" is to recognize the otherness of the other, to understand, in a sense, the fullness of the other that exceeds all knowing, overflows all attempts at circumscription and containment. Derrida writes, "we learn that the other resists the closure of our interiorizing memory. With the nothing of this irrevocable absence, the other appears *as* other" (*Memoires* 34). The absence of the other that cannot be overcome points to a fullness of the other that cannot be recreated by memory or language. The recognition of this loss, this absence that remains is, according to Derrida, a strange type of success, a gesture of respect toward the otherness of the other: "the *failure succeeds:* an aborted interiorization is at the same time a respect for the other as other, a sort of tender rejection, a movement of renunciation that leaves the other alone, outside, over there, in his death, outside us" (*Memoires* 35).

In mourning, one confronts the "remains," the "beyond," that which exists outside of systems of representation, that which resists conscious knowing, resists articulation—that which can only be experienced as loss. But, as Cornell writes, "it is the very failure of mourning as mimetic interiorization that allows us to attempt fidelity to the remains. The inevitable failure of memory to enclose the Other, opens us to the 'beyond'" (73). Mourning thus becomes both crucial and, in a sense, impossible. One must grapple with absence, with the past, knowing that loss can never be eliminated or overcome fully. This painful experience of loss and the resistant residue of otherness opens one to the "beyond," to the recognition of incompleteness, to the recognition of the limitations of signifying systems, and to the frightening yet potentially liberating prospect of other ways of thinking. An openness to or opening of the beyond is the openness to difference, to a different future, a future yet-to-come.[5] Only where the possibility of loss exists can things be found. Cornell concludes that, "the chance for the future . . . is preserved in the work of mourning which ironically remembers the remains through the experience of the limit of interiorization, through the very finitude of memory that makes 'true' mourning impossible, and yet so necessary" (75).

Justice, in Cornell's reading of Derrida, is "our singular responsibility to the Other" (143), and "doing justice" to the *memory* of the other takes place through incomplete mourning, through the absence of the other that remains, through the otherness of the other that resists assimilation to the same. *Beloved*, I suggest, in its attempt to do justice to the memory of the lost and dispossessed, is not about the process of filling in historical gaps, as Caroline Rody contends (93). Nor is it a project of "historical recovery" (Krumholz 395). Both these descriptions imply that a coherent, singular, "truthful" narrative of history could be established if only certain missing pieces could be unearthed. A project of "historical recovery" suggests that history is in some sense an organic body, sick or lost, but potentially sound, whole, and present.[6]

On the contrary, Morrison's narrative suggests that history will not recover, that, as Morgenstern asserts, there is "no easy cure" (117), and I do not believe that *Beloved* is about the "filling in" of anything. I suggest that it is instead about loss, about emptiness, about emptying. To the extent that it is about recovery, it is precisely about first recovering or experiencing the "beyond" as *loss:* the loss of history and history as loss. This process of recovering lostness, as opposed to the filling in of gaps, means to recognize and appreciate gaps as gaps, to recognize the terrifying fact that some things *can* be lost forever. It necessitates a coming to grips with the fact that certainty is never possible, and that action must take place precisely in the *absence* of cognitive mastery. Finally, the idea of filling in gaps which I would describe as the denial of the possibility of loss—is also the attempt to side-step the painful process of mourning—indeed, to avoid the frightening prospect of an interminable mourning that will never succeed fully in "closing the circle" around lost experience. But it is this encounter with lostness and the necessity of mourning that are crucial if the opening of a different future is to be envisioned. Morrison's text, I suggest, in juxtaposing Sethe's "recovery" of narrative with Beloved's breakdown of narrative, proposes that it is only by *having* loss, owning lostness, that one can avoid *being lost* altogether. Ghosts in this sense are symptomatic of failures of mourning, the failure to recognize loss. The ghost points to a gap, a loss, an absence. *Beloved* demands that one mourn the lost as lost, to preserve their lostness, their disappearance, even as one seeks to "resurrect" their stories—to remember the lost in their lostness so as to open the possibility of a different future—a just future, a future of justice yet-to-come.

Necessary Impossible Telling

Alongside of the specific story of Sethe's murder of Beloved, there is another story, a twofold tragedy of disappearance and forgetting—the deaths of the "sixty million and more" Africans during the Middle Passage. Baby Suggs points out to Sethe, "There's more of us they drowned than there is all of them ever lived from the start of time" (244). Of these millions, Morrison writes, "No one praised them, nobody knows their names, nobody can remember them, not in the United States or Africa. Millions of people disappeared without a trace, and there is not one monument anywhere to pay homage to them, because they never arrived safely on shore. So it's like a whole nation that is under the sea" (qtd. in Furman 80). It is from this place of forgetting that Beloved emerges and, as Karla Holloway observes, she is "not only Sethe's dead daughter returned, but the return[ed] of all the faces, all the drowned, but remembered, faces of mothers and their children who have lost their being because of the force of that EuroAmerican slave-history" (ibid.).[7] Or, as Susan Bowers concisely puts it, "Beloved is the embodiment of the collective pain and rage of the millions of slaves who died on the Middle Passage" (66). But Morrison's attempt at reclamation, at remembering the disremembered, at telling the story of the forgotten again raises the issue of her distinction between truth and fact and the issue of the ethics of memory. How can Morrison use fiction in the "fight for the oppressed past"? How can Morrison do justice to the departed? And, in reference to historical catastrophes such as slavery, is it in fact ethical to attempt to reintegrate the events into narrative memory, to force them into stable, communicable, comprehensible configurations? Cathy Caruth raises these same questions in her discussion of *Hiroshima, Mon Amour* when she poses the questions of the ethics of narration and of how not to "betray" the past (*Unclaimed* 27). What Caruth proposes, following Shoshana Felman and Claude Lanzmann, is that the possibility of a "faithful" history arises out of an "indirectness of telling" (27) and a "creative act of listening" (Introduction 154). As numerous critics have noted, *Beloved* provides the former and demands the latter.

Beloved is not a text that progresses from start to finish in a linear fashion. Neither does it have a singular, stable narrator. Rather, like Sethe in her kitchen, attempting to tell Paul D something for which she has no words, for which words fail—why she killed her daughter—the text "circles" around its subjects. Philip Page remarks that "[Sethe] cannot say directly what she did or why, so the narration does tell the story directly. . . . The novel is like the circle Sethe spins, collecting, omitting, repeating fragments. . . . It tends to drop an unexplained fact on the reader, veer away into other matters, then circle back with more information about the initial fact, then veer away again, circle back again, and so on" (140–141). And part of the novel's "obliqueness" (141) is its multiple and overlapping points of view. This "deviousness" (141) of the text, the resistance of the narrative, is most evident during the middle section of the text in which identity dissolves as the voices of Sethe, Denver, and Beloved intertwine, and especially during Beloved's monologue, in which the text itself threatens to unwind altogether.[8]

What Beloved's disarticulated monologue reveals is the impossibility of telling, the impossibility of recovering the stories of the dispossessed, of explaining the horror of the Middle Passage, of articulating death. Morgenstern observes that, "What most needs to be said in the novel defies narrative form" (118), and Beloved's monologue is the moment in the story when the text literally falls apart through the introduction of spatial gaps and the absence of punctuation. Here, where logic fails, the historical power of trauma is experienced in and through the experience of a gap, of a not knowing. Valerie Smith writes that, "this section of the novel resists explication. It prompts, rather, the recognition that what is essentially and effectively unspoken can never be conveyed and comprehended linguistically" (352). Mobley proposes that the literal gaps left in the text during this section "signal the timelessness of [Beloved's] presence as well as the unlived apaces of her life" (362), but they also figure the resistance of trauma to telling, of the secrets of the unknown to being solved.[9] One might wish to consider Beloved's monologue figuring both her individual death and the Middle Passage of slavery as the horrific Middle Passage of both the text and of language itself. Her monologue actualizes on the levels of text and language fears of fragmentation, of exploding and being swallowed up (133). On this leaky ship of language, meaning slips away through the cracks.

However, one may ask, as Derrida does of translation, what if this "disadjustment," this disarticulation of the text, is in fact the very condition of attempting to do justice to the victims—or the memory of the victims—of the Middle Passage? (*Specters* 19–20). What Morrison avoids doing in Beloved's monologue is making any attempt at rendering either Beloved's experience of death or the deaths of millions readily intelligible. Rather than to try to represent coherently horror that exceeds intelligible frameworks, Morrison attempts to convey or transmit horror, to allow the reader to experience horror, through the performative "breakdown" or "breakage of words."

In *Testimony*, Shoshana Felman discusses the resistance of the Holocaust to intelligibility. Any attempt to explain it can only result in reduction. For Felman, it is the "breakage of words" that *acts* (39). When language breaks down, when gaps are introduced, when comprehension is problematized, language begins to act, to enact, to perform, rather than report. Following Felman, one may propose that the "breakage of words" of *Beloved*'s monologue functions performatively to enact and communicate horror without attempting to explain it or reduce it. The textual spaces, the gaps, the play of perspective and voice are all strategies that Morrison employs to fulfill her "single gravest responsibility": "not to lie" ("Site of Memory" 113). To try and speak the horror of infanticide and holocaust, to contain overwhelming emotions and experiences in a structured narrative, would be to betray the past. Paradoxically, Morrison can only speak the truth by not speaking it, and the trauma can only be remembered and mourned through the reader's involvement and witnessing.

What *Beloved* demands is the reader's active participation in the process of constructing meaning and memory. Morrison is explicit concerning this narrative strategy and comments in several different interviews and articles about her partnership with the reader. She observes addressing ambiguities in her texts, "These spaces, which I am filling in, and can fill in because they were planned, can conceivably he filled in with other significances. This is planned as well. The point is that into these spaces should fall the ruminations of the reader and his or her invented or recollected or misunderstood knowingness" ("Unspeakable" 29). In *Beloved*, the reader's participation is pivotal in as much as the reader's piecing together of the textual fragments amounts to the piecing together of a damaged past, functions as a way to "evolve a subjective language with which to attach different meanings to slavery outside the ways in which it has become fixed in historiography and myth" (Keenan 55).

Ultimately, what *Beloved* demands is that the reader, like Ella, "listen for the holes" (92), or, as Dori Laub puts it, the listener to trauma "must *listen to and hear the silence*, speaking mutely both in silence and in speech, both from behind and from within speech" (58). This listening for the holes, listening to silence, is an act of "creative listening," one that allows a story to emerge that the teller cannot know in the process of telling. And the listener, by virtue of the listening, becomes implicated in the event: "By extension, the listener to trauma comes to be a participant and a co-owner of the traumatic event: through his very listening, he comes to partially experience trauma in himself" (Laub 57). The reader's active participation in the construction of *Beloved* functions as a witnessing to the historical trauma of slavery and the Middle Passage and, to the extent that *Beloved*'s "breakage of words" functions as performative testimony, moves the reader to feel the "bewilderment, injury, confusion, dread, and conflicts that the trauma victim feels" (Laub 58), one can say in Caruth's terms that the "falling" or "departure" of the text, its impossibility of telling, *impacts* on the reader—that the "ghost of reference" returns in the very disarticulation of the text itself. In the absence of knowing, one is moved by an epitaph that haunts.

Passing On

The ghost therefore presents an impossible task—to attempt to negotiate an unstable past and to speak what cannot he spoken fully. This dilemma is most forcefully imposed by the radical ambiguity of her thrice repeated insistence that the story of Beloved was and to "not a story to pass on" (274–275)—that suggests simultaneously that the story is one that should not be bypassed and that the story is one that should not be communicated. The paradox of speaking the unspeakable remains unresolved and doing justice to the dead, in the sense of redressing past injuries, impossible. What can be done with the aporetic conclusion of a story not to pass on, of a story that is too painful to remember but must he remembered to prevent it from being repeated? Morrison's answer is a "creative listening" and imaginative revisioning that listens to the silences of traumatic history and, rather than trying to fill them in, appreciates the silences as silences.

To move through *Beloved* is to undergo the ordeal of undecidability. Morrison's ghost Beloved gestures toward these gaps and Beloved's story is a "laying along side" of a different story against the historical record. The injustices done to the dead can never be redressed. However, justice can be done to their memories by remembering their stories in order to open a different future, an always yet-to-come future of justice. And this necessary remembrance is not just the unearthing of facts to fill in gaps in the historical record. Rather, it is an interrogation of the record itself, the constant reminder that one story assumes prominence at the expense of others and that what is necessary to recover these other, forgotten stories is the act of imagining. Truth, Morrison tells us, differs from facts. And justice, Derrida notes, is different from law—and the gap between each is the space in which the ghost returns to open up the possibility of a future-to-come different from what one can imagine in the present.[10]

Although Morrison writes that "By and by all trace is gone, and what is forgotten is not only the footprints but the water and what is down there," the last word of the text, "Beloved," belies this forgetting for the tombstone of the "crawling already?" baby and its overdetermined epitaph remain. To learn to live with ghosts is neither to reject the past, nor to let it overwhelm the present. Rather to live with ghosts is "to be haunted in the name of a will to heal," which means to "allow the ghost to help you imagine what was lost that never even existed, really" (Gordon 57). And this imagining cannot be done alone. In *Beloved*, it is the community that rallies to expel Beloved, and Paul D who returns Sethe to herself, thus opening for her a chance for a future. The last word of the text, which circles back around to the title and the beginning, reminds one that Beloved belongs to each of us individually and all of us together. *Beloved* demands to be read as an epitaph. The starkness of the title and the unspeakable incommensurability of "ten minutes for seven letters" is crushing. The ethical imperative that it sets forth is for one to recognize the immensity and terrifying reality of loss. *Beloved* structures an encounter with lostness and introduces the necessity of mourning the lost as lost so as to open the possibility of a different future. Finally, what Sethe and Denver learn to do, at the end of it all, is to live. And it is a ghost that teaches them how.

Notes

The author wishes to thank Jeffrey Jerome Cohen, Elissa Marder, Marshall Alcorn, Christopher Sten, Robert Samuels, Elizabeth Grosz, and Jean Wyatt, all of whom read various versions of this essay and offered helpful commentary.

1. Scruggs suggests that Sethe's fornication with the stonecutter is not just payment but an act of penance (189), in which case, one may add "guilt" to the list of essential terms manifest in the encounter.

2. However, although Sethe clearly has not forgotten or repressed the past, she also has not "worked through" the trauma of the loss of her baby girl. Caruth's description of trauma survivors as not possessing but "possessed" (Introduction 5) by an event or image is clearly applicable to Sethe who undergoes the "literal return of the event" against her will. Sethe does not remember, but "rememories," relives or reexperiences as flashbacks. For her, "rememory" entails "being there," returning to the site of trauma. I will argue that this phenomenon of rememory, *as distinct from remembrance,* is connected to a failure of mourning and "working through."

3. Wyatt writes that, "The novel withholds judgment on Sethe's act and persuades the reader to do the same" (476). Henderson brings up the question of Sethe's accountability, but concludes that Morrison, within the text, "neither condemns nor condones," but "delivers" her protagonist (82), delivers in the sense of redemption. Morrison herself comments in a 1988 interview with Marsha Darling that "I got to a point where in asking myself who could judge Sethe adequately, since I couldn't and nobody else that knew her could, really, I felt that the only person who could judge her would be the daughter she killed" ("In the Realm" 248). However, Beloved's judgment, one that locks Sethe into a "cycle of impossible atonement and expiation" (Keenan 72) and ultimately necessitates her exorcism from the text, clearly is not a verdict Morrison supports.

4. Here one should recall Morrison's comment in "The Site of Memory" that she journeys to a site of trauma to "see what remains were left behind" (112), to reconstruct what remains unthought or untold through the imagining stimulated by traces. The remains themselves cannot be spoken, but openness to the trace as absence yields the possibility of telling a new story.

5. Derrida writes,

> Memory stays with traces, in order to "preserve" them, but traces of a past that has never been present, traces which themselves never occupy the form of presence and always remain, as it were, to come—come from the future, from

the to come. Resurrection, which is always the formal element of "truth," a recurrent difference between a present and its presence, does not resuscitate a past which had been present; it engages a future. (*Memoires* 58)

In this sense, "memory projects itself toward the future, and it constitutes the presence of the present" (*Memoires* 57). At this point in the text, Derrida also quotes Paul de Man on "this trace of the future as the power of memory." De Man writes, in his reading of Poulet reading Proust, "The power of memory does not reside in its capacity to resurrect a situation or a feeling that actually existed, but is a constitutive act of the mind bound to its own present and oriented toward the future of its elaboration" (*Memoires* 59).

6. As Morgenstern observes, "much of the criticism on *Beloved* celebrates the text as it retells its story as a story of cure" (122, n28).

7. Jessee observes that what slavery and the Middle Passage disrupted were West African conceptions of time and death in which "present" time "encompasses much of the immediate past, including Several generations of ancestors" (199). According to Jessee, Beloved is a "forgotten ancestor" (200) who returns to "initiate the collective sharing of memory" (208), which Jessee figures as a process of healing.

8. The absence of linear plot development has also been associated with Morrison's incorporation of aspects of African American oral traditions as well as with African conceptions of time. See Christol, Gorn, Jessee, Sale, and Traoré.

9. Bouson writes concerning this point that, "Deliberately using a fragmented and repetitive narrative structure to convey the disrupted, obsessive world of the trauma victim, Morrison circles around and around the shameful secrets that haunt her characters" (136).

10. Derrida observes the difference between law and justice in "Force of Law."

WORKS CITED

Benjamin, Walter. "Critique of Violence." *Reflections: Essays, Aphorisms, Autobiographical Writings*. Trans. Edmund Jephcott. Ed. Peter Demetz. New York: Schocken Books, 1978. 277–301.

———. "Theses on the Philosophy of History." *Illuminations*. Trans. Harry Zohn. Ed. Hannah Arendt. New York: Schocken, 1969. 253–264.

Bouson, J. Brooks. *Quiet As It's Kept: Shame, Trauma, and Race in the Novels of Toni Morrison*. Albany: SUNY Press, 2000.

Bowers, Susan. "Beloved and the New Apocalypse." *The Journal of Ethnic Studies* 18:1 (1990): 59–78.

Caruth, Cathy. Introduction. *Trauma: Explorations in Memory*. Ed. Cathy Caruth. Baltimore and London: The Johns Hopkins University Press, 1995, 3-12.

———. *Unclaimed Experience: Trauma, Narrative, and History*. Baltimore and London: The Johns Hopkins University Press, 1996.

Chase, Cynthia. "Reading Epitaphs." *Deconstruction is/in America: A New Sense of the Political*. Ed. Anselm Haverkamp. New York and London: New York University Press, 1995. 52–59.

Christol, Helene. "The African-American Concept of the Fantastic as Middle Passage." *Black Imagination and the Middle Passage*. Ed. Maria Diedrich, Henry Louis Gates, Jr., and Carl Pedersen. New York and Oxford: Oxford University Press, 1999. 164–182.

Cornell, Drucilla. *The Philosophy of the Limit*. New York and London: Routledge, 1992.

Derrida. Jacques. *Memoires for Paul de Man*. Revised edition. Trans. Cecile Lindsay, Jonathan Culler, Eduardo Cadava, and Peggy Kamuf. New York: Columbia University Press, 1989.

———. "Force of Law: the 'Mystical Foundations of Authority'." *Deconstruction and the Possibility of Justice*. Ed. Drucilla Cornell, Michel Rosenfeld and David Gray Carlson. New York and London: Routledge, 1992. 3–67.

———. *Given Time: 1. Counterfeit Money*. Trans. Peggy Kamuf. Chicago and London: University of Chicago Press, 1992.

———. *Specters of Marx: The State of Debt, the Work of Mourning, & the New International*. Trans. Peggy Kamuf. New York and London: Routledge, 1994.

Felman, Shoshana and Dori Laub, M.D. *Testimony: Crises of Witnessing in Literature, Psychoanalysis, and History*. New York and London: Routledge, 1992,

Furman, Jan. *Toni Morrison's Fiction*. Columbia: University of South Carolina Press, 1996.

Gates, Henry Louis, Jr. and K. A. Appiah, eds. *Toni Morrison: Critical Perspectives Past and Present*. New York: Amistad, 1993.

Gordon, Avery. *Ghostly Matters: Haunting and the Sociological Imagination*. Minneapolis and London: University of Minnesota Press, 1997.

Gorn, Elliott J. "Black Spirits: The Ghostlore of Afro-American Slaves." *American Quarterly* 36 (1984). 549–565.

Henderson, May G. "Toni Morrison's *Beloved*: Re-Membering the Body as Historical Text." *Comparative American Identities: Race, Sex and Nationality in the Modern Text* Ed. Hortense J. Spillers. New York and London: Routledge, 1991. 62–86.

Hirsch, Marianne. "Maternity and Rememory: Toni Morrison's *Beloved*." *Representations of Motherhood*. Ed. Donna Bassin, Margaret Honey, and Meryle Mahrer Kaplan. New Haven and London: Yale University Press, 1994. 92–110.

Horvitz, Deborah. "Nameless Ghosts: Possession and Dispossesion in *Beloved*." *Studies in American Fiction* 17.2 (1989): 157–168.

Jessee, Sharon. "'Tell me your earrings': Time and the Marvelous in Toni Morrison's *Beloved*." *Memory, Narrative and Identity: New Essays in Ethnic American Literatures*. Ed. Amritjit Singh, Joseph T. Skerrett, Jr., and Robert E. Hoga. Boston: Northeastern University Press, 1994, 198–211.

Keenan, Sally. "Four Hundred Years of Silence." *Recasting the World: Writing After Colonialism*. Ed. Jonathan White. Baltimore and London: The Johns Hopkins University Press, 1993. 45–81.

Krumholz, Linda. "The Ghosts of Slavery: Historical Recovery in Toni Morrison's *Beloved*." *African American Review* 26 (1992): 395–407.

Laub, Dori, M.D. "Bearing Witness, or the Vicissitudes of Listening." *Testimony: Crises of Witnessing in Literature, Psychoanalysis, and History*. By Shoshana Felman and Dori Laub, M.D. New York and London: Routledge, 1992. 57–74

Lawrence, David. "Fleshly Ghosts and Ghostly Flesh: the Word and the Body in *Beloved*." *Studies in American Fiction* 19.2 (1991): 199–202.

Mobley, Marilyn Sanders. "A Different Remembering: Memory, History, and Meaning in *Beloved*." Gates and Appiah 356–366.

Morgenstern, Naomi. "Mother's Milk and Sisters Blood: Trauma and the Neoslave Narrative." *Differences: A Journal of Feminist Cultural Studies* 8:2 (1996): 101–126.

Morrison, Toni. *Beloved*. New York: Plume, 1987.

——. "A Conversation: Gloria Naylor and Toni Morrison, 1985." Taylor-Guthrie 188–217.

——. "In the Realm of Responsibility: A Conversation with Toni Morrison." Interview with Marsha Darling, 1988. Taylor-Guthrie 246–254.

——. "Interview with Toni Morrison." Interview with Christina Davis, 1988. Gates and Appiah 412–420.

——. "The Site of Memory." *Inventing the Truth: The Art and Craft of Memoir*. Ed. William Zinser. Boston: Houghton Mifflin Company, 1987. 103–124.

——. "Unspeakable Things Unspoken: The Afro-American Presence in American Literature." *Michigan Quarterly Review* 28.1 (1989): 1–34.

Page, Philip. *Dangerous Freedom: Fusion and Fragmentation in Toni Morrison's Novels*. Jackson: University Press of Mississippi, 1995.

Rody, Caroline. "Toni Morrison's *Beloved:* History, 'Rememory,' and a 'Clamor for a Kiss.'" *American Literary History* 7 (1995) 92–119.

Sale, Maggie. "Call and Response as Critical Method: African-American Oral Traditions and *Beloved*." *African American Review* 26 (1992): 41–50.

Scruggs, Charles. *Sweet Home: Invisible Cities in the Afro-American Novel*. Baltimore and London: The Johns Hopkins University Press, 1993.

Smith, Valerie. "'Circling the Subject': History and Narrative in *Beloved*." Gates and Appiah 342–355.

Spillers, Hortense J. "Notes on an Alternative Model: Neither/Nor." *The Year Left 2: An American Socialist Yearbook*. Ed. Mike Davis. London: Verso, 1987. 176–194.

Taylor-Guthrie, Danille, ed. *Conversations With Toni Morrison*. Jackson: University of Mississippi Press, 1994.

Traoré, Ousseynou B. "Mythic Structures of Ethnic Memory in *Beloved:* The Mammy Watta and Middle Passage Paradigms." "*Beloved, she's mine.*" *Essais sur* Beloved *de Toni Morrison*. Ed. Geneviève Fabre and Claudine Reynaud. Paris: Cetanla, 1993. 77–89.

Wyatt, Jean. "Giving Body to the Word: The Maternal Symbolic in Toni Morrison's *Beloved*." *PMLA* 108 (1993) 474–488.

REGINALD WATSON

Derogatory Images of Sex:
The Black Woman and
Her Plight in Toni Morrison's Beloved

Sexual imagery has dominated black literature for quite some time, and when it came down to black male/female relationships, the images have appeared subtly pornographic. Some are works that are explicit in their descriptions of love. In Toni Morrison's *Beloved* there are both positive and negative sexual references related to the black woman and her plight. In this work, Morrison used images of nature, animalistic descriptions, and rape to exemplify how the black woman was exploited sexually during and after slavery. Dysfunction in black male/female relationships was inevitable, as the rape of the black woman by the white phallus set the stage for impotence in terms of physical and psychological development in the black community. In *Beloved*, nature is used to represent the black woman and her relationships. The animal imagery is dominant through the treatment of the black woman and man. Rape is also another dominant motif, especially since the black woman's body is constantly violated by the white phallus of slavery and then by the black phallus of an insecure man.

In *Beloved*, there are explicit, sometimes derogatory and pornographic sexual references when used in connection with the black woman's body, especially when the black male tries to assert his power by raping the black woman's body, mind, and soul. In Morrison's *Beloved*, the black woman is clearly a sexual object, a human mule present to bear the burdens of oppression

CLA Journal, Volume 49, Number 3 (March 2006): pp. 313–335. Copyright © 2006 *CLA Journal*.

from men. Before discussing *Beloved*, however, it would be appropriate to discuss one example of sexual exploitation: Sarah Bartman.

Sarah Bartman, a nineteenth-century Hottetot woman who was literally put on display for her unusual genitalia, is symbolic of how African American women have been the objects of sexual abuse from both black and white societies. Bartman, who died an early death after a long life of exploitation, abuse, and prostitution, had her genitalia removed during autopsy. Like in life, Bartman was exploited in death, which is evident when one sees her preserved sexual parts on display in a French museum. Like Bartman, the black woman in literature is symbolized only by her sexuality. She becomes powerless while her vagina becomes an object of subjugation, exploitation, and abuse.

In *Beloved*, nature is a key symbol because it is used to represent the black woman's growth, whether painful or fulfilling. Africa is often depicted as the motherland, the birthplace of all civilization. However, because of European greed, the continent was raped, exploited for its mineral and human resources. Rape is generally defined as an act that is based on power, not sex, a definition which clearly fits the dilemma faced by black women over the course of history. Like Bartman, black women's sexuality is still on display in the media. Audiences, both black and white, still hunger for and enjoy the sexual exploitation of black women. The myth that black women are highly sexual in nature is still alive in American society. The image of the black woman has, like Sarah Bartman, been relegated to a pickled vagina, put on display for the pleasure of others.

In Toni Morrison's *Beloved*, Sethe is a woman who becomes a sexual object for both white and black society. The images of nature, rape, and animalistic behavior and treatment dominate this neo-slave narrative about a vengeful baby ghost, who, in the form of a young teenage woman, comes back to haunt Sethe, the mother who cut her throat. *Beloved* is a work written to honor the sixty million or more Africans who were lost on the slave ship voyages during the dreaded Middle Passage. This tribute is vividly symbolized when Beloved returns to life via a pond, an appropriate image of rebirth and renewal. According to Deborah Horvitz, "[t]he powerful corporeal ghost who creates matrilineal connection between Africa and America, Beloved stands for every African woman whose story will never be told. She is the haunting symbol of the many Beloveds—generations of mothers and daughters —hunted down and stolen from Africa" (93).

Milk and water imagery is prevalent, representing not only the death that occurred during the Middle Passage, but also the loss of black motherhood. During slavery, the black woman was seen as either only a vagina or womb, objects that were there for sexual gratification or material gain. Her body was used as an assembly line to mass produce more slaves for the plantation. In *Beloved*, each woman, starting with Sethe, has to deal with having her "milk" spoiled by the demeaning forces of slavery. Milk is mixed with blood as black women fight back against their oppression through the act of infanticide, choosing to take the lives of their own children rather than let them be material possessions for the master. Thus, throughout *Beloved*, nature is corrupted, disrupted by rape perpetrated by the white phallus of slavery.

Such oppression sets the stage for murdered youth and dysfunctional family relationships in the black community. It is no wonder that the natural images of black motherhood and manhood are turned upside down in this work. According to Deborah Ayer Sitter, the novel *Beloved* shows how "the meaning of slavery's impact on a people encompasses more than maternal love; it involves the way internalization of oppressors' values can distort all intimate human relationships and even subvert the self" (190). Neither the black woman nor the black man could operate in a "natural way" because, in a sense, they were both exploited for their sexual organs. The black man was the studding animal, used only for the purpose of impregnating black women. Under these circumstances, there was never supposed to be any fidelity or loving bond. Only a human assembly line was necessary when it came to profit for the master. It is no surprise, then, that in *Beloved* and other neo-narratives like it, there was no affection when it came down to sexual relationships. Unfortunately, as seen in *Beloved*, the natural becomes unnatural, the milk becomes spoiled, and traditional becomes untraditional as the white phallus rapes and destroys all that is pure between mother, child, man and wife in the black community.

For Sethe, the rape and the stealing of her milk symbolized the taking of her self-hood, her inner being. As a child, she was denied full access to her own mother's milk. Like her daughter, Beloved, Sethe is starving for mother's milk that is almost always mixed with the blood of slavery. According to Barbara Schapiro, Sethe was emotionally starved as a baby; she was denied "a significant nurturing relationship. That relationship is associated with one's being or essence; if she has no nursing milk to call her own, she feels without a self to call her own. Thus [she is] ravaged as an infant, robbed of her milk/essence by the white social structure" (159).

So in *Beloved*, the rape and exploitation of both the black woman and man set the stage for the unnatural and animalistic behavior that dominates the work. The black woman's sexual organ becomes the one commodity or object of value for the slave master; her reproductive abilities are manipulated and warped as a dollar value is placed on her vagina. According to Marsha Jean Darling, the novel's central themes revolve around the following questions: "What are the entitlements and boundaries of 'mother's love'? Why is the 'precious interior, the loved self, whatever it is, suppressed or displaced and put someplace in the children, in the lover, in the man'? And why do the same women who surrender so much of themselves possess so strongly, even to the point of acting in ways that compromise their in-earnest attempt to love?" (86).

Such questions are never completely answered as the plight of the black woman is addressed in the novel. Yet, one cannot help but to question and feel disgusted when it becomes clear that bonding between mother and child, man and woman are tainted and forever made dysfunctional whenever the white phallus of slavery imposes itself. The institution of slavery and its sexual and psychological oppression of both the black man and woman drove Sethe's mother, Baby Suggs, Ella, and other black women to go beyond acceptable boundaries of mother love.

It is the white phallus of slavery that drives Sethe to murder her baby. It is the white phallus that drove many mothers to commit infanticide both on and off the slave ships. Many would choose death for either themselves or their children. Thus when the novel opens, we find that Sethe's residence on 124 Bluestone Road is "full of baby's venom" (Morrison 3), a haunting from a baby long dead. "Who would have thought that a little old baby could harbor so much rage?" (Morrison 5) are the words that describe Sethe's reflections about her act of infanticide. Eventually, Sethe's two boys run away, while her mother-in-law, Baby Suggs, dies completely insane. Baby Suggs, who wishes to see only color before her death, completely loses her hold on reality when Halle, the one son she had left, is also beaten down by the system of slavery. As will be discussed later, Baby Suggs, like Sethe and other black women in the novel, are victims of rape, reduced to sexual machines that exist only for the master's benefit.

Paul D, like Sethe, is another survivor of Sweet Home, the plantation where most of the black men were named Paul, all of them symbolically castrated. In fact, they were only men when their master declared them as such. Otherwise, Paul D, along with other Sweet Home men, was bereft of any legitimate manhood. Indeed, in a very graphic example of sex, the narration reveals that because of a shortage of women, the black men engaged in having sex with calves. These acts of bestiality are vivid reminders of how black men, made impotent by the white master, are expected to act like animals in the eyes of white society: "And so they were: Paul D Garner, Paul F Garner, Paul A Garner, Halle Suggs and Sixo, the wild man. All in their twenties, minus women, fucking cows, dreaming of rape, thrashing on pallets, rubbing their thighs and waiting for the new girl—the one who took Baby Sugg's place after Halle bought her with five years of Sundays" (Morrison 11). The new girl, of course, was Sethe, who eventually winds up marrying (if it could be called that during slavery) Halle. Before this happens, though, the young black men would dream of raping the young girl named Sethe. These lines by Morrison are again reminiscent of how the white slave master set up an environment conducive to rape. This would continue beyond the boundaries of slavery.

Morrison does a good job in detailing the beginnings of this sad dynamic when she describes the sadistic, sexual thoughts and practices that were born on a white man's plantation, ironically named Sweet Home. In the beginning of the novel, it becomes evident that both Sethe and Paul D are truly surviving victims of a harsh reality. From the start, Paul D is clearly impotent in terms of expressing true emotion. He has not been taught to be a true man. Even though Mr. Garner, his master, proclaimed that "my niggers is men every one of em" (Morrison 10), it becomes painfully obvious that it is an artificial manhood that has no validity outside of the Sweet Home plantation. Thus, when Paul D arrives at 124 Bluestone Road, he arrives sexually inadequate. Just like Sethe, he is castrated emotionally and scarred badly by his experiences at Sweet Home; consequently, Paul D can only express himself through sex, not true love. Still, Sethe is willing to accept him in this way, especially since Halle had disappeared from her life. The sexual imagery at this point of the novel is both beautiful and pornographic. Paul D, the man who once had sex with cows, could now see his rape dreams come true because, on the first night, Sethe allows him into her bed. Both people are sexually starved and both of Sethe's daughters, one alive, the other dead, realize it. Thus, it comes as no surprise that soon after Paul D arrives, the baby ghost acts up and eventually takes on flesh in the form of a nineteen-year-old woman. In the meantime, Sethe feels comfortable and relieved enough to tell Paul D about how she was raped by the white boys on Sweet Home plantation. In a sense, Sethe's story of rape opens up the door for another sexual act because Paul D becomes aroused when Sethe describes how the boys with mossy teeth sucked her breasts and stole her milk while she was pregnant.

Like the cows that had no chance around the black males on Sweet Home, Sethe was milked, treated and whipped like an animal. The whipping brought about a scar in the form of a chokecherry tree on Sethe's back, which is symbolic of her hardships and ability to grow beyond her rape. She is strongly rooted by tradition and experience, and when Paul D hears her story, he holds her breasts and commences to rub his cheek "on her back and learned that way her sorrow, the roots of it; its wide trunk and intricate branches" (Morrison 17). The sexual imagery becomes dominant at this point as Morrison describes how, upon seeing the tree on her back, Paul D felt he would have no peace until "he had touched every ridge and leaf with his mouth" (Morrison 18). Sethe is unable to feel the kisses because her back skin has been dead for years; however, she was heartened that the responsibility, "for her breasts, at last, was in somebody else's hands" (Morrison 18). The ghost-child makes one more attempt to scare away Paul D and his sexual lust, but when Paul D directly confronts the unseen entity, it leaves the scene, but only temporarily, which allows time for Paul D and Sethe to consummate their sexual desires.

As Morrison relates, the two lost no time in getting upstairs. "Over-whelmed as much by the downright luck of finding her house and her in it as by the certainty of giving her his sex, Paul D dropped twenty-five years from his recent memory" (Morrison 20). However, Paul D is tired, battered, and made impotent by slavery and the white phallus of power. His own phallus cannot hold up under the stressful conditions that slavery had created for both him and Sethe. This is made clear in their sexual encounter: "It was over before they could get their clothes off. Half-dressed and short of breath, they lay side by side resentful of one another and the skylight above them. His dreaming of her had been too long ago. Her deprivation had been not having any dreams of her own at all. Now they were sorry and too shy to make talk" (Morrison 20). This scene was revealing because it symbolizes the impotency that characterized many black male/female relationships during and after slavery.

For both Sethe and Paul D, dreams were never realized during slavery, and even in freedom, those dreams can easily turn into harsh realities. In this scene, the sunlight revealed the ugliness and scars that characterized both their lives. In fact, Trudier Harris suggests that Paul D is intimidated from the very first time he enters 124 Bluestone Road. He has, according to Harris, an ancient fear of women: "When he enters the house haunted by Beloved's ghost, it becomes the enveloping enclosure of the vagina; the vagina dentata myth operates as Paul D feels the physical threat of the house" (130). In this interesting analysis, Harris reinforces the sexual themes of the novel by de-scribing Paul D as one surrounded by a femininity he cannot control. It is no wonder, then, that his first sex act with Sethe does not last long. Faced with an emasculated past and an uncertain future with Sethe, Paul D is destined to fail because the artificial manhood created on Sweet Home plantation just will not do. According to Trudier Harris, features of the demonic and the satanic are characteristic of the female body in *Beloved* (129), particularly the female body that Beloved, the ghost, assumes later in the novel. She is, indeed, a true witch, as well as a ghost or devil, one who, as Harris asserts, manipulates those around her (129). However, Beloved's job is not a hard one because Paul D is already vulnerable, weakened by his experiences on Sweet Home plantation.

Paul D's dissatisfying sex act with Sethe opens his eyes to a number of negative things. First, as Harris points out, Paul D feels threatened by the house, which becomes an enveloping vagina. He is also eventually intimidat-ed by not only the ghost-child but by Sethe herself. His impotent behavior is representative of how inadequate he truly is when it comes down to facing certain realities. In the enclosure of the vagina, Paul D cannot "get it up," so to speak. The artificial manhood created on the white man's plantation is no match for the matriarchy represented by a tired mother named Sethe and her two daughters, one living, one dead. Faced with his own insecurities, Paul D tries to find impurity and fault in Sethe, his sex partner. Deborah Ayer asserts that the "nubile maiden Paul D has dreamed of for twenty-five years turns into a hag before his eyes" (193). Her tree, which was so beautiful before his sex with her, is now a clump of ugly scar tissue (21). According to Deborah Ayer, "Paul D's denial that Sethe has a tree on her back is a case of phallic assertiveness masking his insecurity about his own manhood. He imposes his own (male) conception of a tree, measures her 'tree' by it, and finds it lacking" (195).

Paul D, in Morrison's *Beloved,* becomes embarrassed by his animalistic sex with Sethe and starts to remember a tree he named "Brother." It was under this tree that he felt safe, a tree very different from the one he saw on Sethe's back. According to Ayer, "[a]s the metaphor of the tree develops, it becomes clear that the chief barrier to Paul D's committing himself to Sethe is an ideal of manhood which is threatened by the woman she is" (197) Paul D's fear of commitment drives him to fear Sethe's body; he cannot handle the combination of pain and power inherent in those scars. The imprint of a "chokecherry tree" on Sethe's back chokes Paul D to the point that he cannot function in her life or her bed.

Near the end, Paul D fully regains his manhood in the "vagina" of the house on 124 Bluestone Road. It is then, and only then, after the exorcism of the baby ghost, that Paul D will be able to fully understand Sethe's body and her tree of experiences. However, in the beginning, when Paul D "reads" the stories inherent in Sethe's wounds, he closes the "book" and loses his phallic power. It is at that point that Sethe's tree was not inviting, nor was it something he felt he could trust. In a sense, Paul D becomes impotent while outnumbered and overpowered by a matriarchal trinity. In the meantime, Sethe, sensing Paul D's disgust, decides the following: "But maybe a man was nothing but a man, which is what Baby Suggs always said. They encouraged you to put some of your weight in their hands and soon as you felt how light and lovely that was, they studied your scars and tribulations, after which they did what he had done: ran her children out and tore up the house" (Morrison 22). Sethe turned her back to Paul D, not wanting to excite him any further. Paul D also had neither the strength nor the inclination to try again, because the appetite was gone (Morrison 23).

However, the appetite for revenge was not gone for the baby ghost, who ultimately comes back to take possession of the house and Sethe. According to Wyatt, Morrison "links Beloved to the 'Sixty Million and more' by joining her spirit to the body of a woman who died on one of the slave ships" (241). Beloved was a link and a reminder of how black women were not only hunted down, but exploited sexually. In response, Sethe felt that the only way to fight back was to cut the throat of her two-year-old child; her exploitation and rape on Sweet Home drove her to this desperate act, which ultimately sets the stage for the haunting at 124 Bluestone Road. According to Marsha Jean Darling, "Sethe's mother love does and undoes itself; it is nurturing and destructive, empowered and tragically unjust" (86)

Beloved the ghost is a reminder of how the phallus of slavery disrupted all bonds when it came down to the black family. Paul D, the bearer of this bad news, is just another example of how "manless" a black man can become when faced with the horrors of slavery. Like Halle, Paul D was rendered powerless by an iron bit placed in his mouth. In fact, Sethe feels that Paul D really wants to tell his story and how "offended" his tongue must have felt when weighted down by iron (71). Sethe knew many, like Paul D, who were reduced to having "wild looks" in their eyes after they were brought down to the level of helpless, speechless animals. For Paul D, Halle, and the rest of the Sweet Home men, there is no manly voice that they can use in protesting the rape and sexual exploitation of black women. With their manufactured manhood, they can only serve as witnesses to the crime and watch as the "milk" goes sour for the physical, spiritual, and mental well-being of the black family. So it is no surprise that Paul D can offer few words of comfort for Sethe. Animalistic sex and behavior is all he knows in the beginning, and, when faced with the "flesh" of a vengeful ghost, he can only play the role of easily manipulated victim once again.

The mossy mouths of the white boys have indeed soured much more than Sethe's milk because they have also sucked away all hope for bonding between mother and child, husband and wife. Halle, like Paul D, is helpless when it comes down to protecting the sanctity of the mother, and this is made evident in his impotence. Elizabeth House asserts that the character of Beloved illustrates the themes associated with the destruction of family bonds brought about through slavery (118). Beloved's ghost is more than just the reincarnated spirit of Sethe's murdered child. It becomes clear from the girl's disjointed narrative that she is also the ghost of another girl who, along with her mother, was captured in Africa while picking flowers. Both mother and daughter were put aboard the slave ship in horrid conditions, with the result being the mother committing suicide by jumping overboard. So Beloved is a child twice reincarnated, and one who has experienced the loss of not one, but two mothers. It is no wonder that she comes back with a hunger and greed for mother's milk. House is right; Beloved is symbolic of how there was family-breakup and loss, and, unfortunately, the imagery of sex and rape are the tools for this breakup. Beloved is associated with nature; she can be seen as symbolic of Africa, the motherland, and how it, as well as its inhabitants, were habitually raped and exploited. When nature is disrupted, chaos is born, as seen in Beloved's first mother jumping overboard to the sharks and Beloved's throat being cut by her second mother.

Beloved is also symbolic of lost identity, another dynamic that applies to all of the black mothers mentioned in the work. According to Barbara Hill Rigney, we never know Beloved's true birth name because her life was taken before proper labeling could be accomplished. She takes her name from an epitaph on her tombstone. Beloved clearly has no identity because she has "merged with the Sixty Million and more" who suffered the outrage of enslavement (146). The "outrage" is simply the sexual and economic exploitation that drove the black mother to horrendous acts of infanticide and suicide. It is no surprise that Beloved, in trying to get rid of Paul D, uses sex to manipulate and control him. This was all she knew because it was sex and greed that set the foundation for the loss of mother's love and nurturing milk. According to Horvitz, Beloved is an "inter-generational, inter-continental, female ghost-child who teaches Sethe that memories and stories about her matrilineal ancestry are life-giving" (94). It is through these memories that Sethe is reminded of her own nameless mother who, along with other black mothers, was victimized and forced into unspeakable degradation and sexual exploitation in slavery.

Andrew Schopp argues that Beloved, as a figure, "represents a prime example of the unspeakable being spoken" (205), and when Paul D comes up against that "voice" from the grave, he cannot help but to become impotent. According to Harris, Beloved's "very body becomes a manifestation of her desire for vengeance and of Sethe's guilt. She repays Sethe for her death, but the punishment is not quick or neat" (131). As a result, Beloved slowly eliminates Paul D's voice and presence by making herself, physically, irresistible to him. She succeeds in forcing him out, to make him "retreat farther and farther from the territory she has claimed as her own" (Harris 131). Thus, the sexual imagery starts to really become explicit, as the flesh takes over the spirit and the young nineteen-year-old Beloved, in a sense, "rapes" Paul D, sexing him to the point where he falls into deep sleeps around the main house on 124 Bluestone Road. In a revealing scene, Beloved, after lifting up her skirt, makes her intentions clear to Paul D: "I want you to touch me on the inside part and call me my name" (Morrison 116). Paul D, weakly, tries to resist touching the "inside part," but the vagina and the vengeful designs of a murdered child are too much. According to Harris, Beloved uses her body, through three sexual encounters, to drain Paul D both physically and spiritually (132). Ultimately, Paul D becomes a "shadow of his former self," which is evidenced when he becomes an alcoholic.

Harris refers to the nineteen-year-old ghost-child as a vampire because she sucks away Paul D's remaining hold on manhood (131). Once again, Paul D fails as an adequate protector because he opens himself up to be "moved" by the ghost. When she "rapes" him, Paul D can only reflect on his own weaknesses. In a very sexually explicit description by Morrison, Paul D's thoughts become clear indicators that his own "Red Heart" is no match for the greedy young woman. In fact, he felt like a "rag doll—picked up and put back down anywhere any time by a girl young enough to be his daughter. Fucking her when he was convinced he didn't want to. Whenever she turned her behind up, the calves of his youth (was that it?) cracked his resolve" (Morrison 127). According to Harris, Beloved becomes a traditional "succubus, the female spirit who drains the male's life force even as she drains him of his sperm" (131).

After this encounter with Beloved, Paul D starts to see things about his own past. He makes feeble attempts to hold on to his manhood by offering to play father in Sethe's life. He felt that, through impregnating Sethe, he could not only "document his manhood," but break out of Beloved's spell (Morrison 128). His offer fails, of course, and it is not long before his mind goes back to his past sexual encounters and relationships. Paul D reflects back on a woman who fed him pork sausage when he was starving. She also offered her body amidst white cotton sheets where "he fell in with a groan and the woman helped him pretend he was making love to her and not her bed linen. He vowed that night, full of pork, deep in luxury, that he would never leave her" (Morrison 131).

However, he would leave, although "thankful for the introduction to sheets" (131), and Paul D eventually winds up at Sethe's door. He now felt as if he "had been plucked from the face of a cliff and put down on sure ground" with Sethe in his life, but his offer to make Sethe pregnant fell on deaf ears. Sethe was frightened by his offer: "She thought quickly of how good the sex would be if that is what he wanted, but mostly she was frightened by the thought of having a baby once more" (131–132). It is at this point that Sethe mentally builds a case against Paul D. She makes up her mind that Paul D resented her girls, Denver and Beloved, and she decides that Paul D is only in the way.

Ultimately, it is not long before Paul D is pushed out of 124, mentally and physically drained. After becoming a drinking tramp, Paul starts to reflect on how he and the other black men were broken into boys by Mr. Garner's successor, Schoolteacher, on Sweet Home plantation. Paul D then thinks about black men, like Sixo, who managed to retain their manhood and their sanity. It is also at this lowest point for Paul D that another true man named Stamp Paid approaches him and offers help. This was appropriate for Stamp Paid because during slavery he served as the guide who helped others to freedom. So it is no surprise when he tries to guide Paul D back to stability.

Paul D's life is filled with images related to nature, life, death, and revelation. When Paul asked, "How much is a nigger supposed to take?" Stamp Paid responds with "All he can," a statement which makes it clear that black men must always find a way to fight back against the odds. Stamp Paid teaches Paul D that he must try, once again, to reassert himself in Sethe's life. Paul D's red, red heart beats again because Stamp's advice, along with his memories of "true men," motivates him and he regains the "erection" needed to reenter the "vagina" of the house on 124 Bluestone Road. His "erection" is now built upon understanding and revelation, so it is no surprise that, at this point, Paul D's artificial manhood is eradicated. He now truly understands the chokecherry tree on Sethe's back; he is now ready to hold her tired breasts.

Beloved's presence also forces Sethe to reexamine her past, particularly as Sethe gradually finds out that the young, wayward teenager in her home is reincarnated flesh, greedy for mother's attention. Sethe starts to slowly feel guilt and almost allows the ghost to totally consume her. It will take the community of women coming together to save Sethe, an act which is clearly indicative of the strong matriarchal presence in the work. The mothers of the community recognize Sethe's plight because, at one point, they, too, were exploited victims who suffered loss of family. Sethe, like so many African women, committed love-murder because after being victimized by brutal rape and sex, these women felt that they had no choice. Infanticide or blunted affection is, unfortunately, the aftereffect of this exploitation, examples that are brought out through the characters of Baby Suggs, Ella, and Sethe's nameless mother.

Sethe's mother, whose name is never mentioned, is clearly an example of how sexual exploitation and the treatment of black women as only tools for reproduction drove them to desperate acts of retaliation. Sethe is raised by another, a woman named "Nan," who tells the story about Sethe's mother. The story told reveals a woman who, after numerous rapes, had many children black and white. However, Sethe's mother throws away all of her children except the black one: Sethe. So again, it appears that infanticide becomes the black woman's tool against her oppressive rapists. Sethe's mother is like the many nameless faces lost on the Middle Passage, but she fights to have a name carried on through Sethe. Sethe's mother chooses to keep Sethe because her father was black, and as for the whites who repeatedly raped her, Sethe's mother never let them put their arms around her. Treated like an animal, she, in a sense, acts like an animal by brutally destroying her offspring; still, however, she regains control and freedom by taking back lives that would soon be enslaved. Through such acts, Sethe's mother, like Sethe and other enslaved black women, would reassert rights to her own womb. Sethe's mother chose a black man to have as her sexual partner, an event which is told by Sethe's Nan. It was Nan who spoke the language of Africa and was the companion of Sethe's mother on the slave ship that brought them to America. Nan describes how both she and Sethe's mother were "taken up many times by the crew" (Morrison 62), or raped repeatedly, a common practice on the slave ship. Such painful rememories of Sethe's Nan and Sethe's mother are powerful examples of how, through infanticide, African mothers fought back against their sexual oppression through what can be called "love-murder."

In *Beloved,* the black women are all bonded in their exploitation; mother's milk is the only means of nurturing and continuing stability and hope for the future. Sethe's mother, before being killed, lifted her breast to show her daughter the marks of a circle and cross branded into her flesh. This brand of slavery is symbolic of how a black woman's life-giving breasts were constantly violated and her milk spoiled by rape and exploitation. When Sethe sees the mark and asks for one like it, her mother slaps her because she did not want Sethe to carry the same burdens that have plagued her life. In fact, Sethe's mother, like the ghost Beloved, is symbolic of Africa and the sixty million or more lost on the Middle Passage. It is her strength that teaches Sethe, to respect and to remember the importance of motherhood and unity. So it is no surprise that after her mother's demise, Sethe is continually fed off the breast of a black mother named Nan, another symbol of Africa the motherland.

Sethe tells the tale of her physical rape to Paul D, an act that her own husband, Halle, was powerless to prevent. With her breasts full of milk, Sethe talks about the two boys with mossy teeth and "how one sucked her breast, while the other held her down" (Morrison 70). Unfortunately, the mossy mouths of the white boys have indeed soured much more than Sethe's milk because they have also sucked away all hope for bonding between mother and child, husband and wife. Consequently, Halle, like Paul D, is helpless when it comes down to protecting the sanctity of the mother, and this is made evident in his impotence. In addition, the boys' book-reading school-teacher was observing and writing about Sethe's rape in a book. The animal imagery is dominant at this point because Sethe is milked like a cow, while Halle, the only male "somebody" in her life, watches from the barn loft. Sethe's rape and exploitation is too much for Halle. Her rape is his rape because soon after the horrible incident, he loses his sanity.

The phallus of slavery would take its toll on black motherhood. Darling cites an example of how "Legislation like the Virginia statute of 1662 validated white male sexual abuse of black women and ensured the continuing existence of the slave force by using black women as breeders, whether the fathers were black or white men. Law and practice worked together to dismantle the nuclear core of Black families" (86–87). Darling goes on to describe how such laws reduced black women to human baby machines (87), a factor which played a role in why Sethe's mother threw away the offspring of her white rapists and why Sethe chose to cut the throat of her own child.

Baby Suggs is definitely another rape victim of slavery's phallic power. Her life is tragic because she is the epitome of how black women were used as "baby machines," forced into numerous sexual relationships just to make the master rich. Halle, her eighth and last child, was supposed to be a permanent fixture in not only her life, but also the life of her daughter-in-law, Sethe. Unfortunately, when Halle witnesses Sethe's rape and her breasts violated by the mossy-teethed white boys, he loses all phallic assertiveness as a husband and a man. He eventually loses his mind as well and covers himself in clabber and butter, a sign that the "milk" has been spoiled for both him and Sethe. Just as tragic is the fact that Halle was seen as a true man and "somebody" in Baby Sugg's eyes. Like Sethe, Halle is "named," a child considered as truly legitimate because his parentage involves a black man. He was the only ray of hope in what was otherwise a very tragic existence for Baby Suggs. It is no wonder that upon Halle's mental break down, Baby Suggs loses her mind as well, seeing only colors before she dies under Sethe's care. Perhaps she chooses to see color because most of her young and adult life was bereft of hope. Like most black slave women, she never had control over her own destiny.

Baby Suggs is clearly a woman who has been used as a brood sow. True love and sexual pleasure have been gutted by the horrors of slavery. The black woman rarely experienced tenderness and affection in her sexual encounters. For Baby Suggs, sex is without joy, an act committed in the name of power. The black woman's body became an assembly line for the production of more babies. Baby Suggs, along with other black women, had to endure exploitation by both white and black men, which unfortunately would last even after slavery was abolished in this country. It is no wonder, then, that affection between mother and child, woman and man were blunted to the point of dysfunctional behavior.

In most cases, during slavery the black woman had her children taken from her early on, causing many of these mothers to not even bother naming their offspring. These mothers knew that their children were only there to be brought up to be bought out, pawns or checker pieces in a game that only white society could win. This is why Baby Suggs considered herself lucky when she was allowed to keep Halle. Still, the circumstances under which she was allowed to keep him are all too tragic and unfortunate because Halle was given to her, no doubt, to make up for hearing that her two girls, neither of whom had their adult teeth, were sold and gone, and she had not been able to wave goodbye, and to make up for coupling with a straw boss for four months in exchange for keeping her third child, a boy, with her—only to have him traded for lumber in the spring of the next year and to find herself pregnant by the man who promised not to and did. That child she could not love and the rest she would not. "'God take what He would,' she said. And He did, and He did, and He did and then gave her Halle who gave her freedom when it didn't mean a thing" (Morrison 23).

Baby Suggs, like Sethe's mother, refused to love offspring that were products of the white man's rape. This is clearly an example of how affections were blunted between mother and child, especially when that child was conceived through sexual exploitation. In slavery, a black woman was expected to have many daddies for her children, but under such a system, there could be very few fathers. The black man was not expected to have responsibility for the fruit of his loins. He was a studding animal who was supposed to have sex with numerous black women. Fidelity was definitely not expected from the black man. So it is no wonder that Baby Suggs was proud of Halle for several reasons. He was obviously the offspring of a black man, and later in life he became a "somebody son" who would stay "married" to Sethe and father all of her children. Halle, the last child of eight, was Baby Sugg's hope, the checker piece that would not be moved from her life. It is unfortunate, though, that later in life, despite the saving of Halle's body, Baby Suggs could not hold on to his mind, forever lost because of slavery's brutal exploitation of Sethe.

Later, it is revealed through Denver's perspective that Baby Suggs was very conscious of how both white and black people probably looked down on her because her eight children had different daddies. Denver's reflective thoughts on Baby Suggs help to sum up the dilemmas that black women faced on a daily basis:

> Slaves not supposed to have pleasurable feelings on their own; their bodies not supposed to be like that, but they have to have as many children as they can to please whoever owned them. Still, they were not supposed to have pleasure deep down. She said for me not to listen to all that. That I should always listen to my body and love it. (Morrison 209)

To Denver, Baby Suggs was representative of how black women were forced to be "brood sows," animals that were supposed to reproduce for only the master's benefit. Still, before Baby Suggs loses her mind and dies, she teaches Denver that a black woman should learn to listen and love her body, especially when others did not. Denver is truly a ray of hope, a progressive step beyond the harsh indignities that her mother, her grandmother, and other black mothers had to endure. By work's end, it becomes clear that Denver will not be just another victim; her body will not be violated by the phallus of white or black society.

Unfortunately, though, this is not the case for Ella, another black woman victimized by sexual exploitation. In the novel, she is the first to convince the other women in the community that Sethe was in need of help. She was one of the women who thought things through and decided to bring Sethe back within the circle of "folk" by exorcising the vengeful ghost. Ella was glad no one loved her because she considered love a "serious disability." Ella is scarred and raped by the white phallus of slavery. Like Baby Suggs, Ella is used as a sexual object, "shared by father and son," white men whom she considered as the "lowest yet" and who gave her disgust for sex and against whom she measured all atrocities (Morrison 256). Because of this experience, Ella is able to understand Sethe's rage, but not her willingness to kill her children. Still, because Ella thinks things through, she is able to have sympathy for Sethe and her "dilemma," particularly since the two women shared common bonds related to rage and disgust with slavery's raping of their lives. Ironically, then, Ella, who considers love a disability, puts aside her disgust for Sethe's act of infanticide to show love and concern for Sethe's plight. So when Denver comes to her door, Ella does not hesitate to bring in the rest of the community in exorcising Sethe's vengeful child.

On this point, then, it is important to discuss how sexual exploitation of black women helped set the foundation for Morrison's neo-slave narrative. It is this exploitation that leads to the unity of mothers needed by work's end to rid the town of the vengeful ghost. Sethe, Sethe's mother, Baby Suggs, and Ella are all part of these unified, whole, named and unnamed mothers who had suffered the indignities of slavery's phallus. So by work's end it is appropriate that a community of women come together to exorcise the demon ghost. Their unity and power of prayer are powerful tools, symbols that castrate the evil effects of slavery's white phallus. Ironically, both young and old breasts, long dried of mother's milk, come together to nurse Sethe back to sanity. These women help to cleanse and nourish not only Sethe but also her other daughter, Denver. So despite their victimization, these mothers are able to bring about constant renewal, rebirth, and cleansing, a function which is a fitting end considering the many instances of sexual exploitation and animalistic treatment that these victimized women had to endure.

Sethe is reunited with Paul D, and in this reunion it becomes clear that only "this woman Sethe could have left him his manhood like that. He wants to put his story next to hers" (Morrison 273). With manhood restored, Paul D no longer suffers from psychological and physical impotence. With Beloved's ghost gone, the memories of slavery's horrors are gone, at least temporarily. Now, with the circle completed, a black man and woman can come together and truly satisfy each other. Sex is no longer just sex; it is an expression of love that was denied in the chains of slavery. In other words, Sethe's tree can now truly represent growth and love. It is under these circumstances that feeling can now return to Sethe's deadened flesh, as Paul D becomes more secure in his acceptance of her life. By work's end, Paul D is man enough to hold those breasts and gain the nourishment needed for a healthy coexistence with a full-fledged woman.

Sexual imagery in *Beloved* takes many forms: sometimes beautiful, sometimes pornographic. Against the backdrop of oppression, relationships and sex between black men and women would, at times, be expressed through rape and brutality. Through animal images and references to nature, Morrison manages to successfully show how the black woman has been exploited throughout history by both black and white men. Unfortunately, sex as depicted in this novel is, for the most part, not positive for the black woman. Today, there is a carry-over from the slave plantation; dysfunction, with its roots traced to slavery, still exists in black male/female relationships. Black men and women are still stereotyped as being sexual beings, a fact that is constantly made clear in the media. It would seem that we have yet to throw away the pickled vagina of Sarah Bartman because, in this society, it is quite clear that sexual exploitation of the black woman is here to stay.

WORKS CITED

Ayer, Deborah. "The Making of Man: Dialog Meaning in *Beloved*." *Critical Essays on Toni Morrison's* Beloved. Ed. Barbara H. Solomon. New York: G. K. Hall, 1998. 2211–2232.

Darling, Marsha Jean. "The Ties That Bind." *Critical Essays on Toni Morrison's* Beloved. Ed. Barbara H. Solomon. York: G. K. Hall, 1998. 84–87.

Harris, Trudier. "Woman, Thy Name Is Demon." *Critical Essays on Toni Morrison's* Beloved. Ed. Barbara H, Solomon. New York: G. K. Hall, 1998. 127–137.

House, Elizabeth B. "Toni Morrison's Ghost: The Beloved Who is Not Beloved." *Critical Essays on Toni Morrison's* Beloved. Ed. Barbara H. Solomon. New York: G. K. Hall, 1998. 2211–2232.

Horvitz, Deborah. "Nameless Ghosts: Possession and Dispossession in *Beloved*." *Critical Essays on Toni Morrison's* Beloved." Ed. Barbara H. Solomon. New York: G. K. Hall, 1998. 2211–2232.

Morrison, Toni. *Beloved*. New York: Plume, 1987.

———. "The Pain of Being Black: An Interview with Toni Morrison." With Bonnie Angelo. *Conversations with Toni Morrison*. Ed. Danielle Taylor-Guthrie. Jackson: University Press of Mississippi, 1994. 255–261.

Rigney, Barbara Hill. "Breaking the Back of Words: Language, Silence, and the Politics of Identity in *Beloved*." *Critical Essays on Toni Morrison's* Beloved. Ed. Barbara H. Solomon. New York: G. K. Hall, 1998. 2211–2232.

Schapiro, Barbara. "The Bonds of Love and the Boundaries of Self in Toni Morrison's *Beloved*." *Understanding Toni Morrison's* Beloved *and* Sula: *Selected Essays and Criticisms of the Works by the Nobel Prize-winning Author*. Ed. Solomon O. Iyasere and Marla W. Iyasere. New York: Whitston, 2000. 155–172.

Schopp, Andrew. "Narrative Control and Subjectivity: Dismantling Safety in Toni Morrison's *Beloved*." *Understanding Toni Morrison's* Beloved *and* Sula: *Selected Essays and Criticisms of the Works by the Nobel Prize-winning Author*. Ed. Solomon O. Iyasere and Marla W. Iyasere. New York: Whitston, 2000. 204–230.

Wyatt, Jean. "Giving Body to the Word: The Maternal Symbolic in Toni Morrison's *Beloved*." *Critical Essays on Toni Morrison's* Beloved. Ed. Barbara H. Solomon. New York: G. K. Hall, 1998. 2211–2232.

DEAN FRANCO

What We Talk About
When We Talk About Beloved

What are we personally willing to sacrifice, give up for the "public good"? What gestures of reparation are we personally willing to make? What risky, unfashionable research are we willing to undertake?
    —Toni Morrison, "How Can Values be Taught in the University?"

A substantial amount of critical writing about Toni Morrison's novel *Beloved* is invested in the ethically problematic and politically limited discourse of co-memory and co-mourning. This kind of criticism is what I would call "critical wish fulfillment,"[1] a critical projection of real-world ethical and political goals onto the reading scene, allowing readers to facilely identify with the novel's characters and their experiences. However, by passing the prevailing discourse of trauma studies through a more overtly politicized analysis we can arrive at a critical approach that both advances the ethical and political claims a literary text such as *Beloved* has on its readers—the claims of the past on the present—and acknowledges the limits of reader-text identification, or the otherness of text and reader. I begin with an analysis of psychoanalytic approaches to Morrison's novel but end in a very different place, suggesting we read the novel as a contribution to the contemporary national discussion of reparations for slavery and Jim Crow segregation.

MFS: Modern Fiction Studies, Volume 52, Number 2 (Summer 2006): pp. 415–439. Copyright © 2006 for the Purdue Research Foundation by The Johns Hopkins University Press.

109

The critics I survey in this article already presume some sort of ethical project at the center of their own writing, at least insofar as they presume that a study of mourning and healing in literature is on the side of what's good. My analysis here aims to examine what critical, theoretical, and ethical presumptions prevail in the criticism, and to show how psychoanalytic discussions of agency in *Beloved* can be translated into an activist public-sphere. Making this explicit will not undermine the value of such trauma studies readings; on the contrary: Under the adage that where there is quantity there must be quality—or something that is deeply valued—the prevalence of the ethical impulse underwriting so much of *Beloved* criticism tells me that it is a good thing, worthy of clarification and praxis.

That *Beloved* is a ghost story is well known, and it is not hard to imagine how a contemporary novel about a historically distant but nonetheless always present time—the period of American Slavery and Reconstruction—participates in something like mourning for the past. The story is overwhelming, as is its genesis in the real-life incidents of a runaway slave, Margaret Garner, who in 1856 killed her own child to keep it out of the hands of her pursuing owner. In *Beloved* the murder of the child by her mother Sethe is in the past, but Sethe remains literally haunted by her dead daughter, until her ghost materializes as a young woman named Beloved, come to live with Sethe and her other daughter Denver. Sethe's haunting, dispelled at the end of the novel by a stirring exorcism, resonates so awfully because, as the highly applicable formula puts it, the reader is made to experience the presence of the past. Appropriately therefore, scores of critical articles and book chapters have been devoted to describing the machinations of the novel's mourning, its role in cultural healing, its quest to rebury the dead, or its program of redeeming black female subjectivity from the damning criticism of analyses like the Moynihan report and its bastard children, the Reagan-era bashing of "welfare queens" and Dan Quayle's pathologization of single-motherhood.

The tenor of this criticism is well matched to the novel's achievements. But the claims that the criticism makes are far from self-evident, and the performative power ascribed to literature in such claims bears some scrutiny, if not from the point of view of narratology, then from the perspective of cultural criticism, or even metacriticism. The criticism cited in this article claims that novels *do* things, presumably in the world at large. What do novels do and how do we know they do them? If I were to claim that a novel builds a bridge, I could then empirically say, "and look, there it is, right there—the bridge." But we do not claim that novels do things in three-dimensional space, and no such empirical knowledge is available to us. Novels build bridges across time or among cultures, but these are metaphors only, and express what we wish on their behalf. However, if novels build metaphorical bridges, this implicates a wider reading culture in the process. I suggest that mourning, like bridge-building, may likewise be a metaphor that points us not only to what happens in the novel but also to what responsibilities and actions the novel establishes for readers. A theory of how literature participates in cultural transformation needs to tap into the transformative potential in literature in both psychical and material ways. Psychoanalysis or materialism: this suggests a divide in approaches to African American and other ethnic literatures, and to *Beloved* in particular. Activist, Marxist-materialist criticism in African American and ethnic literary critical practice is one way of putting literature into conversation with the social reality of the world "out there"; with postmodern novels like *Beloved*, formal, linguistic-oriented, or psychoanalytic studies suggest a still deeper if less popularly accessible way of relating literature to lived social experience. I'd like to examine how criticism on *Beloved*, informed by the insights of trauma studies, can participate in a wider political activism.

Mourning, Healing, Redeeming

There is a current of literary criticism that advocates for and finds in literature a process that is variously called mourning, healing, working through, or redemption. Characters, history, and cultures are on the receiving end. Texts—usually novels—do the cultural work, while critics serve as attendants, making the literary and cultural work transparent. Nancy Peterson offers a reading of *Beloved* as part of her larger project in *Against Amnesia* of writing counter-histories in contemporary American ethnic fiction by women. Concluding her book, Peterson sums up: "The preceding chapters have emphasized history as wound, history as trauma, in order to call attention to an important dimension of contemporary women's writing: the need for these texts to bear a double burden—and to function as both history and literature. . . . These literary texts, however, are not only about history; they are also about healing the wounds of history" (169). The goal of ethnic literature, according to Peterson, is not only descriptive, but constructive. Her writers "use literature to tell the other side of history and to refashion the narrative so that history comes out right this time" (183). Peterson's analysis is substantially derived from an optimistic reading of Cathy Caruth's theorizing of literary trauma in her justly celebrated book, *Unclaimed Experience*. Quoting Caruth approvingly, Peterson writes,

> the link between trauma and the initial missed experience leads to a model of reference that is not direct and immediate, but belated, displaced, and oblique. For Caruth, such a theory of trauma and its indirect referentiality suggests "the possibility of a history that is no longer straightforwardly referential." Where better to find an obliquely referential history than in literature, which by

virtue of its figurative language constantly exceeds straightforward understanding? (13)

For Peterson then, literature offers a "counter-history" (13).

Besides the disciplinary slide from history to literature, Peterson has subtly translated Caruth's language. A history "no longer straightforwardly referential" is Caruth's beginning description of narrated traumatic experience (Caruth 11), but Caruth concludes, trenchantly and with implied reference to the work of Paul de Man, that surviving to tell the story of trauma means telling *"what it means not to see"* (105).[2] The deconstructive loop in bearing witness to blindness suggests that the experience of historical trauma is rescued from melancholy only insofar as the suffering subject can narrate his or her own melancholic experience. To the extent that history is a "wound," a reimagining of history along the lines Caruth suggests is always in danger of succumbing to a "repetition compulsion . . . [manifest in] allegories of excess, incomprehensibility, and empty utopian hope" (LaCapra, *History* 208). With Caruth's analysis, the "wound" of history always throbs, though Peterson would have the novelist heal it. This obviously endows the literary author with an impressive capacity for power over the past, especially in Peterson's analysis of *Beloved* where the status and meaning of the concepts "history," "memory," and "imagination" are interwoven and ceaselessly give way to one another, while actual people, the subjects and objects of history, are left out of the loop. Can we so facilely collapse linear time in order to recast history? Can we claim that *Beloved* does things with and for culture and history without also claiming that it somehow is involved in and with the past? And in what way: repetition or closure?

Sharing Peterson's critical agenda and conclusions, many critics have credited Morrison's novel with "working through history and memory . . . [and] building new social configurations of family and kin" (Jesser 325). Others go further, arguing that "Morrison constructs history" and that such "history-making becomes a healing process for the characters, the reader, and the author" (Krumholz 395). All are healed because "Beloved is both the pain and the cure" (400). According to Wardi, "By participating in acts of homage and commemoration, [Morrison] resurrect[s] the spirit of those that came before and raise[s] monuments for the dead." In this way, *Beloved* is a "visible marker that provide[s] a resting place for the ancestors" (51). And in her analysis of the "call-and-response" quality of *Beloved,* Maggie Sale argues that "*Beloved* presents a new way of conceiving of history, one that refuses and refutes master versions of history" (43). Sale explains that the novel's "call for communal response is part of the contemporary healing process that this text is involved in" (44). Sale insists on the corrective and therapeutic value of the novel—the novel *does* things—but she credits the reader with participating in the novel's action. Paying more attention to the function of the reader strengthens an overall analysis of how the novel operates in the world at large, but it also raises the question of just what exactly literature and criticism can be said to do.[3]

Sale's discussion of the importance of the reader for realizing *Beloved*'s healing hints at how the novel's achievements—healing, mourning, countering history—may be accomplished in the world outside the pages of the book. I want to trace this insight in another author's analysis of *Beloved* to show the limits of trauma-theory approaches to *Beloved* and to suggest what lies beyond those limits. Kathleen Brogan's analysis in *Cultural Haunting* echoes Peterson's but goes further in theorizing the effects of *Beloved* on its readers. Citing sociologist Robert Hertz's description of a "second burial," Brogan explains that "the movement Hertz describes from preliminary to final burials, in which a dangerous, spiteful ghost is translated into a benevolent ancestral spirit, closely corresponds to the master plot of possession and exorcism that structures so many stories of cultural haunting," including *Beloved* (66). Suggesting that "final burial shifts power from the dead to the living" and "integrates the dead (as newly accessible spirits) into the ongoing life of the community," Brogan nevertheless stops short of claiming that such a ritual has been fulfilled by the end of Morrison's novel (67). The exorcism of the ghost by the community of women reestablishes the claims of the living over the claims of the dead, but importantly, the women, Sethe, and Paul D cannot or will not pass the event on into a symbolic narrative. In this way, "*Beloved* performs the final burial, but leaves the grave open," calling on readers to "join the author in forming a community of mourners who commemorate the dead" (91).

Brogan ephemerally concludes that the novel's haunting becomes the reader's "historical consciousness," but she precedes this with a hint of a more material call for justice: white readers are invited to make "an unpalatable identification with the novel's [hateful] Schoolteacher or well-meaning but condescending Bodwins," and thereby "take responsibility for both the past and the present." Now we're getting somewhere! Taking responsibility takes historical consciousness seriously. We not only remember, nor even "remember." Instead, we are asked to bear some sort of ethical responsibility for the story we read, the story we live. Brogan's assertion that Morrison's novel is an "invitation" to ethics, however, implies an ethics that undermines its own purpose (92). What we are invited to do, we may also refuse. Historical consciousness of this sort separates knowing from doing, inclination from imperative. Avery Gordon offers a more amplified discussion of the compulsion for (and limits of) ethical identification for readers of *Beloved*. As Gordon puts it, readers are not so much invited into relation with the text as *haunted* by it:

To be in the seemingly old story now scared and not wishing
to be there but not having anywhere else you can go that feels
like a place you can belong is to be haunted. And haunting is
exactly what causes declarative repudiations and voluntaristic
identifications eventually to fail, although it must be said that
they can be sustained for quite some time. Reckoning with ghosts
is not like deciding to read a book: you cannot simply choose the
ghosts with which you are willing to engage. To be haunted is to
make choices within those spiraling determinations that make the
present waver. To be haunted is to be tied to historical and social
effects. To be haunted is to experience the glue of the "If you were
me and I were you logic" come undone. Though you can repeat
over and over again, as if the incantation were a magic that really
worked, I am not Schoolteacher/He is not me, the ghostly matter
will not go away. (190)

The tone of Gordon's passage suggests the anxiety of being haunted by the
novel, and the compulsion to take its claims seriously. As Thomas Keenan
puts it, "It is when we do not know exactly what we should do, when the
effects and conditions of our actions can no longer be calculated, and when
we have nowhere else to turn, not even back onto our 'self,' that we encounter something like responsibility" (2). Like Coleridge's "Wedding Guest" we
can neither turn away nor fail "to pass on" (272, 273) the story of *Beloved*.
Or, as Adam Zachary Newton writes, "one faces a text as one might face
a person, having to confront the claims raised by that very immediacy,
an immediacy of contact, not of meaning" (11). Rather than choosing to
identify (or not), we "face" the novel and submit to its claims. For what?
What do we owe it, its characters, its historical antecedent? The "we" of
such questions is a polyglot "we" of the present, a catch-all pronoun that
only makes sense in the language of politics—"we Americans." Of course
there are a plurality of "wes" to consider: black folks, white folks, and others
dissimilarly but simultaneously dispossessed of life and property during the
eighteenth and nineteenth centuries, not to mention African readers who
would reflect on their continent's losses and culpability in the slave trade.
How exactly this responsibility translates is not clear, but this is not beyond
the scope of a critical reading of *Beloved*. Brogan does not follow up with
a materialist analysis of the status of property and the physical claims the
dead might have on the living, but precisely by not doing so, Brogan points
to the breach between a criticism that psychoanalyzes literature and a criticism that drives towards material and political response to literary claims.
Brogan's and Peterson's commitment to psychoanalysis ultimately positions
the text as consciousness itself, acting out, working through, and mourning

its own narrative, but we can follow Gordon's hint to see how the novel participates in the world at large—the world of the reader.

She Has Claim

The word "claim" has shown up in this essay frequently already, and it is prominent in many analyses of *Beloved* for good reason: the novel's plot, its discursive texture, and its characters' development all pivot on the word "claim." The shifting, multivalent meaning of the word "claim" produces a lexicon that complements, if not outright challenges, the discourse of trauma. For example, as all the black characters in the novel come to realize, "freeing yourself was one thing; claiming ownership of that freed self was another" (95). Running away north is freeing, but is owning yourself similarly material, or purely psychological? Or is the psychology of self-ownership necessarily dependent on the material? Perhaps the difference between freeing and claiming is the same as the difference between doing and claiming: "Sethe had done what she had claimed" (165). What Sethe had done is kill her baby; in what way is this claiming ownership? After he sees what Sethe has done, "right off it was clear, to schoolteacher especially, that there was nothing there to claim" (149). Nonetheless, schoolteacher "filed a claim and rode off" (183). In the first instance, schoolteacher sees that among all the blood, terror, and outright refusal, he has lost what he came for, his property. The second instance is more subtly suggestive of Morrison's awareness of the pervasive and ambiguous business of slavery.[4] Apparently, schoolteacher files an insurance claim on his property, cashing in on a policy such as the ones that modern insurance giants like New York Life sold for slaves in Kentucky during the mid-nineteenth century.[5] Nothing to claim/file a claim; doing/claiming; freeing/claiming ownership: In each instance, "claim" is the simultaneously complementary and contradictory term in the pairing, the term that negates the other, even itself. As the narrator says of Beloved, "Although she has claim, she is not claimed" (274). Not claimed because forgotten, repressed, not sought after . . . but what sort of claim does she have, and on whom?

"Claim" is one of those brilliant words that refracts when read through the lens of the Oxford English Dictionary. As both a verb and a noun, it means to demand as one's own or one's due; to assert and demand recognition of (an alleged right, title, possession); an application for compensation; a right or title. Oxford also lists an obsolete definition for "claim": to call for, cry for, beg loudly, and to cry out. Example: "Beloved, she my daughter. She mine" (Morrison 201). In fact, the example is my own, not Oxford's. Or, it is Morrison's example of how difficult it is to sort out reenslaving possession from nurturance and love. Can Sethe use the syntax of the slave-owner, while speaking as a mother? "When I tell you you mine, I also mean I'm yours" (203).

Most readers of *Beloved* skeptically conclude that a property-based epistemology is the root of all the novel's evil. For example, Trudier Harris observes that the characters in *Beloved* consistently think of themselves in monetary terms which are ultimately inadequate or self-negating (333). Building on that observation, Erik Dussere argues that "if liberation is to be had at all for ex-slaves, it is not through the paying of debts or the balancing of books; Morrison deliberately denies the notion of justice implied by such acts" (343). Dussere is at least partially correct. *Beloved* is a novel that consistently pits the status of humanity against the status of property, and no amount of money can justly compensate the dehumanization involved in slavery.[6] However, precisely because the most daring acts of humanity are violations against the laws of property, the discourse of property in slavery is embedded with a dialectical and self-negating discourse of humanity. "Slave" aims to cancel "human," while freeing one's self is always freeing oneself from a state of property. There is no getting around what characters are freeing themselves into, as Houston Baker reminds us: "the creative individual (the *black subject*) must, therefore, whether he self-consciously wills it or not, come to terms with 'commercial deportation' and the 'economics of slavery'" (39).[7] Beyond this dialectic, though, alternative conceptions of property among slaves not only did not cancel humanity but in fact sustained and even *produced* kinship ties. Because legal codes denied a slave's right to property, slaves who had acquired property displayed it publicly, in yards around slave quarters, or with special brands. And because money to buy property was so hard to come by, slaves depended on alliances with kin, or established quasi-kinship with others sharing quarters in order to attain group-owned property.[8] What this means is that there is a way of reading Sethe's property-based discourse outside of the rhetoric of law. Property may ultimately be a material word, but it exceeds the rhetoric of legal codes and requires some form of human recognition to sustain. Rather than dismiss the discourse of property as "the master's language" to be overcome, we can read it as expressing the experience of slavery, including those recurring moments where humanity exceeds the legal codes that would bind it.

Of all the terms associated with property in the novel, "claim" best captures the slippery nature of ownership in the nineteenth century. Claiming is paradoxically performative and redundant: the declaration or act of claim establishes original possession. That is, you acquire the possession in the act of calling it yours. But claiming also means seeking compensation for something lost. As anyone who has filed an insurance claim knows, it is essential to prove your prior possession of what was lost before you can claim it. There's turning the screw of interpretation: how can you claim something you never had, how can you demand something be restored that was not there in the first place? Morrison sustains rather than elides the language of property not to expose how susceptible her characters are to internalized self-perceptions as property, but to turn that discourse against itself, from the inside out. As Hortense Spillers has observed in other emancipatory texts, "the project of liberation for African-Americans has found urgency in two passionate motivations that are twinned—(1) to break apart, to rupture violently the laws of American behavior that make [dehumanizing] syntax possible; (2) to introduce a new *semantic* field to [one's] own historic moment" (226). Making a new semantic field may take on a number of possible revisionary forms, but with *Beloved* the new field is necessarily written across the already existing one. Sethe's murder of her daughter is precisely her claim of ownership for her; breaking the law of slavery is an assertion of the "law of the mother" (Spillers 228). Trauma is experienced as the breaking and re-making of the law, and in this way Sethe's action is an injury to the law, and the one who would claim her, at the same time that it is a trauma to her. Contrary to the way we typically think of injury, it is against the law she breaks that Sethe has claim and produces claim for others around her, because Sethe's humanity and her claim for her family precede the law.

Just as "freeing" and "owning" are words loaded with political, ethical, and material meaning in the novel's setting of Reconstruction, so too is "claim" a word under material and political legislation during the mid- to late-nineteenth century, as Dylan Penningroth explains in *The Claims of Kinfolk*. In 1871, Congress formed the Southern Claims Commission to investigate claims of property loss filed by Southern Unionists who demanded compensation for property stolen by Union soldiers. According to Penningroth, in addition to the thousands of claims anticipated by white southern landowners, the Commission was also inundated by hundreds of ex-slaves filing claims for similarly usurped property. Despite the fact that slaves could not legally have been in possession of property, the Claims Commission recognized alternative definitions of property title and proof, for both black and white claimants. Ex-slaves brought kin and neighbors to testify as eye-witnesses to property possession, and joint claims filed by several members of a family for property were granted. Typically, we think only the state can grant property rights, but in this case the state was forced to recognize or grant the right to property based not on pre-existing title but on hard to pin down claims.

The Southern Claims Commission represents one aspect of a wider re-negotiation of property rights in the US during the mid-nineteenth century. Contemporaneous with the Southern Claims Commission, Congress also passed the General Mining Law of 1872, establishing Federal procedures for staking and filing claims for mineral rights, in concert with previous state-passed laws in 1866 and 1870. The new law, which generally still holds, is remarkably simple: whoever so identifies a precious mineral on previously unclaimed government property may file a claim and thereby take possession of the minerals therein. Administrative fees and proof of "improvement of the claim" are also required.[9] The devil, however, is in the details, as Patricia Nelson Limerick observes: "the events of Western history represent, not a simple process of territorial expansion, but an array of efforts to wrap the concept of property around unwieldy objects" (71). Unwieldy because these objects are minerals that are difficult to access, animals that move, or slaves that run away. In this way, the Fugitive Slave Act of 1850 is one of a number of mid-century attempts to codify property rights over resistant object/agents in a heterogeneous nation. The General Mining Law, as well as the Homestead Act of 1862, can be seen as revisions of the American theory of property law that renegotiated the priority of individuals over things. In "the wilderness," beyond the scope of the law, people needed community to verify claims.[10] At the risk of running far afield from the subject here, it is worth mentioning that Denver—the city whose name is metonymically if not directly attached to Sethe's other daughter, born on the way to freedom in 1855—was founded in 1858, on the eve of the Civil War, by gold prospectors looking to establish a claim district, and during the 1870's—the novel's present time—the city was experiencing its first great population and financial boom due to gold mining.

I offer this information not as evidence so much as resonance in order to suggest how *Beloved*'s historical setting is underwritten by a set of complicated legal and extra legal codes that at least begrudgingly privilege subjects over objects, people over things. *Beloved* is set during a period in history when claiming pillaged property, gold, or your own free self, means establishing that there is something to be claimed in the first place, whether by securing the affirmation of family members, or by digging down deep to uncover what is of value. And because "claim" is one of those redundantly peformative practices—you establish ownership over what is rightfully yours through declaration—it suggests how claiming is less an act of liberation and more an act of restoration, returning yourself to you. Claiming rests on the veracity and verifiability of the "I," and to acknowledge the kinds of claims described so far means recognizing the life and work of the one who makes the claim. Are we back where we started, with another version of working-through? Is this not a material allegory of the Freudian formula, *wo es war, soll ich warden* (where it was, there I shall be—in Lacan's appropriation)—establishing the "I" in the territory of the material, the "it," thereby moving from repressed or absent experience to a worked-through and symbolically mourned trauma?[11] Perhaps so, if we grant what is also new, namely the material, financial implications of the discourse of property.

Property is the point in the novel, and it is where trauma and material possession meet. Drawing out the novel's multivalent utterances of "claim" does not change the subject from trauma to property rights; rather, it points out the novel's particular lexicon of trauma. The experience of the black characters is decidedly the experience of property—stealing or being stolen, freeing or being freed, repossessing, and hauntingly, claiming. Sethe tells Paul D this much near the novel's beginning, when he first observes the raised scars on Sethe's back:

> "They used cowhide on you?"
> "And they took my milk."
> "They beat you and you was pregnant?"
> "And they took my milk!" (17)

The repetitive exchange suggests that "they took my milk" is the clarifying corrective to Paul D's question. The trauma, Sethe tells him and us, is not solely the beating, but especially the taking, not only the whipping but also the stealing of her milk. The operative word in the exchange is "my" as in *mine*. Sethe lays claim to herself, and the product of her own body. Taking, later glossed as stealing (200), means taking what was rightfully hers. Her milk parallels and inverts the production of ink for schoolteacher. Though a formula not of her own design, Sethe mixes the ink just the way schoolteacher likes it (37). With this special-mixed ink schoolteacher records his observations of Sethe and the other slaves. The material rewrites the corporeal, the special ink, synecdoche of individuality, produces the logic by which schoolteacher can later come to claim his property, stolen away to 124 Bluestone, fatefully acting for all the world to see like human beings. Conversely, it is Sethe's own special mix, her breast milk, "enough for all," which impels her, with all the force of human love, to escape from Sweet Home, to claim her right to her own self, a right she has no right to claim (100). In this case the language of material possession is the best register for the expression of being human, the best way to claim humanity. Later, Sethe decides it is time to run when she realizes that her children, the product of her body's own labor, are increased property for schoolteacher.[12] In each case, assertions of self-ownership contradict Sethe's legal status as property, and posit a different sort of claim, where kinship, family, and love produce and define humanity.

This meditation on the relationship between bodily trauma and the body as property, mediated by the language of "rights" and "claiming," points out the flexibility of concepts like injury and redress that constitute the broader field within which trauma occurs. I am negotiating a reading of somatic or psychical trauma with an analysis of proto-legal injury by arguing that a discourse of ownership marks the experience of being a slave; it is through that discourse that Sethe and others are best able to affirm their being-human. As Satya Mohanty puts it, "experiences are crucial indexes of our relationships with our world (including our relationships with ourselves), and to stress their cognitive nature is to argue that they can be susceptible to varying degrees of socially constructed truth or error and can serve as sources of objective knowledge or socially produced mystification" (211). Experiences index objective knowledge when they are indicative of our "objective social location" (216), and they allow for self-knowledge when we are able to read our own experiences in light of our historical and theoretical moment (229). This would mean that Sethe's and other characters' lexicon of property is the result of a conscious analysis of their own experiences—the experience of being raced, dehumanized, or made property.[13] It also suggests a realistic awareness of their social location as subjects and objects in the American capitalist economy.[14]

The discourse of Sethe's emotional and moral experience, performed in trauma-centered analyses of the novel, provides by far the richest possible description of her deep textured humanity. However, in doing so this discourse invariably winds up in impossible ontological problems, especially given the extent to which trauma-theory is wed to deconstructive accounts of being human, a point which Caruth makes clear but which Peterson and others elide. Passing the discourse of psychic trauma through the semantic field of injury and the adherents of materialism and property raises a new question. If the productive response to trauma is working-through and mourning, what is the right response to material loss? Or, to add another twist, is a psychoanalytically conceived effort of working-through adequate to the task when the experience of loss is mediated through the discourse of property?[15]

Reparation

In a study of the intersection of narrative theory and Critical Race Studies, Carl Gutierrez-Jones suggests ways of thinking about how the narrative depiction of trauma may participate in a materialist discourse oriented toward social justice. Gutierrez-Jones reminds us that,

> Simply making power and injury visible in no way guarantees a more liberated society, although of course recognition of these injuries can be a crucial initial step. The key is appropriately mediating between such recognitions and the literacy that governs the interpretation of social and cultural problems generally. Without this mediation, the making visible of injury can easily be co-opted into a project in which conflicts are subdued, or worse yet, completely robbed of their ability to generate "alternative" political thought. (74–75)

Gutierrez-Jones's cautionary gesture points two ways: Mediation means speaking *for* those aggrieved and to a discursive system which sustains oppression; studies of injury need to provide methods of redress in order to be effective, and theories that do not account for material injury do not advance the claims of literature into the "literacy," or discourse, of the world at large. I have been arguing that among the limitations of trauma-studies readings of novels like *Beloved* is that they end up either serving as mute witnesses to a scene of destruction, like Benjamin's so frequently cited "Angel of History," or they end up suggesting that something or someone has mourned and is now healed in or by the text, without adequately exploring just what and how this happens. Working within a psychoanalytic discourse, Gutierrez-Jones associates the first type of analysis with "acting-out" and the second with "working-through" (58). In the case of legacies of historical trauma such as slavery, political measures aimed at producing economic equality between black and white folks may result in reductive and narrow legal redress without addressing fundamental issues of ethics.[16] On the other hand, mourning through literature or other cathected cultural symbols produces a ritual of working-through and perhaps narrative closure, or even the possibility for ethical encounters between black and white as Brogan suggests, but without invoking the clearly central fields of law and property. The reader by now likely anticipates my question: is there a formula, a form of justice, or a rhetoric, that comprehends and enables both mourning and material redress, and that is neither so wedded to the past nor so utopian as to supplant ethics with ideology, resentment, or facile fictions of narrative identification?

I suggest that a discourse of reparation is adequate to the task. To be more and less specific, by "reparation" I mean the idea of reparations for slavery and Jim Crow social oppression and marginalization, though I do not intend to debate the political and philosophical complications here, partly because such complications are so prohibitive, and partly because they are so compelling.[17] Reparation is another provocatively refractable word, meaning restoration, spiritual healing, mending, compensation, and reconciliation. Reparations claims brought forth against participants in the institution of slavery as well as Jim Crow segregation demand money, property retrieval, apology, and institutional redress. In short, the idea within "reparation" includes a combination of psychical and spiritual, as well as material and political redress for wrong done to the injured party. Because the word's meaning toggles between spiritual and material repair it seems to symmetrically address trauma in *Beloved* as the experience of being property and the struggle to claim ownership of one's own self. Precisely because freeing the self is a process requiring, but not wholly facilitated by, the legal documentation of freedom, the up front discussion of compensation for what Margaret/Sethe Garner and her descendants have claim for is part of the process of securing freedom. The materialism of the language associated with reparations may seem off-putting or reductive only when we fail to recognize that Morrison consistently twins the language of spiritual and psychic devastation with the language of material loss and legal injury, giving us a materially textured surface that conforms to the depths of the spirit.

Though there are substantial social and legal obstacles to even engaging a pragmatic conversation about reparations, this does not preclude thinking about the ethics and value of reparations. As J. Angelo Corlett reminds readers in *Race, Racism, and Reparation*, we should not confuse *ought* with *can* regarding reparations (192). In fact, the discourse of reparations is a helpful link between the discourse of trauma and a political and material discourse; furthermore, I suggest that the ethics of reparation underwrites trauma-studies analyses of *Beloved*. By attending to the language of property we may translate a criticism that hails the process of mourning and healing trauma into a critical discussion of the novel's investment in reparative justice. Given the activist sentiment at work in trauma-studies readings of *Beloved*, and given the ethical perspective that accompanies so many of these readings, we find already embedded in this criticism the urge for the novel to participate in something like political reconciliation. Considering too that the novel's own terms for trauma are terms of property, legal redress, and injury compensation, a meditation on reparative justice is well within the scope of any account of the novel that aims to examine how it directly participates in an American context of political race.

A good deal of the intellectual energy for current reparations law suits flows from Boris Bittker's *The Case for Black Reparations*, brought to print in 1973 by Toni Morrison while she was an editor at Random House. It was at Random House that Morrison conceived of and researched the African-American archival project, *The Black Book*, published in 1974, which occasioned her discovery of Margaret Garner's story; the overlap at least suggests that Garner's story and an interest in reparations were drawn from the same intellectual well. Commenting on the recent republication of *The Case for Black Reparations* by Beacon Press, Morrison writes, "publishing Boris Bittker's *The Case for Black Reparations* in 1973 seemed to me an important contribution to the fledgling reparations debate. Now with its focus on the legal hurdles of such compensation, his work is more than significant—it is vital" (Jacket cover). Just as reparations paid to Jewish victims of the Holocaust testify to the presentness of the past, so too should we see the present day lawsuits for black reparations as part of a single trajectory of history that begins with the Middle Passage. Because such lawsuits are class-action and require ancestor tracing, they participate in their own "rememory" project (*Beloved* 36). As Randall Robinson, a leading proponent of reparations, puts it, "even the *making* of a well-reasoned case for restitution will do wonders for the spirit of African Americans" (232). Robinson's point is not so much that African Americans are demoralized and in need of spiritual uplift; rather, the practicalities of filing for class-action lawsuits, including tracing family *and* corporate genealogies, and the genealogy of legal codes regulating slaves and ex-slaves furthers the recovery of our national memory. Thought of this way, reparation is as much an imperative process following horrific and cruel dispossession as is mourning subsequent to trauma. And in the case of *Beloved*, reparation and the work of mourning—namely, working-through—are part and parcel of the same process. Here Dominick LaCapra's description of "working through" (which is rarely cited in trauma theory readings of *Beloved*, but prominent in critical race and new-realist accounts of race and ethnicity) as a process involving "hybridized narrative," and "acting out" for the sake of achieving "critical distance on experience," is most helpful (*Representing* 199–200). LaCapra is refreshingly skeptical of the quasi-mystical analyses of mourning in Holocaust literature, as well as fetishistic narratives of melancholy. Establishing working-through as an historical process, part of but also separate from mourning, LaCapra points to how critical race narratives not only describe and reinscribe legal and political constructions of what we otherwise loosely refer to as "historical consciousness." In LaCapra's terms, the psychoanalytic criticism of *Beloved* together with the novel comprise a "hybridzed narrative," while the present article is an attempt to work through the material implications of such a narrative in order to indeed establish a critical distance from the past.

The novel models one form of reparation near the end, when a group of women who had previously condemned Sethe, first for living so well so soon after manumission, and then for the excess of both her love and her crime directed at her children, come to exorcise the ghost sucking Sethe dry. Ella, who leads the women, was especially appalled by Sethe's "sin" but her sense of justice is keen enough to know that "what's fair ain't necessarily right" (256). I call this act of rescue a reparation in the sense of "restoration," a term also suggested by the circularity of the word "claim"—restoring the self to the self. And if we recall "claim's" gloss as a "shout, an affirmation" and note that the women prayed, sang, and "hollered" (257) for Sethe, we might say that in this way they claim Sethe on her behalf, an act advanced by Paul D's assertion to Sethe that "you your own best thing" (273).[18]

Beloved is a novel that makes the past feel painfully present to readers, as so many of the novel's critics have attested. If such an experience is going to amount to a reckoning beyond haunting, and if we are ever to look up from the open grave constituted by the book in our hands, it is up to the reader to establish "critical distance" between past and present. Revising history means reconstructing a view of the past as well as recharting the future. The dream that the novel makes "history come out right this time" can only come true when we acknowledge just what it is that characters in the novel and the novel itself claim of us. The problematically plural "us" or "we" invoked on behalf of the novel's readers is even more vexed when it comes to the topic of reparations for slavery and segregation. Any reader can imagine some of the more prominent objections to reparations based on America's spectacular racial and ethnic variety and histories, and it is precisely these objections that show us how to extend Brogan's and Gordon's suggestion that all readers identify, willingly or not, with some character or some aspect of *Beloved*. The predictable reactions, "yeah, I'm white, but I didn't own any slaves and neither did my Turkish immigrant grandparents" or "Toni Morrison—she's black and she's got more money than god! What does she need reparations for?" point out how the discourse of reparations is political but also personal and ulti-mately ethical—by what logic do *I owe you*, or *you owe me?*

At the broadest levels of political redress, answers to this question can remain overly general and unsatisfying, but the ethics of narrative encounter produces an intimate as well as compelling answer. Adam Zachary Newton's thesis on narrative ethics, inspired by Emmanuel Levinas, explains a reader-text relation of "facing" where the humanity of the voice of the text preconditions the reading experience as ethical. Newton cites Levinas and interpolates his philosophy into thinking about literature: "The approach to the face is the most basic mode of responsibility. As such, the face of the other is verticality and uprightness; it spells a relation of rectitude. The face is not in front of me but above me. . . . In the relation to the face I am exposed as a usurper of the place of the other" (qtd. in Newton 13). Newton goes on to say that, like Levinas's account of the ethical encounter, "narrative situations create an im-mediacy and force, framing relations of provocation, call, and response that bind narrator and listener, author and character, or reader and text" (Newton 13). *Beloved*'s haunting hails us all, situating us in a subjective yet ethical rela-tion with the book's story, but also our own. From there it is easy to see that braiding the history embedded in *Beloved* with the genealogies of its readers produces an aggregate reading of America, moving us from ethics to politics. Such a movement is implied in many critical analyses of the novel, but in this case psychoanalysis limits the capacity and quality of identification between readers and the text merely to the realm of the psyche. A national discussion on the efficacy and limits of apology, forgiveness, compensation, and broadly conceived social redress begins when readers turn from the private encounter with the novel to the public history the text produces. The desire for his-torically corrective justice transcends but also sustains a free State as well as a state of freedom.[19] Working for justice is the "difficult freedom" Levinas describes that involves continually wrestling with history in order to achieve the present.

Reconciliation and *Ressentiment*

The purpose of recalibrating our critical discourse toward reparations is illustrated by the word "reconciliation," one of reparation's glosses. Reconciliation is a friendly word—conciliation being the state of friendly congress—but it bears nothing less than the weight of history, as it is deployed both ethically and politically, in South Africa for example.[20] Again, avoiding a discussion of the process of such a program, we might consider at least the intended result and compare that against our wish fulfilling dream-readings of *Beloved*. A state of reconciliation may be achieved through recognition or a formal apology. Material compensation is not tied to symmetrical restoration of what was lost, but rather serves a future-oriented project of reconciliation. Indeed, reconciliation is both pragmatically political as well as ethical, meaning the (re)establishment of a state of affairs sufficient for forward progress by reconciling parties into the future.[21] Susan Dwyer's conception of reconciliation as a form of "narrative incorporation" is especially helpful for thinking about how literature might participate in this process: reconciliation means revising our sense of the past based on a full disclosure of what happened, who participated, and how; coherently linking that past to the crises or schisms of the present; and using that narrative to produce a political program for forward progress (102).[22] I suggest that such a narrative is the fullest and most fruitful kind of "historical consciousness" for readers of *Beloved*. The critics I cited here agree that Morrison's novel initiates this narrative by linking past and present, and I am arguing that we take the novel most seriously when we further the narrative through reconciliation ourselves.

Importantly, reconciliation does not demand total compensation for loss, which with slavery is infinite. As James Hans astutely observes, among the central insights of *Beloved* is Baby Suggs's maxim, "good is knowing when to stop" (87), which can be read as an injunction against infinite *ressentiment* (Hans 101). What can be claimed is ultimately unclaimable. Reparation is, after all, a derivation of "repair" or *re-pare*, return to the homeland. In this way, reparation is a concept that negates itself, but for the fact that Morrison provides a language and a conversation-starter adequate for understanding what was lost and what can be gained. Ella's asymmetrical formula, "what's fair ain't necessarily right" releases the present from an infinite debt to the past, and hinges it to a future based on a politics and ethics of responsibility and respect. Both Baby Suggs's and Ella's comments suggest a utilitarian conception of justice over an ideal justice: "knowing when to stop" and "right" replace an infinite "good" or "fair." At least we can talk about it.

Beloved has been called a slave-narrative, a re-memory, and a "counter-history," reenvisioning our past. But it is also our present. The novel we read is the text that reads us, as the saying goes. To the extent that we make reparation a consequence of reading, the book is either our traumatic past, or we are its reconciling future.

NOTES

1. Though I came up with this term originally, I later found Vickroy's citation of Naomi Morgenstern's use of the phrase with regard to *Beloved*. Morgenstern uses the term somewhat differently, calling the novel itself an example of wish-fulfillment for its revision of Margaret Garner's story.

2. Caruth adds, "Through the notion of trauma, I will argue, we can understand that a rethinking of reference is aimed not at eliminating history but as resituating it in our understanding, that is, as precisely permitting *history* to arise where *immediate understanding* may not" (11).

3. Walter Benn Michaels complains that readers of *Beloved* perpetuate racist ideologies of the past when they conflate history with what he considers the novel's "mythology," though he does not pause to consider that amnesia produces its own sort of mythology (188). A more substantive and helpful conflation of the ethics and politics of reading *Beloved* will help us locate our responses to the novel in its true historical moment, the present.

4. See Savitt for a discussion of how the business of insuring slaves produced problems of category and definition for slave owners and courts.

5. According to documents produced by the California Department of Insurance under the directive of former Governor Gray Davis, New York Life Insurance Company's ancestor company "Nautilus" would have been the likely holder of a policy on slaves owned in Kentucky. In response to slave-reparation lawsuits, New York Life has stated on their website:

> New York Life abhors the practice of slavery, historically and currently, and we profoundly regret that our predecessor company, Nautilus Insurance Company, was associated in any way with it, for even a brief period of time. The fact that slavery was legal in certain parts of the United States at the time doesn't make it any less repugnant. Any lawsuit about events 150 years ago faces huge legal hurdles, and we fully expect to prevail in court. We believe it is far more appropriate to judge a company by its values and actions today.

The rhetoric of the statement establishes the present as the negation of the past, and the "move on" attitude is at least ironic in an insurance company.

6. See William Goodell's important and oft-cited *The American Slave Code in Theory and Practice*, published in 1853. Goodell quotes laws establishing the categorical denial of a chattel's right to property, ownership of children, and the right to the term "human." He concludes, "The practice [of slavery] cannot be better than the code itself" (3).

7. Baker is perhaps too celebratory in his analysis of emergent black subjectivity. Saidiya Hartman has examined the economics of manumission and Reconstruction and concludes that for blacks during Reconstruction, "extant and emergent forms of domination intensified and exacerbated the responsibilities and the afflictions of the newly emancipated," primarily because "liberty, property, and whiteness were inextricably enmeshed" (117, 119). Morrison's descriptions of Paul D's experiences with Reconstruction support Hartman's Marxist analysis. I am suggesting that

in such an economic and social environment, ex-slaves such as Sethe and Paul D mediate their experiences through the rhetoric of property and economics in order to strategically assess the dangerous and shifting currents of racism.

8. Despite the categorical prohibition of slaves from owning property, it is quite clear that they did own property, albeit meager, and with the obvious consent of their owners, according to Dylan Penningroth. Garden patches, animals, tools, and domestic implements were more or less owned in an extra-legal sense. See Huston for a macro-history of property rights and the Civil War.

9. *General Mining Law of 1872*, Forty Second Congress, Session II, 10 May 1872.

10. In order to establish at least local procedures for recognizing claims, and to preempt or prosecute fatal acts of "claim jumping," groups of miners formed "claim clubs," organized around local municipal districts.

11. This is the original German, translated by Strachey as "where id was, there ego shall be." Reinhard and Lupton trace the reasoning in Lacan's transformation of "id" to "it" and "ego" to "I," with the "I" emerging out of the "It." Concretizing the "It" as material property is my own suggestion.

12. One interesting confluence: LisaGay Hamilton, who plays the younger version of Sethe at Sweet Home in the film of *Beloved* recently produced a version of Eve Ensler's "The Vagina Monologues," which included Kimberle Crenshaw's reading of her "Black Vaginas"—a monologue suggesting the rational of compensating black women for producing so much productive "property" during slavery.

13. There is substantial evidence that characters do indeed reflect on their social location as property. Consider Baby Suggs's internal meditation on being bought by her son (146), Sixo's lesson learned after stealing the pig (190), Paul D's instruction in his precise monetary value after being caught running away (226), and Sethe's realization that she and her children are her owners' property—an insight that prompts her flight (196–197).

14. Mohanty's analysis of *Beloved* appears at the end of *Literary Theory and the Claims of History*, in which he theorizes an epistemology of reality after postmodernism offering an alternative to reading trauma only or purely from the point of view of psychoanalysis. Mohanty's theory and its companion articulation by Paula Moya in *Learning From Experience* (2002) seem to rely on a problematically tautological presumption that people can evaluate their social experience without that evaluation being somehow part of the experience. Representation—the act of narrative imagination or autobiography—is also an experience of the self writing the self, so it is not clear on what ground of objectivity the post-positivist realist auto-evaluator of experience stands. Unlike Mohanty, I am not arguing that Sethe has "objective knowledge" of her experience, nor do we readers, though we are compelled by the novel to reflect on and reorient our own experiences. For a rich forum on Mohanty's argument see Alcoff, Levine, Buell, Saldívar, Wood, and Anderson.

15. Moving between psychical and materialist analyses is not an either/or choice. Claudia Tate's *Psychoanalysis and Black Novels* makes a persuasive case for a nuanced reading of the black psyche as part of the larger project of exploring social protest literature. The impulse to psychoanalyze is part of the same project of elucidating and advancing the claims of social protest in literature and criticism.

16. Rey Chow's creative and compelling analysis of the "protestant ethnic" suggests the trap of materialist-conceived ethnic identification: Chow concludes by summing up:

> Admittedly, ethnicity continues ... to function in a utopian, Marxist/Lukácsian paradigm of protest and struggle, which is grounded in moral universalisms such as democracy, freedom of speech, and human rights. At the same time, this familiar paradigm seems readily to be transforming into something else, something akin to a systematic capitalist ethos of objectification and reification, whereby what is proclaimed to be human must also increasingly take on the significance of a commodity, a commodified spectacle." (48)

Turning the human into a commodity—the worst kind of cultural violence. Are protests by and on behalf of the oppressed ethnic subject fated to duplicate the logic of oppression-by-comodification, as Chow suggests? Brogan suggests the reader enters the "scene" of the novel, identifying with characters, or standing at the grave, but this is at least potentially narcissistic, a "seen," or act of looking at one's own self and projecting one's own self into the scene. The question I am trying to answer here is, can we imagine a form of criticism that acknowledges the claims that *Beloved* makes on our present without either succumbing to the paralysis of transference, the arrogation of identification, or the assumption of a vocational relation to the text, where criticism requires the traumatized text to support its own critical claims?

17. There are countless legal, cultural, and philosophical texts devoted to the subject of slave reparations, not to mention websites. Boris Bittker's *The Case for Black Reparations* lays out the legal and moral case for reparations clearly and comprehensively. Lecky and Wright's *The Black Manifesto* is a collection of essays on the topic, including the original "Black Manifesto" that gave life to the modern reparations movement. J. Angelo Corlett's *Race, Racism, & Reparations* suggests how Native-American and African-American claims for reparation compare. Janna Thompson's *Taking Responsibility for the Past* is one of many works of political philosophy which discusses reparations. Thompson's work is noteworthy for me because she helpfully moves from the most basic terms and concepts to the complexities involved in a political philosophy of reparation. David Delaney's *Race, Place, and Law 1836–1948* is not about reparations per se, but sets slavery, emancipation, and Jim Crow in a legal history, thereby laying the grounds for individual and class action claims by descendants of slaves against the government. Randall Robinson's *The Debt* is not a scholarly work, but a well-reasoned case for reparations as redress for our current political moment.

18. Ultimately, Sethe has to embrace herself—her "best thing." Ella and the other women, and Paul D can only do so much in this regard. In this way, Ella and Paul D hail Sethe in a way similar to how Baby Suggs hails a community of ex-slaves through her preaching in the clearing, urging them to love themselves. It is debatable as to whether or not Sethe finally claims herself as Paul D suggests she should.

19. Wendy Brown disagrees: "Even as we seek to redress the pain and humiliation consequent to historical deprivation of freedom in a putatively 'free' political order, might we thus sustain the psychic residues of these histories as the animus of political institutions constitutive of our future?" (29). Such a question only has teeth in the realm of theory. Where people really live—schools, jobs, polluted communities—psychic residues would be a fine trade for getting rid of the often physically toxic residues of oppression.

20. The South African "Promotion of National Unity and Reconciliation Act, 1995," which established the historic Truth and Reconciliation Commission,

"provides a historic bridge between the past of a deeply divided society characterized by strife, conflict, untold suffering and injustice, and a future founded on the recognition of human rights, democracy and peaceful co-existence for all South Africans, irrespective of colour, race, class, belief or sex."

21. "A better understanding of reconciliation . . . is that reconciliation is achieved when the harm done by injustice to relations of respect and trust that ought to exist between individuals or nations has been repaired or compensated for by the perpetrator in such a way that this harm is no longer regarded as standing in the way of establishing or re-establishing these relations" (Thompson 50). See Dwyer's realist discussion of why reconciliation is a first-tier moral response to injury and historical trauma.

22. Michigan Congressman John Conyers has sponsored House Bill H.R. 40 as the beginning stage of just this sort of national narrative construction. The Bill aims "to acknowledge the fundamental injustice, cruelty, brutality, and inhumanity of slavery in the United States and the 13 American colonies between 1619 and 1865 and to establish a commission to examine the institution of slavery, subsequently de jure and de facto racial and economic discrimination against African-Americans, and the impact of these forces on living African-Americans, to make recommendations to the Congress on appropriate remedies, and for other purposes."

Works Cited

Alcoff, Linda. "Objectivity and its Politics." *New Literary History* 32 (2001): 835–848.

Anderson, Amanda. "Realism, Universalism, and the Science of the Human." *Diacritics* 29.2 (1999): 3–17.

Baker, Houston A., Jr. *Blues, Ideology, and Afro-American Literatures*. Chicago: Chicago University Press, 1984.

Benn Michaels, Walter. "'You Who Was Never There': Slavery and the New Historicism— Deconstruction and the Holocaust." *The Americanization of the Holocaust*. Ed. Hilene Flanzbaum. Baltimore: Johns Hopkins University Press, 1999. 181–197.

Bittker, Boris I. *The Case for Black Reparations*. Boston: Beacon, 2003.

Brogan, Kathleen. *Cultural Haunting: Ghosts and Ethnicity in Recent American Literature*. Charlottesville: University of Virginia Press, 1998.

Brown, Wendy. *States of Injury: Power and Freedom in Late Modernity*. Princeton: Princeton University Press, 1995.

Buell, Lawerence. "Ethics as Objectivity: A Necessary Oxymoron?" *New Literary History* 32 (2001): 855–857.

California Department of Insurance. 2005. Public Programs: Consumers: Slavery Era Insurance Registry. April 21, 2006 <http://www.insurance.ca.gov/0100-consumers/0300-public-programs/0200-slavery-era-insur/>.

Caruth, Cathy. *Unclaimed Experience: Trauma, Narrative, and History*. Baltimore: Johns Hopkins University Press, 1996.

Chow, Rey. *The Protestant Ethnic and the Spirit of Capitalism*. New York: Columbia University Press, 2002.

"Claim." *Oxford English Dictionary*. 2nd ed. 1989.

Corlett, J. Angelo. *Race, Racism, and Reparations*. Ithaca: Cornell University Press, 2003.

Delaney, David. *Race, Place, and the Law 1836–1948*. Austin: University of Texas Press, 1998.

Dussere, Erik. "Accounting for Slavery: Economic Narratives in Morrison and Faulkner." *Modern Fiction Studies* 47 (2001): 329–355.

Dwyer, Susan. "Reconciliation for Realists." *Dilemmas of Reconciliation: Cases and Concepts.* Eds. Carol A. L. Prager and Trudy Govier. Ontario: Wilfrid Laurier University Press, 2003. 91–110.

Goodell, William. *The American Slave Code in Theory and Practice; Its Distinctive Features Shown by its Statutes, Judicial Decisions, & Illustrative Facts.* London: Clark, Beeton, 1853.

Gordon, Avery. *Ghostly Matters: Haunting and the Sociological Imagination.* Minneapolis: University of Minnesota Press, 1997.

Gutiérrez-Jones, Carl. *Critical Race Narratives: A Study of Race, Rhetoric, and Injury.* New York: New York University Press, 2001.

Hans, James S. *The Golden Mean.* New York: SUNY Press, 1994.

Harris, Trudier. "Escaping Slavery But Not its Images." *Toni Morrison: Critical Perspectives Past and Present.* Eds. Henry Louis Gates Jr. and K. A. Appiah. New York: Amistad, 1993. 330–341.

Hartman, Saidiya V. *Scenes of Subjection: Terror, Slavery, and Self-Making in Nineteenth-Century America.* New York: Oxford University Press, 1997.

Huston, James L. *Calculating the Value of the Union: Slavery, Property Rights, and the Economic Origins of the Civil War.* Chapel Hill: University of North Carolina Press, 2003.

Jesser, Nancy. "Violence, Home, and Community in Toni Morrison's *Beloved.*" *African American Review* 33 (1999): 325–345.

Keenan, Thomas. *Fables of Responsibility: Aberrations and Predicaments in Ethics and Politics.* Stanford: Stanford University Press, 1997.

Krumholz, Linda. "The Ghosts of Slavery: Historical Recovery in Toni Morrison's *Beloved.*" *African American Review* 26 (1992): 395–408.

LaCapra, Dominick. *History and Memory After Auschwitz.* Ithaca: Cornell University Press, 1998.

———. *Representing the Holocaust: History, Theory, Trauma.* Ithaca: Cornell University Press, 1994.

Lecky, Robert S. and H. Elliot Wright, Eds. *Black Manifesto: Religion, Racism, and Reparations.* New York: Sheed, 1969.

Levine, George Lewis. "Saving Disinterest: Aesthetics, Contingency, and Mixed Emotions." *New Literary History* 32 (2001): 907–931.

Limerick, Patricia Nelson. *The Legacy of Conquest: the Unbroken Past of the American West.* New York: Norton, 1987.

Lupton, Julia Reinhard and Kenneth Reinhard. *After Oedipus: Shakespeare in Psychoanalysis.* Ithaca: Cornell University Press, 1993.

Mohanty, Satya. *Literary Theory and the Claims of History: Postmodernism, Objectivity, Multicultural Politics.* Ithaca: Cornell University Press, 1997.

Morgenstern, Naomi. "Mother's Milk and Sister's Blood: Trauma and the Neo-Slave Narrative." *Differences: A Journal of Feminist Cultural Studies* 8.2 (1996): 101–126.

Morrison, Toni. *Beloved.* New York: Plume, 1988.

———. "How Can Values be Taught in the University?" 2000. *University Center for Human Values Tenth Anniversary Celebration.* 23 May 2006. Princeton Web Media. 26 April 2006 <http://www.princeton.edu/WebMedia/special/>.

Newton, Adam Zachary. *Narrative Ethics.* Cambridge: Harvard University Press, 1995.

Penningroth, Dylan C. *The Claims of Kinfolk: African American Property and Community in the Nineteenth-Century South.* Chapel Hill: University of North Carolina Press, 2003.

Peterson, Nancy J. *Against Amnesia: Contemporary Women Writers and the Crises of Historical Memory*. Philadelphia: University of Pennsylvania Press, 2001.

Promotion of National Unity and Reconciliation Act, 1995. South African Parliament, No. 34 of 1995. April 26 2006. <http://www.doj.gov.za/trc/legal/act9534.htm>.

Robinson, Randall. *The Debt: What America Owes to Blacks*. New York: Plume, 2001.

Saldívar, Ramón. "Multiculturali Politics, Aesthetics, and the Realist Theory of Identity: A Response to Satya Mohanty." *New Literary History* 32 (2001): 849–854.

Sale, Maggie. "Call and Response as Critical Method: African-American Oral Traditions and *Beloved*." *African American Review* 26 (1992): 41–50.

Savitt, Todd L. "Slave Life Insurance in Virginia and North Carolina." *Journal of Southern History* 43 (1977): 583–600.

Spillers, Hortense. *Black, White, and in Color: Essays on American Literature and Culture*. Chicago: Chicago University Press, 2003.

Tate, Claudia. *Psychoanalysis and Black Novels: Desire and the Protocols of Race*. New York: Oxford University Press, 1998.

Thompson, Janna. *Taking Responsibility for the Past: Reparation and Historical Justice*. Malden MA: Polity, 2002.

United States Congress. *General Mining Law of 1872*. 42nd Cong, 2nd Session, Chap CLIL, 1872.

———. House Bill H.R. 40. Commission to Study Reparation Proposals for African Americans Act. 101st Cong, 1st Session Nov 20 1989. April 26, 2006 <http://thomas.loc.gov/cgi-bin/query/z?c101:hr3745:>.

Vickroy, Laurie. *Trauma and Survival in Contemporary Fiction*. Charlottesville: University of Virginia Press, 2002.

Wardi, Anissa Janine. *Death and the Arc of Mourning in African American Literature*. Gainesville: Florida University Press, 2003.

Wood, Allen W. "The Objectivity of Value." *New Literary History* 32 (2001): 859–881.

LARS ECKSTEIN

A Love Supreme: Jazzthetic Strategies in Toni Morrison's Beloved

Black Americans were sustained and healed and nurtured by the translation of their experience into art, above all in the music. That was functional. . . . My parallel is always the music, because all of the strategies of the art are there. . . . The power of the word is not music, but in terms of aesthetics, the music is the mirror that gives me the necessary clarity.
—Toni Morrison (qtd. in Gilroy 181)

Music is everywhere and all around in Toni Morrison's novel *Beloved*.[1] In fact, it is so full of music that it seems odd that despite a flood of critical attention, Morrison's intricate tale of the fugitive slave Sethe who killed one of her children to prevent her from being carried back into slavery has seldom been discussed with regard to its musical scope.[2] The novel's most intense "musical" moment certainly occurs towards the end of the tale, when 30 community women succeed in driving out the mysterious and haunting child-woman Beloved from Sethe's home at Bluestone Road 124:

In the beginning there were no words. In the beginning there was the sound, and they all knew what that sound sounded like. . . . [T]he voices of women searched for the right combination, the key, the code, the sound that broke the back of words. Building voice

African American Review, Volume 40, Number 2 (Summer 2006): pp. 271–283. Copyright © 2006 Lars Eckstein.

133

upon voice upon voice until they found it, and when they did it was a wave of sound wide enough to sound deep water and knock the pods off chestnut trees. It broke over Sethe and she trembled like the baptized in its wash. (259–261) [3]

This passage points to the significance of music, not only in the context of *Beloved*, but also with regard to the predicament of the black diaspora at large. The assertion "In the beginning there were no words. In the beginning there was the sound, and they all knew what that sound sounded like," in an ironic subversion of John 1.1, declares the continuity of musical expression in the African American world. The passage refers less to metaphysical implications than to historical conditions, simply putting forth that the—English—word is much younger than the sound patterns of music that originated in African culture. As forms of expression handed down by generations and firmly rooted in the black community, these sounds offer an expressive potential that enables individuals to appropriate the English language and transform it according to their needs: It is the "sound that [breaks] the back of words," and it is in the sound specifically that the self-assured use of language giving voice to formerly unspeakable occurrences becomes possible. And there is a redemptive potential: Sethe and Denver are eventually redeemed of Beloved—who embodies a part of Sethe's unresolved and repressive past—by the sheer force of sound relying on the polyphony of a collective layering of "voice upon voice upon voice."

For Morrison, African American writing fundamentally relies on the sounds and rhythms of black music—as a source of narrative content, but particularly also as an aesthetic "mirror." She notes:

> If my work is faithfully to reflect the aesthetic tradition of Afro-American culture, it must make conscious use of the characteristics of its art forms and translate them into print: antiphony, the group nature of art, its functionality, its improvisational nature, its relationship to audience performance, the critical voice which upholds tradition and communal values and which also provides occasion for an individual to transcend and/or defy group restrictions. (1984, 388–389)

Morrison's narrative approach can be called a "jazzthetic" one. With regard to *Beloved* in particular, her musical scope has received little critical attention. While Morrison's subsequent novel *Jazz* has been acknowledged and praised for its use of musical technique, *Beloved* has rarely been read under similar premises. This critical inattention is surprising since *Beloved*—in which Morrison avoids all kinds of immediate references to written material

—bears rather clearly marked references to musical material and styles.[4] Here I briefly discuss references to the configuration of the main characters Sethe and her daughter Denver. First and foremost, however, *Beloved* takes up jazz in its form, in its "aural" style, and in its performative orientation.[5] Thus, I offer an extensive reading of parts of the novel in the context of John Coltrane's famous 1965 suite *A Love Supreme*. Finally, I examine the ideological implications and motivations of Morrison's adoption of jazz. To begin, however, I clear some theoretical ground on which rests the slightly uneasy relationship between literature and music.

Words into Music—Music into Words

The intimate relationship between African American music and writing has become a commonplace in critical debates. In his essay "Late Coltrane: A Re-Membering of Orpheus," Kimberly W. Benston, for instance, speaks of a shared "notion that black language leads *toward* music, that it passes into music when it attains the maximal pitch of its being" (416). But what exactly happens when language attempts to "pass" into music? How can we conceive of the intermedial dialogue between letters and sound that is so readily posited? Answers to these questions have remained vague in literary criticism, in part because the relationship between verbal language and the musical idiom is, after all, not an easy one. Traditional musicologists, for instance, often strictly deny that words can pass into music at all; they argue that the semiotics of language and of music simply work on premises altogether different from one another. Theodor W. Adorno warns in "Music, Language and Composition": "Music is similar to language. Expressions like musical idiom or musical accent are not metaphors. But music is not language. Its similarity to language points at its innermost nature, but also to something vague. The person who takes music literally as language will be led astray by it. . . . [W]hat is said cannot be abstracted from the music; it does not form a system of signs" (85). Words, Adorno implies, bear reference to things in the world, while music is largely self-referential. If music does not denote anything in particular, it should follow, then, that a translation of literature into music or vice versa is necessarily bound to fail.

More recent approaches in musicology, however, doubt the mutual exclusivity of musical and verbal meanings. First, the notion that music is something "absolute" is firmly grounded in a selective discourse on art music. Adorno's statement is to be seen as a product of a—particularly German— ideological tradition dating back to the nineteenth century, when critics and writers such as Eduard Hanslick, E. T. A. Hoffmann, or Arthur Schopenhauer originally tried to strengthen instrumental music against the (Italian) operatic tradition.[6] As such, the still widely shared, and especially widely taught, conception of music as a self-sustaining structure is a very narrow one that focuses on a limited number of composers of western art music; it operates by an elitist and, at the end of the day, Eurocentric, dismissal of popular, folkloristic, or nonwestern musical traditions.[7]

Moreover, musicologists who insist that music is purely self-referential focus on structural aspects only, thereby neglecting the pragmatic dimension of musical meaning. Recent approaches in musical semiotics and culture (Tarasti, Cook, Frith) emphasise that music cannot be fully understood by looking at an abstract structural entity, but that we have to pay particular attention to the numerous contexts in which music is performed and heard. Like language, musical meaning unfolds not only because it *is*, but also because it *does* things in particular situations. This distinction particularly obtains in performances of black music that fundamentally rely on the antiphonic dynamics between the crowd and musicians, on the expressive release of musical improvisation, and on the signifyin' on other songs and traditions. Adorno's spurious dismissal of jazz, for instance, is partly rooted in an utter incomprehension of such pragmatic aspects in African American art. Yet also beyond specific musical performances, music must not only be understood as a mere aesthetic artifact, but as cultural capital that is appropriated or rejected by individuals and groups for diverse reasons (see Frith).[8] As such, it plays an important part in individual or collective processes of identity formation, and it interacts closely with categories of gender, class, and, last but not least, ethnicity.[9]

In addition, advocates of "absolute" music disregard the fact that even though music may not have stable or fixed signifieds, we may only comprehend or make sense of music by associating sound with personal experiences, which, at the end of the day, are communicated verbally. Such associations are not entirely arbitrary, as musical meaning relies on specific cultural codes and generic conventions shared by particular interpretive communities.[10] More importantly, musical meaning undergoes processes of inter-subjective negotiation, both in the context of immediate experience in a communal performative context, and with regard to processes of distinction and the accumulation of cultural capital. As a result, certain musical styles do indeed denote certain semantic fields. With regard to black music and jazz in particular, Paul Gilroy, for instance, argues that "this music and its broken rhythm of life . . . are a place in which the black vernacular has been able to preserve and cultivate both the distinctive rapport with the presence of death which derives from slavery and a related ontological state that I want to call the condition of pain" (203). Literature may take up such semantic fields—like the death deriving from slavery—by adopting certain musical styles in its verbal framework. As I illustrate below, what Morrison takes up in *Beloved* is precisely what Gilroy refers to as the "condition of pain" that is inherent in African American music, and its particular structural, performative, and expressive conventions to both preserve and transcend it. While Morrison's novel may never fully "pass into" music semiotically, it nevertheless indeed "lead[s] *toward* music." Morrison *musicalizes* her fiction: she charts the origins and traditions of jazz in her particular choice of characters. On a structural level, she carefully incorporates aspects of the formal arrangement of jazz, and pragmatically, she makes use of the performative and expressive scope of black music. By help of such "jazzthetic" strategies, Morrison succeeds in adopting the cultural capital and communal functionality that she associates with a certain type of black music, and makes it work for her prose.

Configuration and the Transcultural Foundation of Jazz in *Beloved*

Morrison associates most of the major characters surrounding Sethe and Denver in *Beloved* with oral or musical styles. Four of them, however, stand out: Baby Suggs, Sethe's mother-in-law; Paul D, Sethe's lover; Amy Denver, the "whitegirl" who helps Sethe during her flight from Sweet Home; and finally Beloved, the mysterious figure who may or may not be a reincarnation of Sethe's two-year-old daughter whose throat she cut with a handsaw.

The character Beloved is obviously steeped in African and African American traditions of oral storytelling. To count these traditions among the "musical" sources of blues and jazz seems justified if one takes into account that the oral tales have always been firmly rooted in the context of communal events of antiphonic performances.[11] Moreover, the transitions from verbal to musical expression are to be seen as fluid because "communicative, performative, creative, expressive, idiomatic and rhythmic characteristics establish [a] continuity within black oral culture" (Putschögl 27, my trans.). In the highly "musicalized" black oral tradition, the "spirit child" who returns after its death to haunt its parents is a core element. It features prominently in West African, particularly Yoruba, mythologies; but also in the African American oral tradition a ghost might occasionally appear among the living, as Trudier Harris points out.

It is difficult to tell whether Morrison had any particular models in mind when crafting Beloved, but one possible source she might allude to is a tale recorded from the Gullah people about "Daid Aaron" (*cf.* Harris 156), who returns to his wife after his death. It is only when one of his wife's new suitors fiddles a fast tune and Aaron starts to dance and eventually fall apart, that peace is restored. Similarly, Beloved visions her own falling apart—"This is it. Next would be her arm, her hand, a toe. Pieces of her would drop maybe one at a time, maybe all at once" (133)—corresponds with the resonating description of Aaron's disintegration: "De fiddleh play mo' loud. An' crickety-crack, down an' back, de dead man go hoppin', an' de dry bone a-droppin', disaway, dataway, dem pieces keep poppin'" ("Daid Aaron" 177).

Baby Suggs, Sethe's mother in law, in turn, clearly evokes the Afro-Christian tradition of sermonising and singing. Her "call" in the Clearing adheres to the typical features of antiphonic sermonizing. These features include, for instance, the use of a "B[lack] E[nglish] rhythmic structure and sounding," a gradual intensification of the expressive effect achieved by a "rhythmical phrasing suggestive of a metrical pattern," and the use of sounding devices that eventually give way to a chanted performance (Putschögl 77, my trans.), all of which are palpable in the aural quality of Baby's sermon: "[I]n this here place, we flesh; flesh that weeps, laughs; flesh that dances on bare feet in grass. Love it. Yonder they do not love your flesh. They despise it. They don't love your eyes; they'd just as soon pick em out. No more do they love the skin on your back. Yonder they flay it. And O my people they do not love your hands" (88). At the end of her call, in a sudden turn to music and dance typical of the sermonising tradition, Baby Suggs "stood up then and danced with her twisted hip the rest of what her heart had to say while the others opened their mouths and gave her the music" (89). In this way, Afro-Christian styles such as the spiritual and gospel are also associated with the character—vocal forms that are partly based on the harmonic material of western hymns, yet have come to be typically "black" forms of expression through their adaptation to the specific patterns of interaction and intonation typical of the African American vocal arts.

If Baby Suggs thus represents an Afro-Christian musical tradition, Paul D clearly embodies the secular tradition of the blues. Paul D, a "singing man," is a blues character, steeped in southern or country blues. Not only do his experiences of slavery in the Deep South, of the chain gang, and of his restless wandering take recourse to typical blues topoi, *Beloved*, moreover, directly quotes from the blues repertoire in Paul D's tunes. The lines "Lay my head on the railroad line, / Train come along, pacify my mind" (40), for instance, reproduce one of the most common motifs in the blues and were immortalized in Bertha "Chippie" Hill's rendering of Richard M. Jones's standard "Trouble in Mind" with Louis Armstrong on trumpet in 1926 (Okeh 8273, reissued Folkways FP 59).[12] The motif perfectly embodies the now painfully serious, now self-ironical performance typical of the blues-mood. A few lines later, after all, Chippie Hill sings: "But when I hear the whistle, Lord, / I'm gonna pull it back." As Ralph Ellison so aptly describes in "Richard Wright's Blues": "The blues is an impulse to keep the painful details and episodes of a brutal experience alive in one's aching consciousness, to finger its jagged grain, and to transcend it, not by the consolation of philosophy but by squeezing from it a near-tragic, near-comic lyricism" (78). It is indeed only in his blues that Paul D is able to express his traumatic past. When Sethe asks for his story, he replies, "I don't know. I never have talked about it. Not to a soul. Sang it sometimes, but I never told a soul" (71).

Ultimately, though, musical expression is not a black privilege in *Beloved*. The "whitegirl" Amy Denver, who massages and encourages Sethe on her flight, and aids her in childbirth, establishes the cross-cultural invocation and generation of the blues. Amy accompanies her "repair work" (80) with a song, humming three stanzas that are quoted in the narrative framework. Cited in full, they assert:

> When the busy day is done
> And my weary little one
> Rocketh gently to and fro;
> When the night winds softly blow,
> And the crickets in the glen
> Chirp and Chirp and Chirp again;
> Where 'pon the haunted green
> Fairies dance around their queen,
> Then from yonder misty skies
> Cometh Lady Button Eyes. (81)

It has been largely neglected in the critical reception of *Beloved* that Amy's tune is not Morrison's own, but literally quotes the first, second, and fourth stanzas of a poem by the white St. Louis poet Eugene Field titled "Lady Button Eyes" (Field 61–63). The sheer otherness of Fields's poem when compared to Baby Suggs's sermon or Paul D's blues is immediately obvious. The use of a stylized Standard English collides with the Black Vernacular English of the blues and the hollers, the strictly trochaic tetrameters clash with the polyrhythmic off-beat phrasings of the work songs and sermon chants, the regular 10-line stanzas with a rigid rhyme-scheme contradict the continuous play with formal conventions in spirituals and folk blues.

Morrison does not employ Field's poem to point to the oppositional nature of African- and European-based music, however, as the tune is clearly seen as a positive in the cautious intercultural encounter of Amy and Sethe. Jazz, Morrison seems to acknowledge here, is not—even though some critics would like to believe so—an autochtonously black form of art. While jazz resists any clear-cut definition, it seems safe to say that it first came into being in the contact zones of the Americas, and developed from certain 18th- and 19th-century forerunners. These precursors certainly are the communal drumming and storytelling sessions in the slave quarters (evoked by Beloved), the Afro-Christian traditions of sermonizing and singing (Baby Suggs), and the manifestations of work songs, field hollers, and other blues (Paul D). These traditions, however, were always negotiated with elements of the European musical tradition, its harmonic structure, its instruments, and of course, with the English language.[13] With Amy Denver, Morrison symbolically acknowledges the western legacy as a legitimate predecessor of modern black art. What is at stake is not so much an opposition of western and African styles, but the integrative power of the black musical culture, which, from its beginnings, adjusted western forms to its own needs.

As a result, one can argue that with the characters Beloved, Baby Suggs, Paul D, and Amy Denver, Morrison indeed symbolically accounts for the essential influences that went into the transcultural making of modern jazz. On these grounds, moreover, they serve as markers of a larger, discursive musicalization in *Beloved* and the employment of "jazzthetic" narrative techniques.

Jazzthetic Technique in *Beloved* and John Coltrane's *A Love Supreme*

More than one narrative sequence in *Beloved* merits close analysis regarding intermedial dialogues with traditions of black music. In a pioneering study, Alan Rice, for instance, looks closely into the rendering of Paul D's chain gang experience and its importance in establishing an ethical and ultimately liberating notion of call-and-response:

> With a sledge hammer in his hands and Hi Man's lead, the men got through. They sang it out and beat it up, garbling the words so they could not be understood; tricking the words so their syllables yielded up other meanings. They sang the women they knew; the children they had been; the animals they had tamed themselves and had seen others tame. They sang of bosses and masters and misses; of mules and dogs and the shamelessness of life. (Morrison 108)

Rice focuses on Morrison's "riffing prose style" in this sequence, and elaborates on how the men in the chain gang use the expressive potential of the musical tradition while making sure as well to "use music as a tool of communication to encode messages between themselves that White men would not be able to decipher" (Rice 164). "The jazz aesthetic," Rice concludes, "is a mode most appropriate for the telling of stories from deep in the past, which Morrison is only just now (at the very moment she does it) telling out loud" (177).

In another sequence, Paul D leaves Sethe, Denver, and Beloved following Sethe's revelation that she killed her child. Immediately after this scene (in a moment often referred to as the "poetic" sequence), Morrison deploys an obviously "jazzthetic" arrangement of the thoughts of the three women left at Bluestone Road 124: their voices assume expressive thrust and performative quality. I want to demonstrate as much by reading the novel alongside a representative piece of jazz music.

For this purpose, it is helpful to focus on John Coltrane's famous 1964 studio recording of the four-part suite *A Love Supreme*, performed by

Coltrane's so-called "classic quartet" with Elvin Jones on drums, McCoy Tyner on piano, and Jimmy Garrison on bass. The choice of this recording is not altogether arbitrary, since it can be argued that Coltrane's classic quartet and Morrison share an awareness of musical and cultural traditions and of community-related performance.[14] *A Love Supreme*, moreover, particularly lends itself to an intermedial reading against *Beloved* since it already negotiates words and music. Thus, in the last part of the suite, "Psalm," Coltrane "reads" on the saxophone a spiritual poem titled "A Love Supreme" (later reproduced on the album cover). Coltrane self-consciously translates verbal language and its emotional substance into instrumental music; as he states in the cover notes: "The fourth and last part is a musical narration of the theme, 'A LOVE SUPREME,' which is written in the context" (see Porter 245–248). But there is also the reverse movement from sound to language. In the first part of the suite, "Acknowledgement," Coltrane spontaneously and verbally takes up the famous four-note blues riff that Garrison has introduced on bass: after his own modulating exploration on sax, he chants the basic theme 19 times using the words "a love supreme," the importance of which was later emphasised by overdubbing the vocal track with several layers of sound. Nevertheless, the choice of Coltrane as a backdrop to reading *Beloved* is not to posit that Morrison must have had this very piece in mind. The suite is to be seen, rather, as representative of a larger, generic reference to African American musical styles.

As an aesthetic foil against which to read *Beloved*, the third and fourth parts of *A Love Supreme* are particularly helpful. Part three, "Pursuance," sets in with a 90-second solo exposition by Jones, which eventually gives way to Coltrane's sounding of the theme to the piece: a stark and simple blues riff in a minor key. Invariably on the basis of Jones's polyrhythmic foundation, the theme is first explored in an exhaustive improvisational flight by Tyner on piano and is then taken up by Coltrane on saxophone, who ends his improvisation by rephrasing the theme twice. From under a drum roll by Jones, a third exploration, this time by Garrison on solo bass, emerges and hesitatingly leads on. Garrison's lyrical contemplation eventually blends in with the polyphonic and polyrhythmic fourth part of the suite, "Psalm," characterised by a largely free play of dialogic calls and responses between the musicians relating to Coltrane's "reading" of the title poem.[15]

The parallels between the suite's musical form and the formal arrangement of the sequence from *Beloved* are obvious. In Morrison's text, we also encounter a fundamental riff or theme that is varied, rephrased, and explored exhaustively in solo-excursions of Sethe, Denver, and Beloved. The core of the theme, here, consists of the phrase "Beloved. She is mine." This decree is first introduced in Sethe's voice: "Beloved, she my daughter. She mine" (200). What follows is a rhapsodic, associative explanation of this statement. The essence of the basic riff, in this context, resurfaces in certain variations—"Beloved. Because you are mine and I have to show you these things" (201)—and in true jazz fashion, Sethe closes her solo flight by returning to a phrasing of the riff in "She came back to me, my daughter, and she is mine" (204).

The next voice to set in is Denver's. She varies the line: "Beloved is my sister" (205), and takes her turn in an extensive improvisational exploration of this motif. The flight of Denver's thoughts also considers the varied theme in new contexts, revolves around them, and finally restates the fundamental riff. Thus, she ends: "She's mine, Beloved. She's mine" (209).

Finally, the third voice at Bluestone Road 124, Beloved's, also comes in. She similarly sets out with a variation of the theme: "I am Beloved and she is mine" (210). Her consequent, tormented reminiscences unfold a dragging rhythm and phrasing. She increasingly throws in lyrical phrases such as "a hot thing" (like Garrison's solo, which intersperses modifications of the four-note "a love supreme" riff established in the first part of the suite). In a subsequent section, then, the fragmentary style is abandoned, and Beloved closes by restating: "I will not lose her again. She is mine" (214).

At this stage, the narrative moves on to a passage that eventually unites all three voices and their characteristics in a polyphonic, collective chorus. The narrative text here faces its own medial boundaries. As Wolf points out,

> music does not only consist of one sequence of sound, but often of several simultaneous sequences, while a work of (narrative) literature is made of one linear sequence of words only. Notably in its polyphonic form . . . music may, on the level of the signifiers, convey several layers of completely different information simultaneously and throughout a whole composition. A similar kind of "pluridimensionality" or "spatialization" can never be fully attained in verbal art. (20)

Still, a polyphonic effect may indeed be "suggested," as it were, by narrative means. Morrison does so by initially establishing a call-and-response pattern involving the by now familiar voices and phrases of the three women. First, a duet between Sethe and Beloved:

> You are back. You are back.
> Will we smile at me?
> Can't you see I'm smiling?
> I love your face. (215)

This duet, in turn, gives way to another call-and-response dialogue between Denver and Beloved:

I watch the house; I watch the yard.
She left me.
Daddy is coming for us.
A hot thing. (216)

In what follows, then, the phrases and phrasings start to blend into each other, and in place of the measured call and response, a collective, intuitive interaction of the voices sets in. The individual voices start to sound together in anaphoric convergences, and eventually seem to blend entirely in the collective incantation of the basic riff:

Beloved
You are my sister
You are my daughter
You are my face; you are me
I have found you again; you have come back to me
You are my Beloved
You are mine
You are mine
You are mine. (216)

The interaction of the characters here—very similar to that of the musicians around Coltrane in "Psalm"—is largely free, yet at the same time strikingly lyrical and emotionally coherent. Even though Sethe, Denver, and Beloved seem to be lost in their very personal thoughts, their voices still come together and resonate as a poetic whole (see Fig. 1).

Within the collective chorus of *Beloved*, the individual voices retain their distinctive qualities. While Denver's voice comes largely in Standard English and conveys a youthful clarity reminiscent of Tyner's handling of the piano, Sethe's voice, in contrast, seems closer to both the hoarse timbre of Coltrane's horn and the warmth of Garrison's bass. There are constant allusions to a spoken Creole, as the frequent omission of verbs and a tendency towards the simple present tense show: "Beloved, she my daughter. She mine. See. She come back to me of her own free will and I don't have to explain a thing. I didn't have the time to explain before because it had to be done quick. Quick. She had to be safe and I put her where she would be. But my love was tough and she back now" (200). The words almost step out from the page. Their aural musicality results from a rhythmical accentuation of certain sounds, as in the word "she," which is first sounded in the opening riff and rhythmically structures the following statement. Longer, floating phrases vary with sudden, exclamational stops, as in "Quick": the overall impression is of an effortless, resonating vocal presence.[16] Not only in its formal arrangement, but also in its improvisational, aural presence, therefore, we are dealing with a jazz-text *par excellence*. But how does the musical quality of Morrison's text function in the larger ideological framework of the novel?

FIG. 1. JOHN COLTRANE, *A LOVE SUPREME* AND TONI MORRISON, *BELOVED*. FORMAL ARRANGEMENT.

A Love Supreme, Parts III–IV	*Beloved*, 200–217
Theme: "Resolution"	Theme: "Beloved. She is mine"
a) First solo exploration (McCoy Tyner)	a) First solo (Sethe): "Beloved, she my daughter. She mine. See. . . . She come back to me, my daughter, and she mine (200–204)
b) Second solo exploration (John Coltrane)	b) Second solo (Denver): "Beloved is my sister. I swallowed. . . . She's mine, Beloved. She's mine" (205–209)
c) Third solo exploration (Jimmy Garrison)	c) Third solo (Beloved): "I am Beloved and she is mine. I see her. . . a hot thing. . . . She is mine"(210–214)
d) "Psalm": free play, call and response, collective improvisation	d) Call and response (Sethe and Beloved) Call and response (Denver and Beloved) Polyphony (Sethe, Beloved, Denver) (214–217)

Music and Trauma: The Functionality of Jazz in *Beloved*

In *The Black Atlantic*, Gilroy investigates what he refers to as the "ethics of antiphony" in black music. He draws particular attention to the communicative design of jazz, rooted in the call-and-response patterns derived from the African musical rhetoric. Beyond the improvisational interaction of groups of musicians, Gilroy argues, black music is also receptive to the input of its audience; it works towards communal identity in a process that is fundamentally rooted in the "experience of performance with which to focus the pivotal ethical relationship between performer and crowd, participant and community" (200, 203).[17] Such a performative thrust is particularly palpable in *Beloved* in its call-and-response structures and aural use of language. More specifically, it is further underlined by explicit addressings to an—implied, as it were—audience, such as in the exclamation "See" in Sethe's solo exploration: "Beloved, she my daughter. She mine. See" (204).

This overt address is crucial since the "ethics of antiphony" are of major importance to the remembrance of personal or collective traumata, of what Gilroy calls the "condition of pain" inherent in black music. Jazz and blues bear an essential expressive potential of traumatic experience, even if, at first sight, they seem to be preoccupied with love and survival rather than death. This expressive potential develops first of all because music was always present in Caribbean or African American history, while the access to literacy and writing was often extremely difficult and paved with problems of censorship. Musical modes of expression were generally seen as less dangerous or subversive by the planters and officials (cf. Walvin 157–175). But it is particularly due to the very nature of antiphonic performances that the expression of trauma succeeds: The backdrop of egalitarian communal support serves as a "safety net" to the individual soloist, who can probe into the abysses of painful personal experience while being sure that the community will eventually force him or her to rejoin the collective chorus. In Sethe's solo excursion, for instance, it is only in the reassuring presence of an audience—of the other characters, but, by extension, also of the sympathetic reading public—that the descent into the traumatic memory of murdering her child is possible. When at the end of the novel, Paul D "wants to put his story next to hers [Sethe's]" (273), Morrison illustrates the dialogic nature of a jazzthetic narrative scope, in which each solo call demands a response.

The encounter with personal trauma is even more dominant in Beloved's solo flight. Phrases such as the repeated interjection "a hot thing," which no longer seems to denote anything in particular, but remains pure, emotion-laden sound, emphasize the musical thrust of Morrison's prose. In the struggle for ultimate possibilities of expression, her language indeed "leads toward music," as Benston would have it, as it "strives to escape from the linear, logically determined bonds of denotative speech into what the poet imagines as the spontaneities and freedoms of musical form" (416). The last seconds of Coltrane's solo in "Pursuance," during which he desperately attempts to reach beyond the limitations of his horn's registers, or else the solo passages in "Acknowledgement" and "Resolution" that are curiously suspended between painful dissonance and ecstatic brilliance, again, provide jazz-aesthetic examples that shed some light on Beloved.[18] The expression of an "excess of love" in Sethe's excursions, as well as the expression of tormenting pain and trauma in Beloved's solo—like Coltrane's explorations in A Love Supreme—expand the frontiers of emotional expressiveness. It is only thus that "unspeakable thoughts" are not "unspoken" (199) in the sense of remaining silent. On the contrary, in a second implication of "unspoken," they are "spoken loose," they are phrased and sounded in a liberating, sublime gesture.

The placement of Beloved in the realm of African American music is Morrison's key to overcoming the speechlessness of trauma and to engaging in a constructive dialogue with painful chapters of the past. The broken beats of the blues, spirituals, and jazz that the novel takes up are so firmly rooted in the African diaspora that they establish a secure foundation for the exploration of suffering and pain. In the expressive tradition of African American music, in the security of its off-beat phrasings, history becomes concrete without being destructive, and its stories can be told. James Baldwin puts it as follows: "Music is our witness and our ally. The beat is the confession which recognizes, changes and conquers time. Then, history becomes a garment we can wear and share, and not a cloak in which to hide, and time becomes a friend" (330). It is in the tension between the individual voice and a collective chorus that the "condition of pain" involved in the Black Atlantic experience can be fully expressed; it is in a culture of antiphony, *Beloved* teaches us, that memory is not self-destructive, and that trauma can be overcome whole.

Notes

1. All references to *Beloved* are to the 1997 Vintage edition.

2. Sethe's memories of her childhood on the "Sweet Home" plantation are framed in song and dance (30–31, 62), there are her husband Halle's tunes (224), and her African friend Sixo sings defiantly at his execution (225–226); her daughter Denver sings at school (120), her lover Paul D sings the blues (39–41, 71, 108–109, 263), Sethe sings for her children, Beloved to herself (88–89), Baby Suggs with the community (88-89), and so on. The neglect of the novel's emphasis on music might change as more scholars and critics engage with Morrison's libretto *Margaret Garner*, based on the same news story as *Beloved*.

3. No other issue has been as vigorously argued in the critical reception of the novel as the "true" nature of the mysterious character Beloved. Three major lines of interpretation can be distinguished. First, Beloved is held to be Sethe's murdered daughter who returns from "another place" to the world of the living (see Edwards and Barnett). A second way of reading Beloved is triggered by the fact that her memories of "another place" bear unmistakable references to an actual slave ship. Beloved, in this reading, cannot be Sethe's daughter; single opinions go as far as to claim that Beloved embodies Sethe's African mother (see Holden-Kirwan). A third version finally argues against metaphysical implications, claiming that Beloved is simply a young woman who has been hidden away and sexually exploited by a sadistic white farmer. As Stamp Paid recounts: "Was a girl locked up in the house with a whiteman over by Deer Creek. Found him dead last summer and the girl gone. Maybe that's her" (235). All versions are given authority in the text, and thus can mutually coexist.

4. Morrison's text foregrounds its intertextuality: *Beloved* is based on documents about the Margaret Garner fugitive slave case, and as such, it has been read in relation to antebellum slave narratives, early African American fiction, but particularly also to western modernists. As a matter of fact, however, Morrison carefully avoids marking pretexts in *Beloved*, even if they appear to be plausible sources of inspiration. Moreover, her attitude regarding the latter group is particularly defensive: "I am not *like* James Joyce, I am not *like* Thomas Hardy, I am not *like* Faulkner. I am not *like* in that sense," she claims. "I know that my effort is

to be *like* something that has probably only been fully expressed perhaps in music" (McKay 152).

5. Morrison characterises her art as "aural literature—A-U-R-A-L—work because I do hear it" (Davis 230).

6. Schopenhauer, for instance, writes in *The World as Will and Idea:* "But it must never be forgotten in the investigations of these analogies [including the expression of human sentiment in the *minor* and *major* keys] that music has no direct, but merely an indirect relation to them, for it never expresses the phenomenon, but only the inner nature, the in-itself of all phenomena, the will itself. It does not therefore express this or that particular and definite joy, this or that sorrow, or pain, or horror, or delight, or merriment, or peace of mind; but joy, sorrow, pain, horror, delight, merriment, peace of mind *themselves,* to a certain extent in the abstract, their essential nature, without accessories, and therefore without their motives" (338). For an excellent study of the emancipation of music from language, see Neubauer.

7. See Born and Hesmondhalgh.

8. The term "cultural capital" is Bourdieu's, and draws on his theories of social distinction; see Bourdieu.

9. It should be noted that this hypothesis is still to be validated empirically. Within the context of a small British town, at least, an empirical study by Ruth Finnegan revealed that correlations between musical taste and categories of class, gender, and race are less significant than previously assumed. See also Born and Hesmondhalgh.

10. As Wolf illustrates by analyzing classical Baroque music: "Music may develop, and in fact did develop in historical times, a codified system of emotional 'expressions'" (32).

11. Baker refers to a "continuum of Afro-American verbal and musical expressive behaviour that begins with everyday speech and popular music and extends to works of 'high arts'" (80).

12. The theme can be found in some of the earliest documents of African American music, for instance, in Leroy "Lasses" White's *Nigger Blues* (1913): "I'm gonna lay my head / Down on some railroad line / Let the Santa Fe / Try to pacify my mind."

13. In his seminal study of *Early Jazz*, Schuller shows how African American music initially developed very much in a Creole fashion. The rhythmic complexity of African drumming, for instance, had been dramatically reduced, while accordingly, the European diatonic scales and Western harmonics were reduced to accommodate better the largely pentatonic structure of African melody; see Schuller 6–26, 38–54.

14. While Morrison propagates a decidedly "black" aesthetic that self-assuredly positions itself in the traditions of oral storytelling, the blues, and spirituals, and at the same time transforms the older models in new configurations and contexts, this occurrence initially has little to do with early forms of jazz and swing. The movement that has come to be known as "swing" was massively influenced by the financial necessity to adapt to the tastes of largely white audiences who exclusively enjoyed dance tunes. It was only with the arrival of bebop in the 1940s that a rediscovery of the complex polyrhythmic phrasings of the African tradition and an emphasis on the blues idiom fundamentally strengthened the expressive potential of African American music. However, bebop musicians relished for quite some time in an exclusive, avant-gardist aura that distanced them from large parts of the black

community. This distance was no longer in place 20 years later with the development of "free jazz," which benefited from all of the artistic novelties of bebop, but also fundamentally engaged with the community and was strongly influenced by political issues. Many of the characteristics of Morrison's narrative art—namely, the explicit articulation from and for the black community, a conscious engagement with older traditions of black expression, and a simultaneous thrust towards aesthetic innovation—are likely to be encountered in "free jazz."

15. "'Psalm,'" Kahn writes, "in fact reveals little structure at all: no metric consistency, no time signature to speak of—completely, purely rubato. And purely emotional" (122).

16. With regard to the second part of the *Beloved*-trilogy, *Jazz*, Morrison stresses the importance of uniting compositional eloquence and inventive ease in her writing, "to blend which is contrived and artificial with improvisation. I thought of myself as like the jazz musician: someone who practices and practices and practices in order to be able to invent and to make his art look effortlessness and graceful" (Schappell 111).

17. In a similar vein, Ellison writes in "The Charlie Christian Story" that "true jazz is an art of individual assertion within and against the group. Each true jazz moment (as distinct from uninspired commercial performance) springs from a contest in which each artist challenges all the rest; each solo flight, or improvisation, represents (like the successive canvases of a painter) a definition of his identity: as individual, as member of the collectivity and as a chain in the link of tradition" (234).

18. Another piece that invites comparisons here—not least due to the similar titles—is Coltrane's "Dearly Beloved," the second track on his album *Sun Ship*, also recorded in 1965 among the "classic quartet." It features among his most spiritual and most intense recordings, and expresses an emotional range from ecstatic exuberance to utterly tormented wailing.

Works Cited

Adorno, Theodor W. "Music, Language and Composition." *Essays on Music*. Trans. Susan H. Gillespie. Berkeley: University of California Press, 2002. 85–113.

Baldwin, James. "Of the Sorrow Songs: The Cross of Redemption." *The Picador Book of Blues and Jazz*. Ed. James Campbell. London: Picador, 1996. 324–331.

Baker, Houston H. *Blues, Ideology and Afro-American Literature: A Vernacular Theory*. London and Chicago: University of Chicago Press, 1984.

Barnett, Pamela E. "Figurations of Rape and the Supernatural in *Beloved*." *PMLA* 112 (1997): 418–427.

Benston, Kimberly W. "Late Coltrane: A Re-Membering of Orpheus." *Chant of Saints: A Gathering of Afro-American Literature, Art and Scholarship*. Eds. Michael S. Harper and Robert Stepto. Urbana: University of Illinois Press, 1978. 413–424.

Born, Georginia, and David Hesmondhalgh. *Western Music and Its Others: Difference, Representation and Appropriation in Music*. Berkeley: University of California Press, 2000.

Bourdieu, Pierre. *Distinction: A Social Critique of the Judgement of Taste*. London: Routledge, 1984.

Coltrane, John. *A Love Supreme*. New York: Impulse, 1964.

Cook, Nicholas. *Music: A Very Short Introduction*. Oxford: Oxford University Press, 1998.

"Daid Aaron," as told by Sarah Rutledge and Epsie Megett. *The Book of Negro Folklore*. Eds. Langston Hughes and Arna Wendell Bontemps. New York: Dodd, Mead, 1958. 175–178.

Davis, Christina. "An Interview with Toni Morrison." Taylor-Guthrie 223–233.

Edwards, Thomas R. "Ghost Story." *New York Review of Books*. 5 Nov. 1987: 18–19.

Ellison, Ralph. *Shadow and Act*. New York: Random House, 1964.

Field, Eugene. "Lady Button Eyes." *Love-Songs of Childhood*. 1894. New York: Scribner's Sons, 1898. 61–63.

Finnegan, Ruth. *The Hidden Musicians: Music-Making in an English Town*. Cambridge: Cambridge University Press, 1989.

Frith, Simon. *Performing Rites: Evaluating Popular Music*. Oxford: Oxford University Press, 1998.

Gilroy, Paul. *The Black Atlantic: Modernity and Double Consciousness*. Cambridge: Harvard University Press, 1993.

———. "Living Memory: A Meeting with Toni Morrison." *Small Acts: Thoughts on the Politics of Black Cultures*. London: Serpent's Tail, 1993. 175–182.

Harris, Trudier. *Fictions and Folklore: The Novels of Toni Morrison*. Knoxville: University of Tennessee Press, 1991.

Holden-Kirwan, Jennifer L. "Looking Into the Self that Is No Self: An Examination of Subjectivity in *Beloved*." *African American Review* 32 (1998): 415–426.

Kahn, Ashley. *A Love Supreme: The Story of John Coltrane's Signature Album*. New York: Viking, 2002.

McKay, Nellie. "An Interview with Toni Morrison." Taylor-Guthrie 138–155.

Morrison, Toni. *Beloved*. 1987. London: Vintage, 1997.

———. "Memory, Creation and Writing." *Thought* 59 (1964): 385–390.

Neubauer, John. *The Emancipation of Music from Language: Departure from Mimesis in Eighteenth-Century Aesthetics*. New Haven: Yale University Press, 1986.

Porter, Lewis. *John Coltrane, His Life and Works*. Ann Arbor: University of Michigan Press, 1998.

Putschögl, Gerhard. *John Coltrane und die afroamerikanische Oraltradition*. Graz: Akademische Druck-und Verlagsanstalt, 1993.

Rice, Alan. "It Don't Mean a Thing If It Ain't Got That Swing: Jazz's Many Uses for Toni Morrison." *Black Orpheus: Music in African American Fiction from the Harlem Renaissance to Toni Morrison*. Ed. Saadi A Simawe. New York: Garland, 2000. 153–180.

Schappell, Elissa. "Toni Morrison: The Art of Fiction." *The Paris Review* 128 (Fall 1993): 83–125.

Schopenhauer, Arthur. *The World as Will and Idea*. Vol. 1. Trans. R. B. Haldane and J. Kemp. London: Trübner, 1883.

Schuller, Gunther. *Early Jazz: Its Roots and Early Development*. 1968. Oxford: Oxford University Press, 1986.

Tarasti, Eero. *Signs of Music: A Guide to Musical Semiotics*. Berlin: Mouton de Gruyter, 2002.

Taylor-Guthrie, Danille. *Conversations with Toni Morrison*. Jackson: University Press of Mississippi, 1994.

Walvin, James. *Black Ivory: A History of British Slavery*. Washington DC: Howard University Press, 1994.

Wolf, Werner. *The Musicalization of Fiction: A Study in the Theory and History of Intermediality*. Amsterdam: Rodopi, 1999.

CHRISTOPHER PETERSON

Beloved's Claim

"I offer a gift of death, I betray, I don't need to raise my knife over my
son on Mount Moriah for that. Day and night, at every instant, on all
the Mount Moriahs of this world, I am doing that, raising my knife over
what I love and must love, over those to whom I owe absolute fidelity."
—Jacques Derrida, *The Gift of Death*

What does it mean to claim one's children as property? When Sethe
declares in Toni Morrison's *Beloved*, "she my daughter. She mine," what is
the difference between *her* claim and the slave master's (200)? That is, how
can we understand the relation between a maternal claim and a property
claim other than in terms of simple opposition and contestation? And what
of Beloved's claim, the claim of a ghost who reaches across time and space,
trespassing the borders that separate the living and the dead? In the closing pages of the novel, Morrison writes: "Although she has claim, she is
not claimed" (274). What does it mean to say that a ghost has claim, that
it claims us with an urgency prior to any claim that we might make on it?
What is this strange sense of possession that emerges anterior to our claim,
as if we do not so much possess our kin—as the vocabulary that permits one
to say *my* daughter or *my* mother suggests—as we are possessed by them?

MFS: Modern Fiction Studies, Volume 52, Number 3 (Fall 2006): pp. 548–569. Copyright ©
2006 for the Purdue Research Foundation by The Johns Hopkins University Press.

Certainly the conventional language of kinship does not suppose that one possesses one's children in the same way that a slave master owns his slaves. Kinship is not identical to slavery. Yet, the conventional opposition of slavery and kinship tends to idealize the latter by insulating it from property relations. Orlando Patterson's seminal work on "social death" is exemplary of this line of thinking. According to Patterson, slavery destroys slave kinship structures, even as it works to justify itself by reintegrating slaves into its own domestic economy. Alienated from all rights or claims of birth, slaves are severed from all genealogical ties to their living blood relatives, and to their ancestors and descendants. For Patterson, then, to oppose kinship to slavery is both to contest the negation of slave kinship relations, and to expose the familialization of slavery that justifies the institution's existence.

While Patterson recognizes that the discourse of paternalism effaces the rigid opposition between kinship and appropriation, this erasure is read as intrinsic to the institution of slavery rather than as a generalizable condition of our relations to others. While the kinship-slavery opposition intends to critique the negation of slave kinship, it also serves to protect the domain of kinship from interrogation. In her influential essay, "Mama's Baby, Papa's Maybe," Hortense Spillers echoes Patterson by claiming that "kinship loses meaning" at the hands of slavery, *"since it can be invaded at any given and arbitrary moment by the property relations"* (74). Like Patterson, Spillers preserves kinship as the sphere of positive affect, bloodlines, love, and connectedness. Although she shifts the terms of kinship away from the patrilineal focus of Patterson's theory of social death toward an exploration of the captive mother's relation to her offspring, Spillers does little to challenge the primacy of what David Schneider has called the "idiom of kinship," that is, the notion that blood ties constitute the privileged domain of social belonging (177). Kinship becomes the foil to the violent negativity of the master/slave dialectic, notwithstanding the possibility that kinship, both paternal *and* maternal, might be implicated in that very negativity.[1] While it may be true that kinship has the potential to undermine the institution of slavery insofar as the recognition of slave kinship would affirm that one's offspring "'belong' to a mother and a father" and not to the slave master, what are we to make of this displacement of one set of property relations for another (Spillers 75)? Although the property relations that obtain between parent and offspring and those between master and slave are certainly not equivalent, they are both property relations nonetheless. As legal scholar Barbara Bennett Woodhouse observes, "our culture makes assumptions about children deeply analogous to those it adopts in thinking about property" (1042).[2] Parental "rights" have historically been upheld under the rubric of the Fourteenth Amendment's guarantee of liberty. This ironic appeal to the constitutional protection of freedom to assert a property claim in one's children recalls the ideology of slavery whereby southerners insisted on their "right" to own slaves. Although children are not considered property in a strictly legal sense (parents do not have the exclusive right to possess, use, transfer, or sell their children), the proximity of property and kinship claims requires that we resist the tendency to oppose slavery and kinship absolutely.

Challenging the kin/property opposition, historian Dylan Penningroth's *The Claims of Kinfolk* overturns the longstanding assumption that slaves were always objects rather than subjects of property. Penningroth details how American slaves made extralegal claims on material property that were customarily recognized not only by other slaves but by masters as well. Despite the absence of written documentation of ownership, former slaves were often successful in receiving compensation from the Southern Claims Commission for property that had been foraged by union armies during the Civil War (73). Both during and after slavery, moreover, black Americans articulated their kinship relations in and through property claims: "Part of property's value for slaves, apart from its capacity to be used or consumed, lay in the social relationships it embodied, ready to be called into action. . . . By bequeathing property, slaves over and over again defined not only *what* belonged to them but also *who*" (91). While Penningroth warns that we should not assume from the existence of such an informal economy of property ownership that slaves were not oppressed, his analysis opens the door for a consideration of the ethical implications of defining kinship through property. What does the intersection of property and kinship suggest about the violence of kinship? To what extent is the violence of appropriation not only a question of corporeal enslavement but of any relation to an other?

According to ethical philosopher Emmanuel Levinas, violence emerges in any dialectical relation to the other in which the other is narcissistically reduced to the same. Against the entire Western philosophical tradition and its thought of being, Levinas locates ethics, and therefore the other, prior to ontology. For Levinas, "I" am always called *to* the other, to whom I am held hostage by an unlimited responsibility, a responsibility that extends to the point of substituting myself for the other. Ontology, on the other hand, promotes a dialectical relation to others that seeks to appropriate and come into possession of the other, and thus ultimately effaces the other's alterity.

Levinas's claim, as it were, is undoubtedly rather hyperbolic in its affirmation of exteriority, of an "absolute other" that cannot be reduced to an object of my comprehension. For Levinas, the other *always* come first, as if the violence of ontology can only be countered through a language that marks a decisive rupture with that tradition: "Ontology as first philosophy is a philosophy of power" (46). Yet, if only a radical reversal of the primacy of being can affirm a non-egological relation to the other, such a claim tends to imagine the other as absolutely outside the same, notwithstanding the notion that appropriation might be both inevitable yet finally impossible.

It is precisely this originary violence that Derrida takes to be the condition of ethics. Despite Levinas's claim that the ethical relation to the other is a relation without relation, that is, a relation in which the other is absolutely other, and not other *than* me, Derrida observes in "Violence and Metaphysics" that "I" am also always the other of the other, which means that the same (the self) is always "other." Given that I am the other's other, the relation to alterity is conditioned by a certain violence that cannot but relate the other to me. For if I were to have no relation to the other, then alterity would be utterly effaced. In order that the other remain other, then, I must still relate that other to me, which means that alterity will always be haunted by the threat of trespass and violence. In *The Gift of Death*, Derrida traces the paradox at the heart of all ethical relations through the aphoristic phrase, *tout autre est tout autre*, which translates as both "every other is absolutely (completely, totally) other" and "every other is (equal to, the same as) every other" (114). If, for Levinas, the other is "absolutely other," for Derrida the other is "irreducibly other," meaning that the other can never be fully reduced either to pure sameness or to pure otherness. In short, violence is necessary for ethics.

Consider that the very term "kinship" denotes what Levinas understands as a reduction of the other to the same. To claim that you are my kin is to say that we are of the same kind. Kinship always poses a relation to others through a language of sameness. Yet, if violence conditions our relations to others, we cannot simply abandon kinship in the name of pure ethics. I want to suggest that this duplicity of kinship is played out in *Beloved* insofar as it moves between a logic of solipsism and possession on the one hand, and an ethics of singularity on the other. 124 marks a site of violence: of Sethe's act of infanticide and of an angry baby ghost, but also of the originary violence that haunts all kinship. One of the fundamental questions that *Beloved* raises is whether there can ever be a pure ethical relation to the other, that is, whether Sethe's maternal claim on Beloved might not in some way repeat the master's (paternal) violence that it seeks to prevent. Because the normative vision of maternity tends to elevate the mother/child relation to an idealized field of ethical action, infanticide is most often read either as an unintelligible aberration from normative kinship, or as an act of pure love, in which case it is thought to be completely *in*telligible. In his *Modern Medea*, Steven Weisenburger observes that the infanticide committed by Margaret Garner, the historical figure on whom Morrison loosely based her character of Sethe, was "used in support of the most poisonous racist theory, or it was a tableau of the most divine mother love" (279). The critical reception of *Beloved*, moreover, has done little to challenge the normative conception of motherly love. When Slavoj Žižek, for instance, argues that Sethe "kills her children *out of* *her very fidelity to them,*" he exorcises maternal love of any specter of violence (154).[3] Sethe may indeed strike at herself with her act of infanticide, as Žižek maintains, but she also *makes a claim* on her child that returns that child *to her.* The murder as *claim* thus returns Beloved to Sethe in advance of this daughter's spectral return. In a similar vein, Homi Bhabha asserts that Sethe "regain[s] through the presence of the child, the property of her own person. This knowledge comes as a kind of self-love that is also the love of the 'other.'" Bhabha then goes on to equate Sethe's act with "an ethical love in the Levinasian sense," attributing to Levinas a notion of self-love that is anathema to his philosophy as well as discounting the violence evinced by Sethe's act (17). As Yung-Hsing Wu observes, the critical reception of *Beloved* has tended to assume that "love is all that interpretation needs because it can comprehend the infanticide and render it understandable" (794). This uninterrogated concept of love understands Sethe's act only as an effect of the invasion of property relations into the domain of kinship rather than as a testament to the violence of love as such.[4]

As Elizabeth Fox-Genovese observes, "all cultures have valued motherhood, but nineteenth-century bourgeois culture raised it to unprecedented heights of sentimentality" (101). Along with this sentimentality came the obligation to exclude violence from the normative view of motherhood, or in the case of Margaret Garner, to absorb the violence of her act into preconceived images of motherly love. Indeed, Weisenburger argues that contemporary responses to Margaret Garner's child-murder most often missed her "absolute singularity and persisted in seeing Margaret as a figure they already knew.... Far more imaginary than she ever was real ... the infanticidal slave mother had by January 1856 become a potent icon signifying everything unnatural and unholy about the 'peculiar institution'" (247). It was almost as if the icon had always awaited and demanded a Margaret Garner.[5] With *Beloved,* Toni Morrison undoubtedly contributes to this imaginary construction of the infanticidal slave mother. As is well known, Morrison was inspired to write her novel after having come across an 1856 newspaper article detailing the basic facts of the murder. Morrison claims she did not do any more research into Margaret's life beyond reading the article because she "wanted to invent her life" ("Toni Morrison").[6] Although Morrison gives only passing attention to the historical details surrounding the case, she clearly grasps the larger political and legal implications involved—namely, the conflict between the Fugitive Slave Law of 1850 and the abolitionist effort to have Margaret tried for murder. Since we know that Sethe does jail time for the murder, we can assume that the abolitionists won out over the supporters of the Fugitive Slave Law in Morrison's version. As Weisenburger shows, however, Margaret Garner's fate was far less happy. Despite the fact that the case marked the

longest fugitive slave trial in American history—an astonishing four weeks—
Margaret was finally remanded to slavery.[7]

That *Beloved* seeks to imagine what might have happened had Margaret
not been returned to slavery is striking, for it suggests that Morrison conjures
up with *Beloved* a certain abolitionist spirit of divine motherly love. Morrison's
significant revision of Margaret Garner's story imagines a triumph over the
Fugitive Slave Law that should caution readers against the almost unanimous
characterization of *Beloved* as a novel of historical recovery rather than of historical invention. As Weisenburger reports, John Jollife, who argued the Garner
case on behalf of the defendants, won only one fugitive slave case out of the
eleven that he argued during the 1850s, a fact that further marks Sethe's story
as anomalous (100).[8] While Morrison's decision not to return Sethe to slavery may indicate a concern with postslavery race relations—indeed, much of
the novel is set in Reconstruction-era Ohio—Morrison is able to situate the
narrative present in a postslavery world only by imagining an alternative past.
Sethe's freedom is therefore conditioned by an imagined abolitionist "success
story" that firmly weds the present (postslavery world) to the very past that
it would appear to have superceded. That this past is dominated by an idealized construction of maternal love means that the narrative present remains
haunted by abolitionist ideology.

Indeed, Sethe tries to convince Beloved throughout much of the novel
that "what she had done was right because it came from true love" (251).
Sethe seeks to make her actions intelligible to Beloved and to the larger community that has made the former into a pariah, indeed, into a sign of abjec-
tion and unintelligibility. To consider her act of infanticide as either wholly
unintelligible or fully intelligible, however, does little to trouble the normative
equation of maternity with ethical non-violence. While the conception of infanticide as an unintelligible aberration leaves the sphere of normative, white
maternity untouched by negativity, so too does its assimilation to ethical love
insofar as it quickly cancels out any trace of violence. For racist ideologues,
slave infanticide is further proof of an animality inherent in black motherhood: a propensity to violence from which white motherhood is exempt. For
abolitionists, slave infanticide emerges both as proof of slavery's evils and of
a mother's love for her children in the face of an institution that disregards
slave kinship. If racist ideologues fail to comprehend slave infanticide because
normative (white) maternity precludes the possibility of violence, abolitionists can claim to understand it fully only by disavowing the violence that is
both the condition and limit of ethical action.

The following reflections seek to uncover the nexus of violence and kinship that the critical reception of *Beloved* has more or less failed to address.
In connection with this interpretive oversight, moreover, I ask how the idealization of maternal love that *Beloved* constructs is redoubled by the novel's

omission of miscegenation from the infanticidal scene.[9] Although Margaret Garner was by all available accounts a mulatta, *Beloved* excludes the possibility of mixed-blood from Sethe's lineage. Rarely has the critical reception of *Beloved* made mention of this omission of miscegenation. One notable exception is Barbara Christian's "Beloved, She's Ours," where she observes how Morrison "eliminates" the "rationale" that Sethe may have been "striking out at the master/rapist" in order to resist "perpetuating the system of slavery through breeding" (41, 42). Christian goes on to note the ubiquity of miscegenation in the novel, but does not pursue the implications of its absence from Sethe's bloodline, that is, how its exclusion further overdetermines the novel's often (though not always) idealized invocations of maternal love. Given that this idealization of maternity tends to ignore how "love," as Christian herself remarks, "can seek to own," it is striking that she does not connect the elision of miscegenation to Sethe's "thick love" (38, 164).[10] Admitting miscegenation into the frame thus complicates any easy distinction between property and kin, ethics and violence. Like Beloved herself, miscegenation emerges as an absent presence that demands to be reckoned with.

Sethe's Gift of Death

That infanticide hyperbolizes a violence inherent to kinship is suggested by Sethe's explanation for the murder: "If I hadn't killed her she would have died and that is something I could not bear to happen to her. When I explain it she'll understand, because she already understands everything already" (200). Sethe kills Beloved so that no one else might kill her. Although seemingly contradictory, Sethe's actions make sense as a form of resistance against the slave master's claim. To kill her own daughter is to claim that daughter as her own over and above the master's claim.

Killing thus becomes equated with claiming. But if to kill is to claim as one's own, then the reverse is also true: the claim of possession is always violent. As Fox-Genovese puts it, Sethe cuts her daughter's throat "to ensure that she could be a daughter—that Sethe could be a mother" (108). The terms of kinship are thus born of violence, which means that the violence of Sethe's claim is not opposed to the explanation that she gives Paul D: that she had to put her children "where they'd be safe." Although Paul D is shocked by Sethe's talk "about safety with a handsaw," this seeming incongruity between love and violence is conditioned by the normative equation of motherhood and ethical purity (164). For Sethe's handsaw is not so much an expression of either aberrant violence or of pure motherly love as it is a reminder of the non-pure ethical relation that is motherhood. As Paul D ruminates: "More important than what Sethe had done was what she claimed" (165). *What* Sethe claims signifies not only her daughter, but also what she claims for her act of infanticide: namely, that it is an act of pure love. To Sethe's notion of pure love, Paul D counters that her love is "too thick" (164). Echoing the familiar trope that blood is thicker than water, Paul D's characterization of Sethe's too-thick love figures that love as excessive, and implicitly connects this excessiveness to violence. Read next to the conventional configuration of blood and kinship whereby the thickness of blood relations marks them as superior to non-blood relations, Paul D's notion of a love that is too thick challenges the elevation of the blood relation to a higher ethical plane.

Thick love is understood as a blood relation that has become excessively possessive, and is further linked to violence by the language that describes the "baby blood that soaked her [Sethe's] fingers like oil" (5). Sethe sheds the thick, oily blood of her daughter in order to save her from a life of slavery. Yet the metonymic chain that links blood, thickness, and violence shows Sethe's love to be implicated in violence from the start. Notwithstanding the formulation that blood is thicker than water, Paul D's notion of thick love relates the blood relation to the violence that the former trope denies. Although Paul D will go on to link Sethe's claim to animality, and therefore seem to reinforce the racist doctrine of slave animality, this seemingly aberrant animality also names the disavowed violence that haunts any relation between self and other. The black slave thus comes to embody the animality that normative whiteness must deny: "The screaming baboon lived under their own skin; the red gums were their own" (199). When Sethe responds to Paul D that "thin love ain't love at all," she reaffirms the equation of thick love with the blood relation at the same time that she suggests that love—by virtue of its thickness—not only carries the threat of violence, but is conditioned by it (164). It is thanks to violence, to the always impure relation to the other, that we have love.

While the explanations that Sethe gives Beloved and Paul D aim at making her actions intelligible, the narrator offers another version that resists intelligibility. It appears in the novel just prior to Sethe's disclosure to Paul D, and is figured as being anterior to the very possibility of explanation:

> Sethe knew that the circle she was making around the room, him, the subject, would remain one. That she could never close in, pin it down for anybody who had to ask. If they didn't get it right off—she could never explain. Because the truth was simple, not a drawn-out record of flowered shifts, tree cages, selfishness, ankle ropes and wells. Simple: she was squatting in the garden and when she saw them coming and recognized schoolteacher's hat, she heard wings. Little hummingbirds stuck their needle beaks right through her headcloth into her hair and beat their wings. And if she thought anything, it was No. No. Nono. Nonono. Simple. She just flew. (163)

This passage is remarkable for how it refuses to explain, to justify, to make intelligible. Sethe simply sees a hat, and hears wings. She does not so much fly as she is flown, propelled by the imagined hummingbirds that lift her up and carry her to perform her deed. Her agency—if we can even say that it finally belongs to her—is figured as independent of conscious thought: "*If* she thought anything, it was No." Although this No would appear to reject schoolteacher's claim on her children, Morrison's language suggests that her No is conditioned by a possible rather than actual thought. That Sethe might have thought nothing suggests that the agency of her(?) actions does not belong to consciousness, that it resides finally in the imagined hummingbirds that stick their beaks into her headcloth. Insofar as her agency emerges from outside, it cannot be attributed to some kind of internal, and therefore maternal, instinct. To claim that Sethe's actions exceed consciousness, moreover, is to refuse the assimilation of the body to the mind *(Geist)*. Indeed, the anteriority of her agency in relation to consciousness reflects the Levinasian doctrine of an ethical responsibility that precedes consciousness, a responsibility that seizes us prior to our acceptance of it—just as the hummingbirds seize Sethe.

The novel thus circles around a primal scene of infanticide that it can never finally explain in rational terms. The impossibility of closing in on this scene, however, does not stop Sethe from trying to explain it. Only by grasping it "right off" and immediately, the narrator suggests, can "anybody who had to ask" come to understand it. Yet, as Derrida reminds us, such an immediate and originary understanding of the other finally effaces that other. Although Paul D is Sethe's immediate interlocutor here, we as readers become Sethe's interlocutors by proxy. We read *Beloved*, in part, so that we too might come to grasp the ethical dimensions of her act: not only why she does it, but whether her actions are justified. Yet Sethe ceases to be other at the very moment that we claim to "get it." Here the language that posits the comprehension of otherness as getting or having affirms understanding and moral judgment as an activity of coming into possession of the other. For the other to remain irreducible to the same (yet not "absolutely" other), however, we must "get it" by allowing for the paradoxical possibility that we can never finally get it completely. Notwithstanding our efforts to comprehend and understand them, then, Sethe's actions finally escape us, they take flight, just like the hummingbirds' wings that propel her to commit her deed.

While the motivations behind Beloved's murder remain opaque, Sethe is unequivocal in her belief that Beloved has "come back to me, my daughter, and she is mine" (204). Returning home to see smoke rising from the chimney, Sethe ponders: "The ribbon of smoke was from a fire that warmed a body returned to her—just like it never went away, never needed a headstone" (198). Here Beloved is figured as a bodily presence that need not be mourned because it was never lost. Given that Sethe exchanges sex for the "seven letters" engraved on her daughter's headstone, the absence and subsequent return of Beloved's body would appear to be implicated in the corporeal loss that Sethe experiences when she "sells her body" to the engraver. That this memorialization is conditioned by Sethe's act of prostitution, and that Beloved's body is imagined not only as having returned to Sethe, but as having never left, never having needed a headstone, suggests a certain revision of Sethe's scene of prostitution. If we follow Sethe's fantasy to its logical conclusion, the act of prostitution that secured her daughter's epitaph would never have taken place: Sethe never would have sold her body. Sethe imagines that her body returns to her, "just like it never went away." Sethe mourns the loss of her body *in* Beloved, which is then fantasized as never having been lost, and therefore not in need of mourning. While Sethe's corporeal loss is narrated through a scene of sexual violence, the mourning of her body as hers also describes the condition of Sethe's relation to others more generally. From the sexual violence that slavery wreaks on her body, to the sacrifice of her body for the lives of her children, to the violent, possessive relation that she affirms with her kin, Sethe's body is always and irreducibly marked as a site of mourning.

Whereas Sethe imagines her dead daughter alternately as a corporeal and spiritual presence, we might also understand Beloved as a specter that gives the lie to the "bourgeois ideology that required martyred slaves to evaporate in some abstract spiritual kingdom" (Weisenburger 258).[11] She is "flesh," as Baby Suggs puts it, "flesh that weeps, laughs." Reversing Christian doctrine, Baby "told them that the only grace they could have was the grace they could imagine. That if they could not see it, they would not have it" (88). When Beloved takes flesh, her incarnation contests the evaporation of slaves that "takes" their flesh, indeed, that steals it away from them. Although Morrison's novel may feed off Christian, abolitionist ideology, the return of Beloved as an angry, fleshy ghost departs considerably from this tradition that "evaporates" slaves into some spirit world. After all, the fleshly presence of the ghost is precisely what inspires its exorcism: "As long as the ghost showed out from its ghostly place—shaking stuff, crying, smashing and such—Ella respected it. But if it took flesh and came in her world, well, the shoe was on the other foot. She didn't mind a little communication between the two worlds, but this was an invasion" (257).

What is most threatening about Beloved is her refusal to be contained within her "ghostly place." She not only takes flesh, but she invades the ostensibly self-contained, insular world of Sethe, Ella, and the other women. Beloved does not respect boundaries, whether spatial or temporal. And if Sethe imagines Beloved to be "a body returned to her," that fantasy of corporeal return—in which spirit and body, as dialectically opposed terms, are always interchangeable—is contested by her spectral uncontainability (198).[12]

Beloved thus emerges as what Derrida calls a specter of spirit, that is, a materialization of an abstract spirit that—while eschewing the evacuation of materiality that bourgeois ideology requires—also refuses any return to the body. As a specter, in other words, Beloved does not correspond solely to Sethe's daughter or Denver's sister. For Beloved is finally, as Denver puts it simply: "—more" (266). To read Beloved only as the daughter or the sister is to miss how she literally fails to embody these terms. That she fails to contain the mourning she emblematizes is made clear in the final pages of the novel:

> There is a loneliness that can be rocked. Arms crossed, knees drawn up; holding, holding on, this motion, unlike a ship's, smoothes and contains the rocker. It's an inside kind—wrapped tight like skin. Then there is a loneliness that roams. No rocking can hold it down. It is alive, on its own. A dry and spreading thing that makes the sound of one's feet going seem to come from a far-off place. (274)

The mourning that can be contained, rocked, and wrapped up inside one's skin is contrasted to a mourning that roams, that cannot be rocked or held down, that spreads beyond the borders of the self-contained body. This illimitable mourning corresponds to a plurality of Beloveds, the "sixty Million and more" to whom Morrison dedicates her novel. Morrison's image of a "loneliness that can be rocked" at first recalls the rocking of a child in the arms of its mother. It then moves to the rocking of a ship, and conjures up Beloved's earlier interior monologue where she "channels" the ghost of a slave woman who died during Middle Passage, and whose body was thrown into the sea. The ship that quite literally contains the bodies of slaves leaves traces of a violence that spreads beyond the boundaries of space and time. In this way Beloved's return marks a spectrality that cannot be contained by the body that Sethe memorializes. The emergence of the ghost from the name that Sethe has engraved on her epitaph affirms that Beloved bears a proximity to Sethe's dead daughter that cannot be denied. Yet "Beloved" also signifies a generalizability that exceeds the (one) body of the daughter.

The (almost) White Face of the Other

To claim Beloved as a sister or a daughter or as an historical or literary property will always perform a certain violence: a desire to make her ours. If to read is to make intelligible, and thus in some sense to own or possess what one reads (as in the colloquial expression, "what did you *get* from reading. . . ?"), then reading will always betray its own violence. We must begin, then, by avowing this violence as the condition of our reading. Beloved is no more ours than she is Sethe's. Yet, from the celebration of *Beloved* as a novel that bears witness to aspects of slave life "too horrible and too dangerous to recall," and that therefore allows readers to reclaim and come into possession of facts omitted from "official" histories, to Oprah Winfrey's purchase of the film rights to the novel, to the recent on-line publication of Joanne Caputo's *Diversity of Love*, which claims that Caputo is the reincarnated child whom Margaret Garner murdered in 1856—the reception of Morrison's novel and of Garner's child-murder is the history of this proprietorial violence (Christian 40). This is not to say that one does violence to a text in the same way that one exercises violence over another person. Yet the asymmetry between interpretative violence and violence committed against another does not mean that there is no relation between these two registers. If there is a violence of reading, it lies in the reduction of the text, this *other* other, to the self: hence, Winfrey's insistence that she not only own the rights to the film adaptation of *Beloved,* but star in it as well, that she might say, with Sethe, "Beloved, she my daughter. She mine."[13]

In *Diversity of Love,* Caputo claims to have established a new genre that she calls "historical spiritual non-fiction," which, in addition to more traditional historical research, "includes information Caputo received directly from the deceased Garner and eight (8) other spirits with whom she has been communicating since 1997" (1). Although such a claim seems rather dubious, it is not altogether clear that Caputo's claim is finally distinguishable from the many other claims that have been made on this story of child murder. The headline of Caputo's press release—"Writer Claims Murdered Slave Child Past"—could describe any one who has written about Margaret Garner or her various reincarnations, and has therefore made certain claims about her or even on her. While Caputo is perhaps unique in the literality of her claim, it only signals a fantasy of possession pushed to its absolute limit. *Caputo is Beloved and she is hers.* Indeed, the fantasy of reincarnation names the ultimate act of appropriation insofar as it fully collapses the distinction between self and other. Although Caputo anticipates that readers will resist her claim because she is white, it is less Caputo's whiteness than the claim of reincarnation that is most suspect here. For the "historical" Beloved was described in the Cincinnati *Gazette* as "almost white," a "little girl of rare beauty." The *Gazette* also surmised that her mother Margaret was a "mulatto, showing from one-fourth to one-third white blood," and that her only other living daughter, Cilley, was "much lighter in colour than her mother, light enough to show a red tinge in its cheeks" ("National"). The specter of miscegenation haunted Margaret Garner's fugitive slave trial from the beginning, but only at the close of the proceedings did it fully materialize in a speech given by the abolitionist and feminist, Lucy Stone. After the court had adjourned to await the judge's verdict, Stone addressed the audience as to the evils of slavery and the "depths of a mother's love," before finally acknowledging what everyone present already knew too well but refused to admit:

> The faded faces of the negro children tell too plainly to what degradation the female slaves submit. Rather than give her little daughter to that life, she killed it. If in her deep maternal love she felt the impulse to send her child back to God, to save it from coming woe, who shall say she had no right to do so? That desire has its root in the deepest and holiest feelings of our nature— implanted in black and white alike by our common father. (Coffin 565)

While the audience was undoubtedly scandalized by this public admission of miscegenation, as well as the explicit connection made between mixed-race children and the open secret of sexual relations between slave masters and their female slaves, the *double entendre* of "our common father" certainly brings the point home. Stone's language ostensibly means to explain the origins of maternal love in a God who instills in both black and white the desire to protect one's children. Although more than likely lost on the assembled crowd, the subtext of Stone's language reveals (perhaps unintentionally) the slave master as this "common father" who plants his seed in "black and white alike." The pun thus aligns the slave master with the Christian father/spirit, and implicitly sexualizes these "deepest and holiest feelings of our nature." Posing God as white, the conflation of father/master figures this God as a miscegenator by analogy: a spirit who becomes a specter through the mixing of his seed with black blood.[14]

Of course, it was never proven that Mary Garner was fathered by Margaret's master, Archibald Gaines. Not surprisingly, however, does Caputo claim that the spirit of Gaines came to her and all but confessed his paternity to her. Nowhere in Morrison's *Beloved* is it suggested that Sethe's daughter was fathered by schoolteacher. Yet Morrison's text is certainly not silent on the issue of miscegenation. We know that Ella gives birth to "a hairy white thing, fathered by 'the lowest yet,'" and, refusing to nurse it, lets it die of starvation (259). Baby Suggs's "eight children had six fathers," many of them white (23). Nan tells Sethe after the death of her mother that Nan and Sethe's mother, who knew each other from the sea, "were taken up many times by the crew. 'She threw them all away but you. . . . You she gave the name of the black man. She put her arms around him. The others she did not put her arms around. Never. Never'" (62). But Sethe "had the amazing luck of six whole years of marriage to that 'somebody' son who had fathered every one of her children" (23). What is most striking about the treatment of miscegenation by the text is that it excludes Sethe and her offspring from what it nonetheless presents as a rather wide-spread practice. Although we are told that four women in the novel (Sethe's mother, Nan, Ella, and Baby Suggs) gave birth to mixed-race children, these children are otherwise absent from the narrative. That Sethe was the only child born to her mother who was not fathered by a white man, and that she would in turn have had the "amazing luck" of giving birth to four children who were all fathered by the same black man, suggests that the text's exclusion of miscegenation from Sethe's blood line is more or less an active effacement.

Halle's parentage, however, does remain somewhat unclear. We know that he is the last of Baby Suggs's eight children, and that at least some of her children were fathered by white men. Yet absent any textual proof that either Sethe or Halle carry any white blood, Beloved's race would not appear to be in question. Given Morrison's public statements that she limited her research on Margaret Garner to the barest details of her child murder, it is difficult to determine if she was even aware of Mary Garner's "almost white" skin at the time that she wrote Beloved.[15] The effect, however, of referencing Sethe's "amazing luck" is to redouble the novel's idealization of love. The text acknowledges the ubiquity of miscegenation only to exempt Sethe and her offspring from it. Considering the numerous other atrocities that Sethe suffers at the hands of slave masters, her exemption from bearing mixed-race children seems almost too good to be true. Indeed, Sethe is raped when she is already pregnant with Denver but still nursing Beloved. In one of the novel's most disturbing lines, Sethe understates the violence perpetrated against her, telling Paul D that they "took [her] milk" (17). Beyond excluding the possibility that Sethe could have conceived a child as a result of the rape, the effect of this passage is also to pose sexual violence and rape as a foil to the sanctity of motherhood. The theft of milk stands synecdochically for a certain violence perpetrated against motherhood, thus burdening the rape with the weight of all violence, indeed, of all that ostensibly conflicts with Sethe's "instinct" to bring milk to her child. Thus, the sacralization of maternity is intensified not only by excluding miscegenation but also by opposing this scene of aberrant violence to that most cherished of scenes: a mother breastfeeding her child.

To trace race in Beloved is to encounter something like the inverse of what Morrison identifies in Absalom, Absalom! where Faulkner "spends the entire book tracing race, and you can't find it. No one can see it, even the character who is black can't see it." If, as readers of Faulkner, we are "forced to hunt for a drop of black blood that means everything and nothing," Beloved's exclusion of white blood from Sethe's lineage sends us on a search to identify its presence, to trace those textual moments where it appears only to disappear ("Art" 101). Excluding the specter of miscegenation from the scene of Sethe's infanticide, however, the text does so in the spirit of pure, motherly love. In an odd reversal, whiteness itself becomes a contaminating threat to the purity of this love.

If miscegenation is what the novel must foreclose in order to purify Sethe's act of infanticide, this is not to suggest that this purification amounts to what some might be tempted to call "reverse racism." The novel certainly does not invoke whiteness as a threat to the future of the black race, as in some odd corollary to Shreve's fantasy in *Abaslom, Absalom!* of having "sprung from the loins of African Kings" (302). Although it turns out that some black people may have indeed sprung from the loins of some white, American presidents, it is not so much the threat of miscegenation per se as its erasure from the scene of infanticide that is at issue here. For the novel dramatizes an incessant conflict between the spirit of maternal love and the specter of miscegenation that is never finally resolved. To admit miscegenation into the frame of slave infanticide would be to allow for a much more ambivalent master/slave dialectic, a relation in which the distinction between one's kin and one's property becomes all the more difficult to determine. If Margaret Garner "saved" her daughter wielding the same handsaw with which she destroyed the master's progeny, her excessive violence, her too-thick love, allegorizes the irreducible violence that haunts any and every kinship relation.

Of Kinship and Cannibalism

The critical silence on *Beloved*'s elision of miscegenation thus reflects a proprietorial violence analogous to that which we have been tracing in the novel itself. Reducing Sethe's actions to an idealized portrait of maternal love, critics have come into possession of the infanticidal mother only at the risk of effacing her altogether. As Lucy Stone's statement at the Garner trial demonstrates, however, the acknowledgement of miscegenation in no way guarantees the demystification of motherly love. For Stone brought the issue of miscegenation to light in the very service of the abolitionist paradigm. Similar to contemporary critics, she rendered Garner's actions intelligible only at the price of reducing them to maternal instinct. But what if the entrance of miscegenation on the critical stage could multiply rather than reduce the scenes of interpretation? Or, to use the novel's own metaphor, what if the emergence of miscegenation allowed us to widen rather than narrow the circle of interpretation that Sethe tells us can never finally be closed? That we can never "close in" or "pin it down" would mean that we must resign ourselves as readers to not fully understanding Sethe's act. To shatter the silence on miscegenation, then, is not to claim that we have finally "got it." How might we abandon our will to possession and allow the text to remain *other*, to remain, that is, a specter? And how might this specter resist both the Levinasian injunction to "absolute otherness" and the temptation to claim the text as ours?

When Weisenburger notes Garner's "absolute singularity," he gestures toward the necessity of affirming the alterity of the other. Indeed, a non-possessive relation to the other is what Sethe is given to learn when Beloved, her "best thing," evaporates and becomes "just weather" (275). While 124 Bluestone Road is quite literally haunted by the language of possession, "non-sensical" speech from which Stamp Paid can make out only the word "mine," the novel also shows how the failure to affirm a pure, non-violent relation to the other paradoxically engenders a certain success (172). It "succeeds" where it fails to affirm a non-violent relation to the other, and where it fails to in-corporate the other that it must necessarily cannibalize. As Derrida observes: "The moral question is thus not, nor has it ever been: should one eat or not eat . . . but since *once must eat* in any case . . . *how* for goodness sake should one *eat well* (282)? Ethics always involves a certain cannibalization of the other, an impossible incorporation of the other as "mine."

If to eat or not to eat is *not* the ethical question, but rather, how to eat well, then we might ask: is the exorcism of Beloved an example of eating well? Judging from Morrison's language in the closing pages of the novel, this com-munity of black women eats rather too well. There is nothing left of Beloved, no waste, no excrement: "By and by all trace is gone, and what is forgotten is not only the footprints but the water too and what is down there. The rest is weather" (275). Beloved's demand for recognition finds itself in tension with the will of a community that seeks to exorcise her, to "disremember" her. The women quit their claim on Beloved: they dismiss, release, or otherwise absolve themselves of it. For Morrison, disremembering names a process of incorporation by which the "chewing laughter swallow[s] [Beloved] all away" (274). To disremember is thus to *dismember,* indeed, to cut the other up into incorporable, digestible pieces. But perhaps it is not a question of eating well, of historical digestion, but rather, of indigestion, of allowing some trace to remain unincorporable and unmournable. Beloved, however, remains both too buried within and too far outside their rememories:

> They never knew where or why she crouched, or whose was the underwater face she needed like that. Where the memory of the smile under her chin might have been and was not, a latch latched and a lichen attached its apple-green bloom to the metal. What made her think her fingernails could open locks the rain rained on? (275)

Is Beloved trying to get in or get out? Does she remain trapped by rusted locks in something like Paul D's tobacco tin, entombed under the sea with the rest of the "underwater face[s]" of Middle Passage, or has her exorcism cast her out, leaving her to scratch at the doors, begging to be readmitted to their rememories (275)?

Addressing our continuing relation to others whom we have lost, Pascale-Anne Brault and Michael Naas observe that, "in mourning, we must recognize" that the other "is now both only 'in us' and already beyond us, in us but totally other" (11). Although we most often think of mourning in terms of the loss of an other who, by virtue of death, is now totally other and removed, Brault and Naas observe that the loss of the other carries with it the paradox that the dead other is now closer to us than ever before, existing only in us. Might this overproximity explain part of the dread that attends mourning the other who no longer exists outside us, and who therefore lodges inside us like a guest who has overstayed its welcome? As Derrida puts it in *Specters of Marx*, "one welcomes them [ghosts] only in order to chase them. One is only occupied with ghosts by being occupied with exorcising them, kicking them out the door" (141). And this welcome is precisely what Sethe's community rescinds at the end of the novel. "So, in the end they forgot her too. Remembering seemed unwise" (274). The novel concludes with the ambiguous exhortation: "This is not a story to pass on" (275). The story is thus at once not to be neglected or put aside, not to be transmitted or repeated to others, and not to be allowed to die. In other words, Beloved is not to be negated, preserved, or superceded in the name of some Hegelian dialectic, but rather, to persist precisely as a specter who resists assimilation, who remains long after the chewing laughter has swallowed her all away.

NOTES

1. Unmasking the ideology of paternalism, Patricia Williams (like Spillers) notes the exclusion of slaves from the family only at the risk of opposing violence and kinship: "Folklore notwithstanding, slaves were not treated 'as though' they were part of the family. . . . Those who were, in fact or for all purposes, family were held at a distance as strangers and commodities" (161). While not denying the pernicious force of paternalism, the present essay seeks to show that this estrangement and alterity is not reducible to slavery, but is also a general condition of kinship.

2. For more on this analogy, see also Merry Jean Chan.

3. Also writing within a psychoanalytic frame, Jean Wyatt argues that *Beloved* imagines a "maternal symbolic" that contests the paternal substitution of "the word" for the lost maternal body. While she alludes to Sethe's lack of separation from her children as an "oppressive plenitude," and further links the novel's vocabulary of possession to the language of the slave master, Wyatt does not explore how a maternal symbolic might still carry the threat of its own violence (237): "The hope at the end of the novel," Wyatt concludes, "is that Sethe, having recognized herself as subject, will narrate the mother-daughter story and invent a language that can encompass the desperation of the slave mother who killed her daughter" (249). Maternal violence emerges as an anomaly driven *only* by desperation within an otherwise non-violent mother-daughter dyad. If there is any violence to be found in

the maternal symbolic, this argument seems to suggest, it would have to be an effect of what Spillers characterizes as the invasion of property relations into the domain of kinship. See also Rody. Rody contends that the "historical project of the novel is in a profound sense a mother-quest, an African-American feminist 'herstory' that posits a kind of 'mother of history'" (97).

4. In recent years, critics have become increasingly interested in problematizing the ethics of Sethe's act. In addition to Wu, see Phelan and Reinhardt.

5. Weisenburger later notes that the more recent discovery of Sudden Infant Death Syndrome (SIDS) and its higher prevalence among slave populations (largely due to poor diet and hygiene) casts doubt on the long-held belief that infanticide was widely practiced by slave mothers. This revelation lends credence to the notion that the "imaginary" infanticidal slave mother fed the abolitionist cause by reinforcing the bourgeois image of motherhood.

6. Morrison came across the 1856 article while editing *The Black Book*. See "A Visit to the Slave Mother Who Killed Her Children," reprinted in Middleton Harris.

7. Much of Margaret's case hinged on whether a prior visit with her master across the border into Cincinnati necessarily released her from bondage. Because she did not come into the state as a fugitive on this first visit, the master could not make a claim under the Fugitive Slave Law. The law usually required, however, that the slave claim his or her freedom while on free soil, something that Margaret had failed to do. See Yanuck, 47–66; and Hawkings, 119–136.

8. For a reading that departs from the trend toward historical recovery see Heffernan.

9. While the invention of the term "miscegenation" in 1864 postdates Margaret Garner's act of infanticide, Morrison's novel begins in 1873 (some years after Beloved's murder, and thus, after the historical emergence of "miscegenation"). The 1987 publication date of *Beloved* only adds to this sense of historical discontinuity. I thus invoke the term miscegenation as a sign of a broader pattern, unconfined by strict historical periodization. For more on the origins of the term, see Kaplan; Sollors; Spickard; and Hodes.

10. In an essay that reads *Beloved* against historical accounts of Margaret Garner, Angelita Reyes argues that Garner's escape from Kentucky challenged the traditional characterization of the tragic mulatta as weak and fragile. Despite her careful attention to the politics of miscegenation, however, Reyes does not pursue how Morrison—by excluding the possibility of miscegenation—misses the opportunity to counter the image of the tragic mulatta through her invention and development of Sethe's character. See Reyes, 464–486.

11. As Russ Castronovo has shown, both antislavery and proslavery narratives tend to equate freedom with death, and thus depend on an ideology that effaces the materiality of slavery suffering. See Castronovo.

12. For more on the dialectical relation between spirit and body, see Vidal.

13. Winfrey, who purchased the film rights to *Beloved* in 1987, has stated her identification with Sethe in countless interviews. "I've always thought I could play Sethe, from [the time I read] the first page. I don't know how to explain it: instinct. From the moment I read [the book], I always knew that I was Sethe, and that Danny Glover was Paul D" ("Odd Couples").

14. As I have argued elsewhere, the imagined contamination of miscegenation curtails the master's aim of transcendent continuity, a project tacitly modeled on

the Christian father/spirit's incarnation in a finite son whose death/resurrection conditions the father's immortality. See Peterson.

15. Whether or not Morrison was aware of Margaret's mixed-race status, we would be mistaken to attribute the significance of this elision entirely to Morrison's authorial intentions. Regardless of her intentions, in other words, it is the effect of this exclusion (the idealization of maternal love) that should concern us here. Morrison's recent libretto for Richard Danielpour's opera, *Margaret Garner* (which, like *Beloved*, is only loosely based on the historical personage), is also silent on the possibility that Margaret or her children are the product of interracial sex. While Act One concludes with the rape of Margaret by her master, Edward Gaines, no children are produced from the rape. This would not, however, exclude the possibility that some or all of Margaret's children could have been fathered by Edward Gaines's brother (from whom Edward inherited Margaret and her children), though this likelihood is never explicitly acknowledged during the opera. See *Margaret Garner: A New American Opera*.

Works Cited

"A Visit to the Slave Mother Who Killed Her Children." *American Baptist* 12 Feb. 1856. Rpt. in *The Black Book*. Ed. Middleton Harris. New York: Random, 1974.

Bhabha, Homi. *The Location of Culture*. New York: Routledge, 1994.

Brault, Pascale-Anne and Michael Naas, eds. *The Work of Mourning: Jacques Derrida*. Chicago: University of Chicago Press, 2001.

Caputo, Joanne. *The Diversity of Love*. 25 Jun. 2002 <http://www.yellowsprings.com/margaretgarner>.

———. "Writer Claims Murdered Slave Child Past." Press Release 24 Jan. 2002.

Castronovo, Russ. *Negro Citizenship: Death, Eroticism, and the Public Sphere in the Nineteenth-Century United States*. Durham: Duke University Press, 2001.

Chan, Merry Jean. "The Authorial Parent: An Intellectual Property Model of Parental Rights." *78 N.Y.U.L. Rev.* (2003): 1186–1226.

Christian, Barbara. "Beloved, She's Ours." *Narrative* 5.1 (1997): 36–49.

Coffin, Levi. *Reminiscences*. New York: Arno, 1968.

Derrida, Jacques. "'Eating Well,' or the Calculation of the Subject." *Points . . . Interviews, 1974–1994*. Stanford: Stanford University Press, 1995.

———. *The Gift of Death*. Trans. David Wills. Chicago: University of Chicago Press, 1995.

———. *Specters of Marx: The State of the Debt, the Work of Mourning and the New International*. Trans. Peggy Kamuf. New York: Routledge, 1994.

———. "Violence and Metaphysics." *Writing and Difference*. Trans. Alan Bass. Chicago: University of Chicago Press, 1978). 79–153.

Faulkner, William. *Absalom, Absalom!* New York: Vintage, 1986.

Fox-Genovese, Elizabeth. "Unspeakable Things Unspoken: Ghosts and Memories in *Beloved*." Ed. Harold Bloom. *Modern Critical Interpretations: Beloved*. Philadelphia: Chelsea, 1999. 97–114.

Harris, Middleton. *The Black Book*. New York: Random, 1974.

Hawkings, William G. *Lunsford Lane*. New York: Negro Universities, 1969.

Heffernan, Teresa. "*Beloved* and the Problem of Mourning." *Studies in the Novel* 30.4 (1998): 58–73.

Hodes, Martha. *White Women/Black Men: Illicit Sex in the Nineteenth-Century South*. New Haven: Yale University Press, 1997.

Iyasere, Solomon O., and Marla W. Iyasere, eds. *Understanding Toni Morrison's Beloved and Sula*. Troy, New York: Whitston, 2000.

Kaplan, Sidney. "The Miscegenation Issue in the Election Year of 1864." 1949. *Interracialism: Black-White Intermarriage in American History, Literature, and Law*. Ed. Werner Sollors. Oxford: Oxford University Press, 2000. 219–265.

Levinas, Emmanuel. *Totality and Infinity*. Trans. Alphonso Lingis. Pittsburgh: Duquesne University Press, 1969.

Margaret Garner: A New American Opera. 2005. 9 Sept. 2005 <http://margaretgarner.org>.

Morrison, Toni. "The Art of Fiction." Interview by Elissa Schappell. *Paris Review* 128 (1993): 83–125.

——. *Beloved*. New York: Plume, 1987.

The National Anti-Slavery Standard. 23 Feb. 1856.

"Odd Couples." *Philadelphia City Paper* 15 Oct. 1998. 25 Jun. 2002 <http://www.citypaper. net/articles/101598/critmas.odd.shtml>.

Patterson, Orlando. *Slavery and Social Death*. Cambridge: Harvard University Press, 1982.

Peterson, Christopher. "The Haunted House of Kinship: Miscegenation, Homosexuality and William Faulkner's *Absalom, Absalom!*" *New Centennial Review* 4.1 (2004): 227–265.

Penningroth, Dylan. *The Claims of Kinfolk: African-American Property and Community in the Nineteenth-Century South*. Chapel Hill: University of North Carolina Press, 2003.

Phelan, James. "Sethe's Choice: *Beloved* and the Ethics of Reading." *Style* 32 (1998): 318–332.

Reinhardt, Mark. "Who Speaks for Margaret Garner? Slavery, Silence, and the Politics of Ventriloquism." *Critical Inquiry* 29 (2002): 81–119.

Reyes, Angelita. "Rereading a Nineteenth-Century Fugitive Slave Incident: From Toni Morrison's *Beloved* to Margaret Garner's *Dearly Beloved*." *Annals of Scholarship* 7 (1990): 464–486.

Rody, Caroline. "Toni Morrison's *Beloved:* History, 'Rememory,' and a 'Clamor for a Kiss.'" Iyasere and Iyasere 83–112.

Schneider, David. *A Critique of the Study of Kinship*. Ann Arbor: University of Michigan Press, 1984.

Sollors, Werner. *Neither Black Nor White Yet Both: Thematic Explorations of Interracial Literature*. New York: Oxford University Press, 1997.

Spickard, Paul. *Mixed Blood: Intermarriage and Ethnic Identity in Twentieth-Century America*. Madison: University of Wisconsin Press, 1989.

Spillers, Hortense. "Mama's Baby, Papa's Maybe." *Diacritics* 17.2 (1987): 65–81.

"Toni Morrison, In Her New Novel, Defends Women," *The New York Times*. 26 Aug. 1987. 19 July 2002. <http://www.nytimes.com/books/98/01/11/home/14013.html>.

Vidal, Fernando. "Brains, Bodies, Selves, and Science: Anthropologies of Identity and the Resurrection of the Body." *Critical Inquiry* 28 (2002): 930–974.

Weisenburger, Steven. *Modern Medea: A Family Story of Slavery and Child-Murder from the Old South*. New York: Hill, 1998.

Williams, Patricia. *The Alchemy of Race and Rights*. Cambridge: Harvard University Press, 1991.

Woodhouse, Barbara Bennett. "'Who Owns the Child': Meyer and Pierce and the Child as Property." *33 Wm and Mary L. Rev. 995*. (1992): 996–1122.

Wyatt, Jean. "Giving Body to the Word: The Maternal Symbolic in Toni Morrison's *Beloved*." Iyasere and Iyasere 231–257.

Wu, Yung-Hsing. "Doing Things With Ethics: Beloved, Sula, and the Reading of Judgment." *Modern Fiction Studies* 49 (2003): 780–805.

Yanuck, Julius. "The Garner Fugitive Slave Case." *Mississippi Valley Historical Review* 40.1
     (1953): 47–66.
Žižek, Slavoj. *The Fragile Absolute or, Why is the Christian Legacy Worth Fighting For.* New
     York: Verso, 2000.

ANITA DURKIN

Object Written, Written Object: Slavery, Scarring, and Complications of Authorship in Beloved

In the vast wealth of criticism on Toni Morrison's *Beloved*—and there is an astounding amount of criticism on *Beloved* given that the novel is still less than 20 years old—many scholars rightfully and fruitfully devote extensive analysis to Morrison's use of the African American tradition of orality. Contrarily, relatively little criticism has analyzed the equally important examination of *writing*, which likewise occupies a central place in the novel's construction, as is evident in both Morrison's emphasis on the scarred bodies of slaves as *textual* bodies and in the yet more obvious fact of *Beloved*'s status as written object. The disproportionate attention allotted to the oral character of the novel subsequently veers dangerously close to a subordination of written to oral, a subordination that can, in turn, close off the many interesting questions about the US literary canon and the Eurocentric/white examination of the canon that Morrison's metafictional attention to the subject of writing in *Beloved* raises.

Moreover, this concern is not limited to *Beloved* alone; in fact, questions about white literature, white American authorship, and white criticism are the primary inquiries of two of Morrison's most penetrating critical works, "Unspeakable Things Unspoken: The Afro-American Presence in American Literature" and *Playing in the Dark: Whiteness and the Literary Imagination*. Published in 1989 and 1992 respectively, each of these works appeared shortly

African American Review, Volume 41, Number 3 (Fall 2007): pp. 541–556. Copyright © 2007 Anita Durkin.

after *Beloved* and wrestles the hardly self-evident issues of identity and African American authorship that the novel, too, addresses in its own illuminating medium. As Morrison writes in "Unspeakable Things Unspoken," "the present turbulence seems not to be about the flexibility of the canon, its range among and between Western countries, but about its miscegenation" (205). In her use of the (never apolitical) word "miscegenation," Morrison situates her study of American literature in the context of the irreducibility of identity, suggesting that white American authors (and critics) have constructed their works, their aesthetics, and even themselves as authors in, on, and through the uncertainties of racial identification.[1] Morrison elaborates this uncertainty with greater specificity in *Playing in the Dark*. As she notes, "Africanism is the vehicle by which the American self knows itself as not enslaved, but free; not repulsive, but desirable; not helpless, but licensed and powerful; not history-less, but historical; not damned, but innocent; not a blind accident of evolution, but a progressive fulfillment of destiny" (52). Constructing this sentence in the form of a dichotomous categorization, a polemic in miniature, Morrison elucidates the manner in which white American literature and white American authorship have constructed themselves on the oppositional attributes assigned by whites to the black American population as a means of differentiating, of defining whiteness itself. One can identify the American literary canon as miscegenous, then, through the inextricability of these terms: if whiteness needs blackness for definition, how can whiteness ever fully disentangle itself from blackness?

It is precisely in this white-dominated, Eurocentric construction of American literature—one that takes the presence of African Americans as a kind of blank (that is, of course, never blank) through which whiteness can imagine itself, a key point in *Playing in the Dark*—that the emergence of African American authorship becomes problematic.[2] In her essay "Language That Bears Witness: The Black English Oral Tradition in the Works of Toni Morrison," Yvonne Atkinson posits the difficulty of "[f]itting the intricate oral tradition of language into a written form" (14). This fit is one facet of the difficulty—that is also, of course, the strength—of African American authorship: "Written language does not contain symbols to represent the inflection, tone, and non-verbal gestures of Black English" (14). In other words, as Atkinson suggests, writing inherently is not a medium readily conducive to the African and African American traditions of orality; as a result, the African American author's entrance into writing demands some negotiation between the legacy of oral narrative, of storytelling, and publication in written aesthetic forms. More importantly in *Beloved*, since writing in the United States is a form dominated by white authors who imagine themselves and their work through the constructed binaries that Morrison identifies in *Playing in the Dark*, there is always a danger that orality—and with it, black culture and identity—will be subsumed by the form that can only define itself in opposition to blackness.

Given these problematics, African American authorship necessitates a balance between the oral and the written, for this balance stands in large part as the allegorical emblem of the questions of identity construction that questions of authorship and canonicity entail. In her representation of scarred bodies that are also textual bodies, Morrison sustains such metafictional concerns throughout *Beloved*, through her representation of the forced objecthood of slaves by slave owners, expressed in the novel through the encoding of black bodies by whites through whipping, beating, and ultimately, scarring, actions that at once force enslaved African Americans to become the object of white narratives and the text on which those narratives are inscribed.

Written on and written about, Morrison's characters thus grapple with the past that denied them selfhood and search for a means by which to express their dehumanizing, self-less past. And though there is little resolution of these difficulties by novel's end, Morrison, in her construction of both spaces in the novel (geographical and domestic) and the space of the novel (its structure, its language, its status as written object), suggests a mode of African American authorship that directly challenges both the absence of African Americans in works by white American authors and contemporary literary theories (namely, Barthes's "The Death of the Author") that insist on the neutrality of the space of writing. In so doing, Morrison, throughout *Beloved*, comments on the critical folly of reading texts by African American authors through the same theoretical scopes, the same traditions, applied to the study of literature by whites and, in the process, posits the possibility of reading African American literature "on its own terms," according to its own conventions ("Unspeakable Things Unspoken" 209).

The issue of speaking, of self-expression, is hardly new to analyses of *Beloved*. In fact, many scholars examine the different implications of narrative and narrativization within the novel. For example, in "Toni Morrison's *Beloved*: Bodies Returned, Modernism Revisited," Cynthia Dobbs elucidates the relationship between narrative and the novel's events, noting the "characters' efforts to relink the flesh, desire, and narrative," both to reclaim and to rename narrative through their bodies (566). In Linda Koolish's reading, "Fictive Strategies and Cinematic Representations in Toni Morrison's *Beloved*," narrative functions as a kind of object, in need of reclaiming. For her, the novel's resolution depends on Denver's ability to "take away from [schoolteacher] the power to define African-Americans and make their history in a way that steals their past, their souls, and their humanity" (405). In their discussions of narrative in *Beloved*, however, both Koolish and Dobbs focus solely on the use of oral tradition within *Beloved*, the means by which it provides Sethe, in particular, access to storytelling, specifically, the telling of her own story. While these interpretations are more than valid—the novel almost begs, at times, to be read aloud—they tend to consider the novel in isolation from its *written* form, and to appreciate fully the ways that *Beloved* comments on and questions contemporary modes of criticism, it is imperative to recognize the central place of writing within it.

Indeed, unlike many examinations of the relationship between oral culture and writing in the works of various African American authors, examinations of Morrison's use of orality in *Beloved* often neglect the significance of the novel as a written object *as well as* an example of traditional storytelling.[3] Though *Beloved* is a novel that certainly, in both structure and language, reproduces some of the conventions of the oral tradition, it is also *a novel.* To ignore this fact is to subsequently ignore Morrison's ability to invoke both oral and written traditions throughout the book, to produce a written text that is somehow, at the same time, an oral text, as contra-logical as such a phrase may seem. In reconstructing the simultaneity of orality and writing as it appears in *Beloved,* I hope to draw attention to the manner in which the novel reads itself as both a part of the African American literary canon and a part of American literature in general. For, as I hope to show, it is through the combination of written and oral that the novel gestures toward one of its central concerns: the difference, the uniqueness, of African American writing, its complicated inheritance from the constructed leviathan of white American literature. In other words, through this construction, Morrison preserves, even as she writes, the oral tradition at the heart of African American storytelling.

It is not only the construction of the novel that suggests the importance of writing as a principle theme of *Beloved;* the emphasis on black bodies, *scarred* black bodies, likewise indicates the predominance of inscription in the text. For Francois Pitavy, in his essay, "From Middle Passage to Holocaust: The Black Body as a Site of Memory," it is the scars that formerly enslaved characters (most notably Sethe) bear that act as an impetus to tell, to narrativize the past: "To those who have been deprived of language, those scars are precisely the words they have to tell, the unerasable site of their memories. The slaves' narratives are inscribed on their bodies, it has become the text of their stories and the most powerful signifier of their personal and communal histories" (62). While Pitavy astutely links the scarring, the beating of African Americans with writing, he does not fully elucidate what this relationship entails. In *Body Works: Objects of Desire in Modern Narrative,* Peter Brooks provides valuable insight into this topic, suggesting that, in literature, "It is as if identity, and its recognition, depended on the body having been marked with a special sign, which looks suspiciously like a linguistic signifier. . . . Signing or marking the body signifies its passage into writing, its becoming a literary body, and generally also a narrative body" (3). According to Brooks, then, the marking of the human body, scarring, functions as a means of identification and, in this sense, acts in a manner very similar to that of the linguistic sign, an inscription to be read by the viewer/reader. In scarring, the human body thus becomes the site of writing. If this text-making ensues thusly, the human body, through the process of scarring, does not only bear the mark, the signifier of its identity, but also literally becomes a textual body. It becomes, in other words, both the object written and the written object, a phenomenon that, given *Beloved*'s emphasis on Sethe's scars, is emblematic of the difficulties of African American writing in the novel.

For there is nothing usual about these scars: as a physical, visible legacy of slavery, they attest to the brutal dominance of white slave owners over enslaved African Americans. These scars, especially in their 19th-century context, suggest multiple meanings. Referencing the use of scars as a device of recognition in Greek tragedy, Brooks suggests that physical marks on the body, especially in literature, signify the identity of the body (3), on the one hand.[4] This use of the scar, especially in the act of branding, was quite common in American slavery, as the circle and cross burned into the chest of Sethe's mother indicates. She says to Sethe, "This is your ma'am. This" (72). Here, the mark appears not only as a sign of identity, but in the phrasing of Sethe's mother, as identity itself since she points to the scar, to the "this" as she speaks. In making this gesture, Sethe's mother points, really, to the fact that in slavery, this brand, this mark *is* the identity of the slave, or, more accurately, it is so in the estimation of white slave owners. Sethe's mother thus points as well to the mark as an imposed identity, a construction and an invention of the whites. To put it another way, the mark here acts as both signifier *and* signified since it announces to other white slave owners who the slave is, that she is property; and announces to whom she belongs (signifier) while at the same time, the "identity" that the scar supposedly distinguishes is little more than the mark itself, little more than the ownership that it signifies.[5] In this description of her brand, Sethe's mother subsequently indicates the ways that white writing on black bodies, scarring, is both a signifier of identity and the construction of identity.[6]

On the other hand, the act of branding suggests not only the construction, or, more accurately, the invention of black identity by whites, but also the creation of white identity, since identification of the "other" is also an identification of the self. In the novel, Garner's naming of the Sweet Home men as men and the beatings from other slave owners that result clearly indicate this process of self-identification.[7] As Morrison writes, "Garner came home bruised and pleased, having demonstrated one more time what a real Kentuckian was: one tough enough and smart enough to make and call his own niggers men" (13). What is especially significant here is that in naming the "other," Garner literally marks himself: his bruises are a physical indication to other whites that he is Garner, the crazed slave owner who calls his slaves men, the "real Kentuckian." But unlike the marks, the scars and brands, savagely inflicted on slaves by whites, Garner's bruises are only temporary, a condition that emphasizes his relative autonomy as a white man in 19th-century America, for while other slave holders have marked him as a misfit among them, the marks will not last more than a week, at which point Garner may choose (or not) to re-mark himself in whatever manner he likes. At the same time, however, Garner's ability to "make" his identity is also severely limited as long as he continues to call the Sweet Home men "men," for this label is his oddity among other whites, his distinguishing characteristic, and in this sense, Garner remains a "marked" man.

The act of scarring as an act of writing, insofar as it involves a marking of the body that functions in a manner very similar to that of the linguistic sign, introduces an interesting wrinkle to the construction of identities, both black and white, by slave owners. For if the marks on a body function as linguistic signs, then the body here transforms into a site of writing, into the written object; it becomes, in other words, a *textual* body. The body itself, in that it bears writing, may be read like a text; in its function (in the function that whites ascribe to it), it *is* a text. In terms of slavery, this consideration of the body as text is especially important to Morrison's project in *Beloved,* for if the inscription, the scarring, of black bodies by white slave owners produces, invents, white identity, then in this instance, the text in a sense creates the author.[8] In other words, while it is certainly true that these white "authors" invent the identities that they inscribe on the bodies of slaves, it is equally true that they use these inscriptions to define themselves, much as Garner does.[9] As such, the text determines the author, and what is especially significant is this development's similarity to the construction of the American literary canon as Morrison describes it in "Unspeakable Things Unspoken." As she writes, "Canon building is Empire building. Canon defense is national defense. Canon debate . . . is the clash of cultures" (207). In this passage, Morrison identifies the political impetus behind canonicity—the solidification and enshrinement of white identity—and in so doing, suggests how canonicity is something of a self-fulfilling prophecy: in willfully excluding African Americans from the study of American literature, contemporary critics fail to recognize the ways that white authors construct themselves and their texts against blackness, thereby reinforcing a canonical construction built on, certain of, the exclusion it perpetuates. To put it another way, white American authors encode the exclusion of African Americans in their texts, and critics, in reinforcing this exclusion, define "quality" literature as that which excludes, so that the "standard" of American writing becomes the impetus to ignore, to "ghost" the African American presence. The white American author thus defines himself, the quality of his work, against the "elitist" conventions that he himself has invented, the conventions that appear in his own texts.

Despite this "ghosting" of African Americans in canonical literature, the African American presence is, even still, very much a part of American literature. In *Beloved*, Morrison points to this presence in her descriptions of Sethe's scarring, of her inscription as text: "Nor was there the faintest scent of ink or the cherry gum and oak bark from which it was made. Nothing" (6). Intriguingly, Sethe here identifies the branches that schoolteacher's nephew uses to beat her as the main ingredients of the ink that schoolteacher forces her to make. While this link between the branches that act as whip and ink clearly exemplifies the relationship between scarring and writing, since the nephew uses the source of ink, *ink* itself, to inscribe Sethe's body, it also shows how thoroughly Sethe's presence is imbued in this act of "writing." Although indirect, the equation Morrison makes between the branches used by the nephews to mark Sethe, to permanently scar (to mutilate) the flesh of her back, suggests the role that Sethe (unwillingly) plays in textual production.[10] Morrison makes this concept even more apparent in schoolteacher's transcription of his nephews' rape of Sethe's breasts, for as this horrific trauma takes place, schoolteacher is "watching and writing it up" (83). In her emphasis on Sethe's role in the production of the ink that schoolteacher and his nephews use to inscribe her, Morrison thus suggests the manner in which black bodies literally contribute to the production of white texts as both narrative object and "ghosted" subject.

But Sethe's scar is by no means limited to my general interpretation of it as a particularly brutal kind of writing meant to encode black identity, to name flesh by assaulting flesh. As is evident in the various and insightful interpretations of the scar, Sethe's "tree" bears the fruit of multiple resonances, and for some scholars, these resonances often suggest the scar as an emblem of communality, of Sethe's interactions with others. In "Devastation and Replenishment: New World Narratives of Love and Nature," Wendy Faris, for example, focuses on the scar's power to link Sethe with Amy Denver in an unusual relationship of female healing: "The curing powers of a female relatedness to nature are celebrated in the cobwebs Amy applies to what she calls the chokecherry tree on Sethe's whipped back" (178). For Faris, Sethe's injury, soon to be her scar, acts as a locus drawing Amy, namer of the scar, and Sethe together. Similarly, Caroline Rody reads the scar as a generational bond between Sethe, her mother, and Beloved. As she writes, "Sethe carries the family tree on her back . . . Morrison's portrayal of the lost mothers of African-American history inscribes indelibly the daughter's reckless willingness to bear the mark of the mother's pain" (99). Here, the scar carries the double connectedness of Sethe to her literal kin and to her broader family, perhaps adequately read as the "Sixty Million / and more" of Morrison's dedication.

Michele Bonnet, too, in "To Take the Sin Out of Slicing Trees," notes the relatedness—to the immediate community and to the broader community of people of African descent—signaled by Sethe's scar: "Yet the most convincing evidence that Sethe's tree is of the genealogical type is the strategic importance of the family theme in the novel, one of whose major, if not essential, messages is that the individual is not self-sufficient" (47). Once again, the scar acts as an emblem of community and connection, *not* the isolation and separation forced on African American families by slavery.

While these positive interpretations of Sethe's scar certainly bear merit, the scar, like the oral/written duality and the enslaved/free duality that echo throughout the novel, is never clearly, certainly one thing or another. For Susan Corey, in "Toward the Limits of Mystery," its simultaneous signification is evident in that, "like many grotesque images its effect is both repulsive and attractive, signifying the complexity of Sethe's relationship to the past" (34). As such, the scar at once marks the beauty and the pain of Sweet Home. Moreover, insofar as Bonnet rightly identifies the scar as "an active, living tree with an irrefutable power and reality of its own," as a scar, it is also literally *dead* skin (146). And perhaps most important to this discussion, even as the scar signifies communality, it further suggests Sethe's individuality, and marks her as identifiably *Sethe*. In this sense, it is not unlike the brands outrageously burned into the flesh of so many slaves, including Sethe's mother. As Patrick O'Donnell says, "Sethe's mother bears a mark—the brand of the slaveowner—that both proclaims her as one of an unnumbered, nameless mass, and identifies her historical specificity as Sethe's mother, the only one" (325). Identifiable, yet nameless, individual, yet communal, living, yet dead, engrossing, yet repulsive: all of these (non)dualities resonate simultaneously from Sethe's scar.

Since the resonances of the scar *cannot* be limited, cannot be contextually cut off, the scar's function for the whites who inflict it (schoolteacher and his nephews) is never singular, never *controllable*. As Pitavy astutely observes, Sethe "gets beaten, and the inscription of the beating on her back marks her for life. . . . [B]y making those marks, by outraging that flesh, the master has precisely created the visible and ineradicable signs of what he wants to suppress—the black identity and consciousness" (53). What Pitavy thus remarks is the manner in which the scars of formerly enslaved African Americans function beyond the control and intentionality of whites as a communal marker, a sign of black identity. However, what is especially compelling about Pitavy's reading, as well as the many varied readings of Sethe's scar, is not so much the *reading* itself as it is the scar's *capacity to be read*. For it is in the act of reading Sethe's scar that the scar both manifests itself as text and, perhaps more significantly, reveals itself as that which binds Sethe to others, to a community, since the scar's location on "that part of her body which she cannot see" demands always the interpretation of someone else (Bonnet 48). Under slavery, as economic signs passing between slave owners and as warnings of punishment passing from slave owner to slave, scars like that borne by Sethe mark the conceit of men like schoolteacher who seek not only to administer the mark, but to control its interpretation as well. Beyond slavery, as the readings of Sethe's scar by Amy Denver, Baby Suggs, and Paul D (among others) show, the scar's context, its meaning, opens to redefinition and reinterpretation, a kind of overwriting of the slave owner's text.

By no means, however, is the scar, even under slavery, limited to the interpretation of whites. This is evident in schoolteacher's *own* overwriting of the rape scene, one that suggests the manner in which so many 19th-century whites sought to control their texts by violent reinscription. Assuming that schoolteacher writes faithfully what he sees (or, at least, writes as faithfully as rampant bigotry allows), the scene reveals one of the foremost methods used by white Americans and likewise white American authors to exclude African Americans: the willful distortion of black bodies, black identities, into degrading, ridiculous stereotypes. This scene, in which one of schoolteacher's nephews holds Sethe down while the other nurses her, is a literal reenactment of Mammy-ism. Sethe, pregnant with Denver and still nursing the crawling already? baby girl who (maybe) later calls herself Beloved, must relinquish the milk intended for her children to feed the monstrous white boys, just as slave owners forced African American mothers to nurse the white babies of the master, even if doing so entailed deprivation of breast milk for the woman's own children, and even if this forced sacrifice of the enslaved mother necessitated hideous violence and degradation. As she is at once brutalized, treated as an animal, schoolteacher records Sethe functioning (albeit superficially) as a Mammy, thereby *writing over* the text of her scarred body, doubling his inscription in an attempt to delimit its meaning. Schoolteacher's note-taking is necessary as long as the meaning of the scar is variable. Not only can the scar identify Sethe as a slave and a Mammy (schoolteacher's "intended" text), a text that, as the aforementioned interpretations show, is itself variable; it also, even as it identifies Sethe, implicitly identifies the whites who inflict her scars as violent, brutal, all the characteristics, in essence, that schoolteacher assigns to Sethe. It is this somewhat "accidental" construction of white identity by slaveholders constructing black identity that consequently necessitates the *writing over* that schoolteacher performs in the rape scene, necessitates the creation of a *second* text (Mammyism) to obscure the first (rape perpetrated by whites against an African American woman) and thereby distort the brutality of whites.

Schoolteacher's act of writing, of recording this scene, thus gestures toward the tendency of white American authors to absent African Americans from their texts by writing instead an invented, grotesque caricature that likewise obscures the violence and brutality of the white authors themselves. In this scene, then, Morrison calls attention to the Mammy as an invention by contrasting the smiling, doting Mammies of white literature with the role of Mammy as one *forced* on enslaved African American women, an identity thrust on them, and she underscores that this role is/was also an erasure of the violence enacted by whites as a means of constructing black identities, including that of the Mammy.

And yet Morrison herself does not abstain from writing over other narratives in her composition of *Beloved,* narratives such as Margaret Garner's history and the white-dominated American literary canon that condemned, distorted, martyred, and mutilated slave women like Margaret Garner, an Africanist presence. In some ways, this revision of narrative perfectly fits Morrison's use of orality in *Beloved* since an oral tradition almost always includes multiple retellings of known narratives. In *Speaking Power: Black Feminist Orality in Women's Narratives of Slavery,* DoVeanna S. Fulton writes, "The very nature of orality diverges from Western favored concepts: it emphasizes oral rather than written forms; it stresses cyclical over linear structures through retelling; and retelling also allows modification, which contrasts with the singular 'logic' written texts often present" (13). Given this emphasis, Morrison's "overwriting" may be seen as a *version* of select white narratives, a version that provides Margaret Garner a history, a life that far surpasses the boundaries of a newspaper clipping, a version of white American literature that takes African American characters as more than merely "surrogate selves" on whom an author could "[meditate] on problems of human freedom" (*Playing in the Dark* 37). Read through Morrison's employment of orality in *Beloved,* the overwriting of narrative appears as a retelling of white narratives that in some sense is also a revision of white narratives.

At the same time, though, *Beloved* is a novel, a written text that therefore, by virtue of its form, flirts with the "singular 'logic'" that Fulton identifies as endemic to writing. It is the fact of form, the fact that *Beloved* exists in a written medium, that suggests the complicated issue of inheritance for African American authors, an issue left latent in some ways by analyses focused exclusively on orality in the novel. Whereas Fulton's orally-centered reading stresses the "often nonreproducible" tone of Morrison's storytelling, a reading rooted in the written suggests the *reproducibility* intrinsic to print, especially the novel, and subsequently expands the scope of orally-focused readings to include the difficult question of how African American authors can work in a medium with a legacy of denying and distorting their existence (105). Read in this manner, *Beloved*-as-writing suggests not only a *revision* of white narratives, but also a *supplementation* of white narratives not unlike the Derridean concept of the supplement as that which is constantly, and usually violently, deferred.[11] In other words, Morrison's novel stands not in opposition to, not necessarily as counterargument to white American literature, but *in relation to* this literature. Insofar as *Beloved* tells the story of African Americans "imagining ourselves" as "subjects of our own narratives, witnesses to and participants in our own experiences, and, in no way coincidentally, in the experience of those with whom we have come in contact," it responds to the violent ghosting, the brutal limitation of context inherent in schoolteacher's overwriting with a writing-over that *expands* the context, offers space and voice to African American authors to be read alongside the canon that has traditionally denied them ("Unspeakable Things Unspoken" 208).[12]

Into this foray of scarred, mutilated, and tortured bodies enters the scarred, adult body of Sethe's dead child, Beloved.[13] Though fully grown, Beloved seems to remain ensconced in Freud's pre-Oedipal stage, neither fully a self nor fully undifferentiated. Morrison makes this quite clear in the characteristics that she assigns Beloved, specifically, her faltering language, her strong desire to at once possess and to be Sethe, and the general fluidity of her self, a result of disrupted individuation. As Beloved reveals in her monologue, "there is no place where I stop her face is my own and I want to be there in the place where her face is and to be looking at it too a hot thing" (248). Here, Beloved reveals her obsessive desire for Sethe ("a hot thing") while at the same time speaking of Sethe's face and her own face as interchangeable, one in the same thing, an exchange of identity that temporarily succeeds while the women are quarantined in 124. As Denver observes, "the thing was done: Beloved bending over Sethe looked the mother, Sethe the teething child" (294). Yet Sethe's is not the only identity that Beloved assumes: at various times, she takes on the wants, the desires, even the histories of other characters, seems to, in fact, embody them. Almost immediately following her arrival, she takes on Baby Suggs's dedication to color: "She [Beloved] seemed totally taken with those faded scraps of orange, even made the effort to lean on her elbow and stroke them" (65). Not long after, she assumes Denver's sweet tooth, an appetite that, in the beginning of the novel, impels Denver, "slowly, methodically, miserably," to eat her bread and jelly (23) and to find herself "soothed by sugar" at the carnival (58). And finally, in her monologue, she assumes the guise of Sethe's mother, saying that, "it is the dark face that is going to smile at me the iron circle is around my neck she does not have sharp earrings in her ears or a round basket," a description that may also suggest Beloved's representation of the millions of Africans killed during the passage from freedom to slavery (250–251).[14] Each of these embodiments thus amplifies the permeability of Beloved's selfhood and the lack of individuation characteristic of the pre-Oedipal stage that allows these embodiments to take place.

This permeability of self is not, in itself, a particularly bad thing. In fact, in *Beloved,* Morrison writes a multiplicity of identity, a realization and acceptance of the role of the "other" in identity formation as a means of entering into a space of writing that, contrary to white American literature, does not oppress, maim, distort, and destroy the "other" as a means of inflating itself into a preposterously singular identity. And yet this violence that is so apparent in the construction of white identity is precisely the danger of Beloved's mutable self, for, as David Lawrence notes in "Fleshly Ghosts and Ghostly Flesh: The Word and the Body in *Beloved*," "In her insistence on absolute possession of her mother, Beloved resurrects the slave master's monopoly over both word and body, enforcing the internalized enslavement that has become a legacy of institutionalized slavery" (240). That is, the closer Beloved gets to an identity, Sethe's identity, the more violence she inadvertently commits against her, the more she assumes the role of the white slave owner who declares his identity through violence against black bodies. In the novel, as the volatile relationship between the two women reaches a crescendo, Morrison writes that Beloved "ate up her [Sethe's] life, took it, swelled up with it, grew taller on it" (298). Like the whites, then, Beloved solidifies her identity only through the destruction of her mother, the original "other" in Freudian analysis.

Even so, this permeability of self is not characteristic of Beloved alone. As a former slave, Sethe similarly lacks, or, more accurately, is denied, a stable sense of self, a continuity of the self. Betty Jane Powell makes a similar suggestion in "'will the parts hold?': The Journey to a Coherent Self in *Beloved*": "In *Beloved* Toni Morrison writes about the need for victimized people to form an integrated self in the face of a fragmented and unacceptable existence. . . . Morrison sets about the difficult task of fusing such fractures, initiating the possibility of coherence and recognition for the characters in *Beloved* through freedom and alliance with the communities" (143). What is especially interesting about this movement toward coherence—insofar as coherence is possible for any self—are the complications that discourage Sethe's storytelling, specifically, the fragmentation of the individual as a result of the trauma of slavery and, perhaps even more difficult to overcome, Sethe's estrangement from the community. Still, it is at the same time crucial for Sethe to come to terms in some fashion with her selfhood and, with it, her status as both the subject and object of narrative. In other words, telling her stories requires Sethe to inhabit the unusual space of autobiographical writing/storytelling, one that places the writer/speaker in the dual position of both narrator and object of narrative at once. It is the latter that is especially difficult for Sethe as a former slave, given the extraordinary objectification that white slave owners inflicted on their slaves and the subsequent anxiety that emerges from the prospect of assuming the role of object, even in one's own story. This objectification of African American slaves by slave holders, who, with full permission of the law, defined their "possessions" according to whim, is evident in Paul D's reveries about Sweet Home. As schoolteacher's brutal chastisement of Sixo shows, "definitions belonged to the definers—not the defined" (225); that is, slave owners possessed full authority (however dubious, however shameful) to construct the identity of their slaves and to ensure the "stability" of that identity through extremely violent means in the event of a slave transgressing her or his assigned identity, as Sixo does with his logic, and as Sethe's mother did with her rebellion. Further, schoolteacher's "correction" of Sixo is also a re-inscription, for with Garner dead, the slaves inherited by his wife fall under the authority of her brother-in-law, who is then free to re-define and re-inscribe the Sweet Home men through beatings masquerading as legitimate punishment. This incident subsequently points to the fragility of African American identity under slavery: if definitions, including definitions of self, belong solely to the slave owner, then the identity of the slave is completely dependant on the slave owner. As a result, this identity may, in the event of the slaveholder's death and/or indebtedness, require a re-inscription, a re-identification of the slave by her/his new owner. Paul D describes this situation aptly when he tells Sethe, "Mister was allowed to be and stay what he was. But I wasn't allowed to be and stay what I was. Even if you cooked him you'd be cooking a rooster named Mister. But wasn't no way I'd ever be Paul D again, living or dead. Schoolteacher changed me" (86). Thus Paul D suggests the instability, the context-dependence of slave identities as they are defined by the white slave owner, the ever-present possibility of being sold, of the slave owner's death, and the subsequent encounter with a new master who, too, may create the slave's identity according to his whim.

Morrison's description of Baby Suggs' experience of slavery indicates a similar lack of selfhood. Like Paul D, Baby Suggs "knew more about them [her children] than she knew about herself, having never had the map to discover what she was like" (165). Unlike Paul D, however, Baby Suggs, almost immediately on her "escape" from slavery, begins to seek a self, to define it, through her body. She preaches in the Clearing: "'Here,' she said, 'in this here place, we flesh; flesh that weeps, laughs; flesh that dances on bare feet in grass. Love it. Love it hard" (103). As many critics note, Baby Suggs's sermon attempts to redefine African American identity through the flesh, to transform the inscriptions inflicted by whites into a radical self-love of the African American body. Dobbs identifies Baby Suggs's project as an attempt to heal, to re-interpret the identifies imposed by whites on African American bodies: "'Flesh' itself is not allowed to remain in the abstract; instead, the sermon breaks it down into individual parts—each despised by the white slave culture, each in need of claiming by these former slaves" (566). While Dobbs's assertion that Baby Suggs, as preacher, attempts to heal the scars of her congregation, to undo the inscriptions inflicted on them, she does not make much of Baby Suggs's designation of whites as out "yonder." As Baby Suggs says, "Yonder they do not love your flesh" (103). The "they," of course, here refers to whites, and I find this significant precisely because in the novel, whites are never out "yonder"; rather, through the dominion of their laws and the impetus of ownership, they are a constant presence. Even the clearing, which Linda Krumholz identifies as a "space to encounter painful memories safely and rest from them," is imbued with the presence of whites (397). Their presence is evident in the aftermath of Baby Suggs's death when the law (that is, the law of whites) prohibits Sethe from burying Baby Suggs in the Clearing (*Beloved* 201). Insofar as it is fair to understand whites' lawful dominion over the Clearing as a kind of presence, the burying of Baby Suggs's body confirms that in 19th-century America, there are no "safe" places, no spaces in which whites can truly be placed out yonder. This notion is reinforced by Baby Suggs's twice repeated explanation of her absence from the Clearing (after Sethe's attempted murder of her children) to Stamp Paid: "I'm saying they came in my yard" (211). There is an element of shock and disbelief in this phrase, a sense that Baby Suggs has learned too late that no place, no space, is free of white dominance and, with it, white presence.

124 is no exception to this rule: owned by the Bodwins, the resident white abolitionists of Cincinnati, the house, like the Clearing, is "possessed" by them, is both their literal property and a place where their presence, through virtue of ownership, is constant. Ironically, 124 is also the place where Sethe quarantines herself and her daughters as a means of escaping from, willfully ignoring, white folks. Morrison writes, "She didn't want any more news about whitefolks; didn't want to know what Ella knew and John and Stamp Paid, about the world done up the way whitefolks love it. All news of them should have stopped with the birds in her hair" (222), and "When Sethe locked the door, the women inside were free at last to be what they liked, see whatever they saw and say whatever was on their minds" (235). Sethe's description of the house, of being *in* the house, almost precisely matches Roland Barthes's description of the space of writing. In his (in)famous essay, "The Death of the Author," Barthes describes writing as, "that neutral, composite, oblique space where our subject slips away, the negative where all identity is lost" (142). Mirroring Barthes's emphasis on writing as both timeless and identity-less, Sethe desires to "hurry time along and get to the no-time waiting for her," a line that suggests her desire to escape time, and, alongside her denial of the "other," the whites, to negate identity (225). In creating this parallel between Barthes's description of writing and Sethe's quarantine in 124, Morrison thus links Sethe's intentions in 124 (denying the existence of white people) with the insidious project of white American literature: the "ghosting," the "quarantine" of black Americans. In other words, by echoing Barthes's phrasing through Sethe, Morrison ironically questions the conceit of American literature and of critics such as Barthes, who reinforce, presumably inadvertently, its predominant project of exclusion. For 124 is anything but a neutral space:

not only is it filled with the voices of "the black and angry dead" (234); it is also filled with the unidentified presence of the Bodwins as owners, as well as the ghosts of a "mother, grandmother, an aunt, and an older sister" (305) who died in the house. Might these voices, these presences, also be a part of the melee that encompasses 124? Given Morrison's indication in the novel that there are no neutral spaces, no places free from the presence of whites, it is fair to assume that they are.

And given also Morrison's exhortations against the deliberate absenting of black bodies from white literature in "Unspeakable Things Unspoken" and *Playing in the Dark,* it is possible to read Sethe's quarantine as conceit: staying within the house that looks suspiciously like Barthes's space of writing apparently "protects" Sethe and her daughters from the influence of whites, as a near repetition of the patterns of white literature. This possibility, one that, like American literature, risks distortion and violence against the "other," is evident in Sethe's attack against Edward Bodwin. A replay of the novel's central trauma (Sethe's murder of Beloved), this scene depicts Bodwin stopping near 124 to retrieve Denver, an act that, for Sethe, is too close to schoolteacher's trespass for her to bear standing still.[15] For Krumholz, Sethe's second attack (this time on the encroaching white man "threatening" her daughter, rather than on the daughter herself) marks a definite progression from the first. As she writes, "Sethe can act on her motherlove as she would have chosen to originally. Instead of turning on her children to save them from slavery, she turns on the white man who threatens them" (403). While a seemingly logical conclusion to draw, Krumholz's interpretation of the Bodwin scene rests on a problematic assumption: that "originally," Sethe never *intended* to murder her children, that there was nothing deliberate, or powerful, about this act.

On the contrary, one may read Sethe's attempt to murder the children—which is also her successful murder of Beloved—as a (very courageous) attempt to give them an identity beyond the identity of "slave," the identity imposed on them by whites. To draw an uneven but nonetheless helpful analogy, Sethe scars the bodies of her children, *marks* them, as the slaveholders also scar the bodies of enslaved African Americans to identify these men and women as slaves. Significantly, however, Sethe's marking of the children is not a signification of a particular identity so much as it is a *negation* of another loathed identity, a sign declaring that these children are *not* slaves. In other words, Sethe's attack on her children is literally an act of erasure, as most clearly shown, perhaps, by the red scar on Beloved's throat. As a sign of identity, Beloved's scar stands as an anomaly: it is the mark of her death, even though, dead since infancy, she has no flesh. Indeed, the anomaly of Beloved's scar is the anomaly of Beloved herself, for neither fully a ghost nor fully a fleshly human being, she inhabits a scarred body on the cusp of life and death at once.[16] What Beloved exhibits, then, is a central concept of identity: the production of the identity of "one" depends on the construction of an "other," such that the "one," being dependant on the "other" for its existence, is also at the same time the "other." Similarly, Beloved is both alive and dead, as though the one term could not fully *quarantine* itself from the other, and the bright red scar on her throat assuredly attests to this indeterminacy.

Read in conjunction with Sethe's attack on Bodwin, Beloved's scar spotlights the impossibility of erasure. A mirror—but not quite—of the murder scene, Sethe's threat to the white "abolitionist" is again, ironically, a threat to her children. For, if by murdering her children, Sethe meant to mark them as *not* slaves, and if identity necessitates the presence of an "other" to exist at all, then Sethe's inscription of her children's identity is likewise an inscription of the presence of whites, just as the naming of black identity by white slaveholders is also, in fact, the construction of white identity. Yet in Sethe's attempt to murder Bodwin, which may be read as the culmination of her quarantine, the symbolic act of total erasure of whites, lies also the erasure of *Sethe's* identity, as well as *Denver's* identity, since there can be no identity without the presence of an "other." To thus literally ghost her "other" (Bodwin as schoolteacher), much in the way that white American literature has historically ghosted the African American presence that is necessarily present within it, entails a concomitant ghosting of Sethe and Denver, an entrapment of the two women not unlike the limbo of Beloved, for the absence of the "other" is the impossibility of identification, the floating inertia of being neither dead nor alive, neither slave nor free.

Certainly, Sethe must be rescued from this erasure of Bodwin, not only to spare herself the prison time and probable execution that would inevitably follow it, but also so that she may come to terms with the presence of whites, the reality that there are no neutral spaces.[17] Denver intimates the relationship between storytelling/writing when she says, "What was more—much more—out there were whitepeople and how could you tell about them?" (287). This question is one of many lines in the novel that begs to be spoken (thereby exemplifying Morrison's use of oral tradition in her writing): on the one hand, it straightforwardly expresses Denver's fear of whites, of their inscrutable, unfixed collective identity. In this sense, the line acts as a counterweight to Sethe's attempted murder of Bodwin since Denver's anxiety about judging (and misjudging) whites suggests the multiplicity of white identity, its indeterminacy, and thus hints at the violence, the "dismemberment" required to limit it and, more importantly, to erase it. (This is, again, a repetition, but not quite, of the violence perpetuated by white slave holders as a means of usurping the right to define black identity.) On the other hand, shifting the emphasis of Denver's phrase to the word *tell* (as a narrator, in the oral tradition, might do as a way of illuminating hidden meanings) returns this line to the issues of storytelling and writing. That is, "how could you *tell* about them?", differently stressed, highlights Denver's (and Sethe's) inability to narrativize white folks, to speak about them. Still, it is necessary to speak about them, to narrativize them, for white folks, especially in Sethe's case, are an integral part of her story. And to resist the same pull of violence employed by whites against blacks as a means of exclusion from stories necessitates Sethe's coming to terms with the influence whites have had on her life, especially on her role as object.

For to tell her own stories (orally or in print) requires Sethe to place herself in the dual role of subject and object at once, and as a former slave, it is her role as object that is especially troubling, since it is the role that whites have assigned to her. This anxiety of objecthood returns at the end of the novel when the first thing Sethe says to Paul D on his appearance is, "I made the ink, Paul D. He couldn't have done it if I hadn't made the ink" (328). Like many assertions in *Beloved*, this one resounds with significance: by focusing on the ink, Sethe returns intellectually to the role of object ascribed to her (and inscribed on her) by schoolteacher. At the same time, she also emphasizes her role in its production and with it, her role in the production of schoolteacher's texts, both in the notebook and on her body. Though Sethe seems to here indict herself as complicit, and though this, too, is an open psychological scar, her admittance, her vocalized recognition of her role in schoolteacher's objectification of her opens the possibility of her coming to terms with that objectification, of realizing the overlap between white identity and its forced construction of black identity. This realization is necessary for Sethe to overcome her anxiety about making herself the object of narrative, the object of her own stories, since to ignore schoolteacher's influence in defining her and to ignore with it her own role in this definition, this inscription, is to accept the white model of identity construction as a strict binary, a dichotomous classification that rigidly distinguishes the writer and the written. The desire of Paul D to "put his story next to hers," as well as the "exorcism" performed by Ella and the women further complicates this binary mode of identification, since the base possibility of Sethe's *self*-identification is in large part relational, the result of multiplicities rather than strict hierarchies (322). And while there is no indication in the novel that Sethe succeeds in her reestimation of identity as multiple and overlapping, her final words, a repetition of the first person object pronoun, "Me? Me?" (322) suggest the possibility of her reclaiming herself as both subject and object, a reclaiming that thus allows her the prospect of telling, of writing, her own stories.

But how can Sethe, being illiterate, write her stories? And how can *Beloved*, then, be a story about writing? While writing in the space of the book is not a skill available to Sethe, Morrison's emphasis throughout the novel on the inscription of bodies, the writing of texts, certainly seems to indicate writing as a central theme of *Beloved*. Furthermore, Sethe's struggles with identity, subjecthood, and objecthood, as well as her impetus to tell her stories, shows narrative as another primary concern. These two aspects of the novel, taken together, intimate the possible characteristics of African American authorship, its unique development, that Morrison highlights through the interplay between writing and the compulsion to narrativize, writing and the practice of storytelling. In fashioning her story in this way, Morrison gestures toward the interaction in African American culture between orality and writing, a combination that distinguishes African American writing, including her own. Morrison brings this fact home (so to speak) in the near-repetition of the novel's final chapter: "It was not a story to pass on," "It was not a story to pass on," and, finally, "This is not a story to pass on" (323–324).[18] These lines, which critics interpret variously, strongly evoke the oral tradition in their capacity to be read aloud, for the meaning of these lines alters considerably with a shift in the speaker's emphasis. Three possible interpretations might include, "It was *not* a story to *pass on*" (not a story to repeat), "It was not a story to *pass on*" (not a story to overlook), and "It was not a story to *pass on*" (not a story to die, to be forgotten). In their ambiguity, these lines subsequently suggest the orality of Morrison's writing, the ways that the novelist uses the oral tradition. At the same time, being written, the writing avoids the fixedness of meaning possible through the storyteller's emphasis.

And yet it *is* writing, and Morrison draws attention to this fact with the change in the final "repeated" line: "This is not a story to pass on." Still retaining all the ambiguity of the lines that precede it, the meaning of which arguably depends on how they are spoken and/or read, this line both shifts to the present tense and changes the uncertainty of the "it" to the more definitive "this." In other words, it calls attention to the physical object, the book, the "this," in the reader's hands, almost as though the story itself were entering the space of the reader.[19] This possibility is enormously significant, for here, Morrison both draws attention to the fact of her writing, to the written text, while at the same time preserving the tone and fluidity of the oral tradition. This confluence of writing and orality highlights the significance of writing in the novel and the ways that this centrality of writing remarks and questions American literature in the twentieth and twenty-first centuries, since it is through her use of the oral that Morrison negotiates the complex inheritance of African American authorship in a written medium. Not that one form is privileged over the other; rather, the problematics of authorship suggested in *Beloved*'s focus on the written are answered and illuminated by an oral praxis, one that preserves African American and African culture in a medium mired in repression of those identities.

This concern with writing and the ways that white American literature constructs itself against blackness, as well as the ways that African American authors transcend these patterns of exclusion, are central to *Beloved*. Too often read solely in light of its oral aesthetic, this aspect of the novel, this obsession with writing and with written bodies, is a conspicuous absence in current scholarship, conspicuous precisely because it is a blindness not unlike the leviathan of white literary criticism that refuses to see the ways that white American authors construct themselves and their texts by the codes and conventions of exclusion. In *Beloved,* Morrison addresses this issue through her indictment of the conceit of singularity assigned to white characters as well as in her re-imagining of the emergence of African American writing within the prescriptions and restrictions of its 19th-century setting. The appearances of such concerns in the works of African American authors, the ways that many authors negotiate the anxieties of an alien medium, are perhaps the critical loci articulated in both "Unspeakable Things Unspoken" and *Playing in the Dark* that receive considerably less attention than the larger project of revisiting the major works of white canonical authors, including Melville, Poe, Hemingway, and Hawthorne, in search of the Africanist presence. That these concerns occupy such a critical place in Morrison's best known and most honored novel suggests the manner in which *Beloved,* in transcribing its own complex heritage, in exhibiting the possibilities of how such a heritage may be worked through and worked over, effectively gestures toward the difficulties of authorship perhaps necessarily transcribed in many African American texts.

Notes

1. Since Morrison's essays focus primarily on 19th- and early 20th-century white American authors, I use the phrase "white American authors" to likewise refer to the white American authors of these periods. This is not to say that the ghosting of African Americans that Morrison describes has not been perpetrated by mid- and late 20th-century white American authors and contemporary white American authors as well.

2. I use the term "authorship" here to denote its most common, though by no means most accurate, definition as the state of one who has produced a *written* text.

3. This uneven focus on orality extends beyond *Beloved* and is especially well-debated in analyses of *Song of Solomon.* To suggest only one example of critical privileging of oral over written, Joyce Irene Middleton, in "From Orality to Literacy: Oral Memory in Toni Morrison's *Song of Solomon,*" writes that "Morrison's readers observe how literacy, a means to success and power in the external, material, and racist world, alienates Macon Dead's family from their older cultural and family rituals, their inner spiritual lives, and their oral memories" (24). While interesting and insightful, such a reading, in its stark division of oral and written, necessarily maintains a dichotic separation of the two that threatens to turn at any moment into a hierarchical construction.

4. Interestingly, in "Unspeakable Things Unspoken," Morrison identifies Greek tragedy as a genre in which she feels "intellectually at home" because of "its

similarity to Afro-American communal structures . . . and African religion and philosophy" (202).

5. That is, to the white slave owners who are primarily the readers of brands, insofar as they and not African Americans are invested in this distinction of ownership, the differentiation of slaves by these scars need not encompass any more than the slave's status as property.

6. Sethe's mother (and to some degree Sixo) also resists the mark that identifies her by the rebellion for which she is presumably executed. It is also interesting to note that the reaction of whites to the irrepressibility of the mark is to "erase" the mark—or, more accurately, to erase the flesh that bears the mark, the flesh that continually menaces interpretations different from those intended by the white authors, the slave owners.

7. While Garner's beatings are more directly the result of his "affront" to feminine honor, that is, his suggestion that he would not let the Sweet Home men near the wives of his contemporaries, they are more indirectly, but still fairly, the result of his naming practices.

8. At least, it is especially important to the aspect of her project that involves a writerly critique of contemporary literary modes.

9. However, it should be noted that Garner himself does not scar the bodies of his slaves. It is fair to suggest that he scars their psyches, perhaps, but in his case, the identification, the inscription, of the Sweet Home men is a matter of naming, an act that functions almost exactly as the inflicting of physical scars.

10. I do not mean that Sethe is somehow complicit in her scarring. Complicity requires volition, and slavery, as an institution, systematically sought to deprive slaves of volition.

11. See *Of Grammatology* and/or *Limited Inc.*

12. In this sense, the possibility that Morrison's overwriting commits the same violence against white identity that schoolteacher perpetuates against black is muted by a particular narrative detail: unlike the African Americans marked as schoolteacher's text, schoolteacher and whites generally already have presence in American writing, presence that Morrison's expansion, as opposed to schoolteacher's limitation, cannot ghost.

13. This is not to say that Beloved is in any way singularly or definitively Sethe's dead daughter. As several authors note, Beloved as easily represents the "Sixty Million/and more" of Morrison's dedication as she does Sethe's child, nor is the possibility that her appearance at 124 is simply coincidental ever fully dispelled. Even so, I read Beloved primarily as the child whose tombstone bears the word, an identity that does not negate or close the possibility of the several other identities she inhabits or, at least, may inhabit. This view of Beloved is valid both in that it focuses centrally on Sethe, who certainly views the girl as her deceased baby, and because so many other characters, especially the women who ultimately cast out the pregnant woman, also perceive Beloved in this way.

14. The combination of the circle of iron and the lack of both Sethe's earrings and her mother's "round basket" for collecting rice suggests that Beloved at this point has moved from embodying Sethe watching her mother to embodying Sethe's mother.

15. Whether Sethe sees Bodwin as Bodwin, or Bodwin as schoolteacher, remains ambiguous in the novel.

16. That she calls herself "Beloved," the word on her tombstone, and that she bears the scar on her throat both suggest that Beloved, though moving like the living, and acting like the living, is nonetheless dead.

17. Many critics have suggested that to reach this realization, Sethe must witness the exorcism of Beloved by the community of women, must witness the casting out of her (maybe) daughter as something to be expelled, something extraneous, even poisonous. Other critics have suggested that what needs casting out is not the girl herself, but, rather, the girl as a representation of Sethe's own ousting from the community. In this sense, Beloved's expulsion is a negation of Sethe's expulsion from the community, an act of forgiveness in which the women finally drive away the ghost of their own guilt, the cause of their own "quarantine."

18. This repetition, interestingly, both invokes Morrison's complicated authorial heritage from white authors such as Faulkner—and in fact, as O'Donnell writes, Morrison in many ways "revisits Faulkner in order to revise him" (323)—as well as the oral tradition she invokes as a legacy of her African-American inheritance. See, for example, J. Middleton on *Song of Solomon*.

19. In this sense, the conclusion of *Beloved* echoes the conclusion of *Jazz*.

WORKS CITED

Atkinson, Yvonne. "Language that Bears Witness: The Black English Oral Tradition in the Works of Toni Morrison." Conner 12–30.

Barthes, Roland. "The Death of the Author." *Image, Music, Text*. New York: Hill & Wang, 1977. 142–148.

Bonnet, Michele. "'To Take the Sin Out of Slicing Trees . . .': The Law of the Tree in *Beloved*." *African American Review* 31 (1997): 41–54.

Brooks, Peter. *Body Works: Objects of Desire in Modern Narrative*. Cambridge: Harvard University Press, 1993.

Conner, Marc C., ed. *The Aesthetics of Toni Morrison: Speaking the Unspeakable*. Jackson: University Press of Mississippi, 2000.

Corey, Susan. "Toward the Limits of Mystery: The Grotesque in Toni Morrison's *Beloved*." Conner 31–48.

Dobbs, Cynthia. "Toni Morrison's *Beloved*: Bodies Returned, Modernism Revisited." *African American Review* 32 (1998): 563–578.

Faris, Wendy B. "Devastation and Replenishment: New World Narratives of Love and Nature." *Studies in the Humanities* 19.2 (1992): 171–182.

Fulton, DoVeanna S. *Speaking Power: Black Feminist Orality in Women's Narratives of Slavery*. Albany: SUNY Press, 2006.

Iyasere, Solomon O., and Maria W. Iyasere, eds. *Understanding Toni Morrison's* Beloved *and* Sula: *Selected Criticisms of the Works by the Nobel Prize-Winning Author*. Troy, NY: Whitston, 2000.

Koolish, Lynda. "Fictive Strategies and Cinematic Representations in Toni Morrison's *Beloved*: Postcolonial Theory/Postcolonial Text." *African American Review* 29 (1995): 421–438.

Krumholz, Linda. "The Ghosts of Slavery: Historical recovery in Toni Morrison's *Beloved*." *African American Review* 26 (1992): 395–408.

Lawrence, David. "Fleshly Ghosts and Ghostly Flesh: The Word and the Body in *Beloved*." *Toni Morrison's Fiction: Contemporary Criticism*. Ed. David Middleton. New York: Garland Press, 1997. 231–246.

Middleton, Joyce Irene. "From Orality to Literacy: Oral Memory in Toni Morrison's *Song of Solomon*." *New Essays on* Song of Solomon. Ed. Valerie Smith. Cambridge: Cambridge University Press, 1995. 19–39.

Morrison, Toni. *Beloved*. New York: Vintage, 1987.

———. *Playing in the Dark: Whiteness and the Literary Imagination*. New York: Vintage, 1992.

———. "Unspeakable Things Unspoken: The Afro-American Presence in American Literature." *Modern Critical Views: Toni Morrison*. Ed. Harold Bloom. Philadelphia: Chelsea House, 1990. 201–230.

O'Donnell, Patrick. "Remarking Bodies: Divagations of Morrison from Faulkner." *Faulkner, His Contemporaries, and His Posterity*. Ed. Waldemar Zacharasiewicz. Tübingen, Germany: Francke, 1993. 322–327.

Pitavy, Francois. "From Middle Passage to Holocaust: The Black Body as a Site of Memory." *Sites of Memory in American Literatures and Cultures*. Ed. Udo J. Hebel. Heidelburg, Germany: Universitätsverlag, 2003. 51–63.

Powell, Betty Jane. "'will the parts hold?': The Journey Toward a Coherent Self in *Beloved*." Iyasere and Iyasere 83–112.

Rody, Caroline. "Toni Morrison's *Beloved*: History, 'Rememory,' and a 'Clamor for a Kiss.'" Iyasere and Iyasere 83–112.

CYNTHIA LYLES-SCOTT

A Slave by Any Other Name: Names and Identity in Toni Morrison's Beloved

Names and naming play an important part in Toni Morrison's *Beloved: A Novel,* which won the 1987 Pulitzer Prize. The story is set in 1873, a decade after the Civil War, but much of it is told through memories and flashbacks of the time when the main characters, Baby Suggs, Paul D, and Halle, were slaves. Morrison's story demonstrates differences in both intent and result when names were issued by slave owners as opposed to names bestowed by Black people themselves.

Toni Morrison's *Beloved* is an example of many different types of literature. It is a supernatural tale about a slain daughter who comes back to life. It is a love story about two people who find one another after nearly twenty years have passed. And it is a familial tale about three generations of women and how their lives were and are affected by the institution of slavery. As Patricia Waugh wrote in *Feminine Fictions,* 'Toni Morrison's novels explore the racial history of black people in terms of how their oppression is lived out through relationships within their family and yet how these same relationships carry the possibility of human dignity and connection' (213). While there are many aspects of *Beloved* that could be argued as important within the context of the novel, the one I am focusing on here is the act of naming or nicknaming as a way of reclaiming one's self and one's identity.

Names, Volume 56, Number 1 (March 2008): pp. 23–28. Copyright © 2008 Maney Publishing.

195

At the beginning, readers get an idea of the special nature of names when they are introduced to the major characters of the novel. Sethe's name has masculine origins while the *D* at the end of Paul's name denotes his being fourth in a succession of male slaves all named Paul. These facts help readers realize that the characters' names are as much a part of the novel as is the plot. As Genevieve Fabre noted in 'Genealogical Archaeology or the Quest for Legacy in Toni Morrison's *Song of Solomon*':

> Names are an essential part of the legacy (of black people), and names have stories which, incongruous, preposterous as they are, must be cared for . . . Blacks receive dead patronyms from whites . . . names are disguises, jokes or brand names—from yearnings, gestures, flaws, events, mistakes, weaknesses. Names endure like marks or have secrets they do not easily yield. (108–109)

Morrison's characters are named aptly and specifically. For example, Sethe was named for a black man, the only one who did not have forced sexual relations with her mother, or 'Ma'am,' as Sethe calls her. As her wet nurse Nan tells Sethe, her mother abandoned or 'threw away' her other children while saving Sethe. The difference is that she chose to have sexual relations with Seth's father. In the other situations she was raped; and rape is never a choice. 'The one from the crew she threw away on the island. The others from more whites she also threw away. Without names, she threw them. *You* she gave the name of the black man,' who most likely was Sethe's father (62). The way Sethe's mother abandoned her mulatto children draws a direct link to the rape of black slave women as a consequence of the institution of slavery.

Sethe's mother goes unnamed in the novel except for the moniker *Ma'am*, which is given to her by Nan, the black wet nurse. She is also identified by a brand consisting of a circle with a cross burned into her flesh beneath her breast. Barbara Rigney wrote in 'Breaking the Back of Words: Language, Silence, and the Politics of Identity in *Beloved*,' that marks like the one Sethe's mother has serve to distinguish their racial identity. The marks are either 'chosen or inflicted by the condition of blackness itself, by the institution of slavery which "marked" its victims literally and figuratively, physically and psychologically' (145). The purpose of these marks was not only to identify slaves, but to brand them literally and figuratively as the property of someone else. In a similar way, Rigney notes that, a slave's name, such as Paul D's and the other Pauls, did not designate an individual as self so much as a 'segment of community, an identity larger than self' (145). Moreover, Rigney observed that Sethe's name is unique because she was not named by a white slave master or overseer. Sethe's name was given to her by her mother and as such 'is a mark of blackness and of acceptance into tribe and culture' representing 'a sense of heritage and a context of relational identity' (146).

Also significant is the fact that Sethe's two daughters, Denver and Beloved, have names which come from black slave mothers—from Sethe herself and from Sethe's mother-in-law, Baby Suggs. Denver is not named geographically for the mile-high city but for the young, white girl—Amy Denver—who helped Sethe deliver her baby when as a runaway slave Sethe went into labor on her journey to Baby Suggs' house at 124 Bluestone Road. In a way, Denver has a 'white' name, but the point is that her mother chose to give it to her. And, as Rigney writes, 'Beloved, whose birth name we never learn, takes her identity from the single word on her tombstone and from the love her mother bears her' (146). In the story line the only other designation Beloved receives is the nickname, *Already Crawling Girl.*

In 'Reconnecting Fragments: Afro-American Folk Tradition in *The Bluest Eye,*' Trudier Harris, observed that 'in their studies of nicknames in black communities, scholars have focused on the tremendous value they have, the special recognition they bestow upon an individual for a feat accomplished, a trait emphasized, or a characteristic noticed' (72). The nickname, *Already Crawling Girl,* identifies Beloved for a feat she accomplishes at an early age and thus falls directly into this category of nicknaming which indicates a kind of acceptance and love. Of course this inclusion in the black community occurs before *Already Crawling Girl* is killed by her mother, an act which ostracizes both Sethe and Denver from their community.

The black male characters in the novel, including Paul D and Stamp Paid, are also affected by the lack of identity that slavery produced. On page 11, readers are told 'and so they were: Paul D Garner, Paul F Garner, Paul A Garner, Halle Suggs, and Sixo (meaning: Six Zero), the wild man.' On page 91, readers meet Stamp who introduces himself with 'Name's Stamp, Stamp Paid.' As mentioned earlier, Paul D is one of a series of Pauls, named in alphabetical succession by the previous slave master who owned them before they were sold to Mr Garner. By being given the same first name, with only an alphabetical character to distinguish between them, the Pauls are effectively dispossessed of their individuality and their own distinctive claim to an identity. Their names do not celebrate accomplishments, personality traits, or family conventions. The designations are solely for the benefit of the slave masters and not the self-identification of the male slaves.

However, Stamp Paid, who was given the birth name of Joshua, renounces his slave name and renames himself. He is the only former slave in the novel to accomplish this, but once he has his freedom, he still questions his self-made identity. As Morrison states:

Perhaps . . . he [Stamp Paid] had misnamed himself and there was yet another debt he owed. Born Joshua, he renamed himself when he handed over his wife to his master's son . . . With that gift, he decided he didn't owe anybody anything. Whatever his obligations were, that act paid them off. (184–185)

This passage not only questions the symbolic freedom from the debt of slavery, but demonstrates that, even with his supposed freedom, Stamp Paid continually suffers under the institution of slavery because the single act of handing 'over his wife to his master's son' deprived him of his dignity and his manhood. Because of this self doubt, Stamp Paid continually pays, and will continue to pay with his self-inflicted misery for his freedom and his name.

In an interview with Thomas Le Clair of *New Republic* magazine, Morrison discussed her use of names in her novels. 'I used the biblical names to show the impact of the Bible on the lives of black people, their awe of and respect for it coupled with their ability to distort it for their own purposes.' Morrison continues, 'I also used some pre-Christian names to give the sense of a mixture of cosmologies' (259). But more than just discussing her use of names, Morrison also goes on to detail the psychological and historical factors behind her choices:

I never knew the real names of my father's friends. Still don't. They used other names. A part of that had to do with cultural orphanage, part of it with the rejection of the name given to them under circumstances not of their choosing: If you come from Africa, your name is gone. It is particularly problematic because it is not just your name but your family, your tribe. When you die, how can you connect with your ancestors if you have lost your name? That's a huge psychological scar. (259)

Lean'tin L. Bracks concurred in her essay, 'Toni Morrison's *Beloved:* Evolving Identities from Slavery to Freedom,' where she wrote that there are many stories like Sethe's, Paul D's, Denver's, Stamp Paid's, and Beloved's in historical research and in the retelling of slavery. Knowing them helps us 'decipher the code they lived and died by' (76). But Bracks believes that personal worth and possessions owned by slaves took on meanings of the 'self-actualization' manifested in loving oneself and others like oneself. She writes that it was freedom that removed limits and allowed slaves to choose their own identities and their own names. Sonia Weiss has found that after the conclusion of the Civil War, one of the first things that many freed slaves did was to cast aside the names that had been forced upon them by their former masters and adopt such new names as Freedman or Freeman to reflect their new status. Some celebrated by adopting the full forms of their shortened names. Others embellished their former names by adding prefixes or suffixes (such as an *m* in front of Edgar, resulting in the name given to civil rights leader Medgar Evers). Still others changed the spelling of their names to further distinguish them from the ones used by whites (131–133). Bracks says that the freedom to choose one's own name was symbolic and 'allowed one to choose possibilities in one's own ability, instead of pinning one's hope on the efforts of others' (61).

However, altering their outlook was a challenge for many blacks as slavery had brought a great deal of suffering and misery into their lives. For instance, the loss of loved ones and family members, made attaining freedom the only way many slaves had to ensuring the lives of those who they had not lost yet, since they could no longer care for the ones they had lost. Bracks concludes that to reconstruct the image of the self, slaves had to embrace the history of their enslavement, which served to express and explore the boundaries of choice or the lack thereof, as well as pay tribute to

> the potential and power that lies within the oppressed and opens the door to love that can heal or bring hope to the lost, damaged, and repressed. It is through this process of embracing the past in all its pain and glory that identities evolve to form a healthy people. (76)

Of all the characters in the novel, Baby Suggs becomes perhaps the most self-identified, self-aware, and self-possessed. In fact, Baby Suggs's definitive 'self' is a direct result of her rejecting the name given to her by white patriarchy and accepting black patriarchy. Readers learn that Baby Suggs is the only character in the novel named by and for a black male. In the exchange between Baby Suggs and Mr Garner, which takes place as he is delivering her into her freedom, bought and paid for by Sethe's husband, Halle, who was Baby Suggs' last-born child and the only one ripped from her arms and sold as a mere toddler:

> 'Mr. Garner,' [Baby Suggs] said. 'why you all call me Jenny?'
> 'Cause that what's on your sales ticket, gal. Ain't that your name? What you call yourself?'
> 'Nothing,' she said. 'I don't call myself nothing.' (141)

According to Rigney, during the exchange between Baby Suggs and Mr Garner, when Baby Suggs answers 'with her lack of name'—'Nothing . . . I don't call myself nothing'—it is a testament to the 'desolated center where the self that was no self made its home.' Rigney goes on to write 'Baby Suggs has no frame of reference by which to establish one, no family, no children, no context' (145). However, I disagree. I think this scene reveals Baby Suggs to be the most self-claimed and self-identified character in the novel:

> 'Suggs is my name, sir. From my husband. He didn't call me Jenny.'
> 'What he call you?'
> 'Baby.'
> 'Well,' said Mr. Garner, going pink again, 'if I was you I'd stick to Jenny Whitlow. Mrs. Baby Suggs ain't no name for a freed Negro.'
> Maybe not, she thought, but Baby Suggs was all she had left of the 'husband' she claimed. (141)

The previous passage demonstrates that Baby Suggs never suffers from a loss of identity because of slavery; she simply did not answer to white patriarchy's identification of her *Jenny Whitlow,* but instead identified herself by the name given to her by husband Suggs. He called her 'Baby' and she in turn completes this identity by naming herself Baby Suggs in his honor.

Morrison supports the idea of Baby Suggs being self-possessed or self-owned, when in one of Sethe's flashbacks, Morrison writes as the omnipotent author about how Baby Suggs suddenly comes alive unto herself and claims her body and soul after being freed from enslavement at the hands of Mr Garner. 'Suddenly she [Baby Suggs] saw her hands and thought . . . "These hands belong to me. These *my* hands." Next she felt a knocking in her chest and discovered something else new: her own heartbeat' (141). In fact, it is from Baby Suggs, her teachings, and her example, that many other characters in the community of freed former slaves, as well as her family and loved ones, take the steps to reclaim their own identities. Baby Suggs tells the rest of the black community that 'the only grace they could have was the grace they could imagine' (88), meaning that as freed men and women, it was only their own autonomous rights and wishes that they had to fulfill, and no longer their master's. And if they could not or would not realize this, then they would remain only freed slaves; free yes, but still enslaved by their own mentality.

For example, the way Baby Suggs leads the rest of the black community of escaped and fugitive slaves in a spiritual gathering in the Clearing reveals Baby Suggs' 'self-actualization.'

> 'Here,' she said. 'in this place, we flesh; flesh that weeps, laughs . . . dances on bare feet in grass . . . *You* got to love it, *you!* . . . Flesh that needs to be loved . . . So you love your neck; put a hand on it, grace it, stroke it and hold it up . . . and the beat and beating heart, love that too . . . For this is the prize.' (88–89)

Baby Suggs's role in helping others become more self-actualized, as when Sethe reclaims her self through living at 124 Bluestone Road, as well as when Suggs delivers her sermons in the clearing, further demonstrates the actualization of Baby Suggs. Morrison writes, 'Bit by bit, at 124 and in the Clearing, along with the others, [Sethe] had claimed herself. Freeing yourself was one thing; claiming ownership of that freed self was another' (95).

More than just your average literary narrative, Toni Morrison's *Beloved* works on many levels to achieve a balance as a slave chronicle and a story of the loves, suffering, and spirituality of three generations of black women, whose lives were devastated by the institution of slavery. *Beloved* centers on the theme of reclaiming identity and achieving self-actualization. The motivating factor at the heart of this tale of self-actualization is the theme of naming and nicknaming, through which many of the characters of the novel lose and reclaim their identities. However, from Morrison's perspective, as developed in *Beloved*, the institution of slavery remains so devastatingly powerful that even the characters who are now free, whether through running away or through actual emancipation, have yet to overcome their own mental enslavement. Many, as illustrated by the character of Stamp Paid, are riddled with so much self-doubt and despondency over those whom they have lost, that they are rendered impotent to progress or advancement.

Works Cited

Bracks, Lean'tin L., 1998. 'Toni Morrison's *Beloved:* Evolving Identities from Slavery to Freedom,' *Writings on Black Women of the Diaspora: History, Language and Identity,* New York: Garland Publishing, Inc., pp. 55–81.

Fabre, Genevieve, 1988. 'Genealogical Archaeology or the Quest for Legacy in Toni Morrison's *Song of Soloman,' Critical Essays on Toni Morrison,* by Nellie Y. McKay, pp. 105–114.

Harris, Trudier, 1988. 'Reconnecting Fragments: Afro-American Folk Tradition in *The Bluest Eye,' Critical Essays on Toni Morrison,* by Nellie Y. McKay, pp. 68–76.

Le Clair, Tom, 1983. 'An Interview with Toni Morrison,' *Anything Can Happen: Interviews with Contemporary American Novelists,* ed. by Larry MacCaffery, Urbana, IL: University of Illinois Press, pp. 252–261.

McKay, Nellie Y., ed., 1988. *Critical Essays on Toni Morrison,* Boston, MA: G.K. Hall & Co.

McKay, Nellie Y., Barbara Christian, and Deborah McDowell, 1999. 'A Conversation on Toni Morrison's *Beloved,' Toni Morrison's Beloved: A Casebook,* ed. by William L. Andrews and Nellie Y. McKay, New York: Oxford University Press, pp. 203–220.

Morrison, Toni, 1987. *Beloved: A Novel,* New York: Random House.

Rigney, Barbara Hill, 1988. 'Breaking the Back of Words: Language, Silence, and the Politics of Identity in *Beloved,' Critical Essays on Toni Morrison's Beloved,* ed. by Barbara H. Solomon, New York: G.K. Hall & Co., pp. 138–147.

Waugh, Patricia, 1989. 'Postmodern Persons?' *Feminine Fictions: Revisiting the Postmodern,* London: Routledge, pp. 209–217.

Weiss, Sonia, 1999. 'Finding Our History: African American Names,' *The Complete Idiot's Guide to Baby Names*, Indianapolis, IN: Alpha Books, pp. 131–140.

Chronology

1931	Toni Morrison born Chloe Anthony Wofford on February 18 in Lorain, Ohio, the second child of George Wofford and Ramah Willis Wofford.
1953	Graduates with a B.A. in English from Howard University, changes name to Toni during years at Howard.
1955	Receives M.A. in English from Cornell University for thesis on the theme of suicide in William Faulkner and Virginia Woolf.
1955–1957	Instructor in English at Texas Southern University.
1957–1964	Instructor in English at Howard University.
1958	Marries Harold Morrison, a Jamaican architect.
1964	Divorces Morrison and returns with her two sons to Lorain.
1965	Becomes editor for a textbook subsidiary of Random House in Syracuse, New York.
1970	Morrison's first novel, *The Bluest Eye*, published; takes editorial position at Random House in New York, eventually becoming a senior editor.
1971	Associate Professor of English at the State University of New York at Purchase.

1974   *Sula* published and an edition of Middleton Harris's *The Black Book.*

1975   *Sula* nominated for National Book Award.

1976–1977   Visiting Lecturer at Yale University.

1977   *Song of Solomon* published, receives the National Book Critics Circle Award and the American Academy and Institute of Arts and Letters Award.

1981   *Tar Baby* published.

1984–1989   Schweitzer Professor of the Humanities at the State University of New York at Albany.

1986   Receives the New York State Governor's Art Award.

1986–1988   Visiting Lecturer at Bard College.

1987   *Beloved* published and is nominated for the National Book Award and the National Book Critics Award.

1988   *Beloved* awarded Pulitzer Prize in fiction and the Robert F. Kennedy Award.

1989   Robert F. Goheen Professor of the Humanities at Princeton University.

1992   *Jazz* and *Playing in the Dark: Whiteness and the Literary Imagination* published.

1993   Awarded Nobel Prize in literature.

1994   Awarded Pearl Buck Award, Rhegium Julii Prize, Condorcet Medal (Paris), and Commander of the Order of Arts and Letters (Paris).

1996   Awarded Medal for Distinguished Contribution to American Letters, National Book Foundation.

1998   *Paradise* published.

1999   *The Big Box* published with her son Slade Morrison.

2001   Awarded National Humanities Medal.

2002   *The Book of Mean People*, with her son, Slade Morrison, published.

2003   *Love* published and *The Lion or the Mouse?* and *The Ant or the Grasshopper?* both published with her son Slade Morrison.

2004   *The Poppy or the Snake?* published with her son Slade Morrison.

2005   *Remember: The Journey to School Integration* published; wins Coretta Scott King Book Award.

2008   *A Mercy* and *What Moves at the Margin: Selected Non-Fiction* published.

Contributors

HAROLD BLOOM is Sterling Professor of the Humanities at Yale University. He is the author of 30 books, including *Shelley's Mythmaking* (1959), *The Visionary Company* (1961), *Blake's Apocalypse* (1963), *Yeats* (1970), *A Map of Misreading* (1975), *Kabbalah and Criticism* (1975), *Agon: Toward a Theory of Revisionism* (1982), *The American Religion* (1992), *The Western Canon* (1994), and *Omens of Millennium: The Gnosis of Angels, Dreams, and Resurrection* (1996). *The Anxiety of Influence* (1973) sets forth Professor Bloom's provocative theory of the literary relationships between the great writers and their predecessors. His most recent books include *Shakespeare: The Invention of the Human* (1998), a 1998 National Book Award finalist; *How to Read and Why* (2000); *Genius: A Mosaic of One Hundred Exemplary Creative Minds* (2002); *Hamlet: Poem Unlimited* (2003); *Where Shall Wisdom Be Found?* (2004); and *Jesus and Yahweh: The Names Divine* (2005). In 1999, Professor Bloom received the prestigious American Academy of Arts and Letters Gold Medal for Criticism. He has also received the International Prize of Catalonia, the Alfonso Reyes Prize of Mexico, and the Hans Christian Andersen Bicentennial Prize of Denmark.

STEVEN V. DANIELS is associate professor of English, emeritus, at Southern Methodist University. He says he is "currently pondering the shifting understanding during the nineteenth century of what the soul is and does," and he is attempting to popularize the samba in Dallas.

NANCY KANG is postdoctoral fellow in the Department of English at the University of Toronto, with a concentration on African American literature. Her 2006 dissertation was "'A Lot of Indian in His Face': The Native American Presence in Twentieth-Century American Autobiography."

TERESA N. WASHINGTON is associate professor of English at Grambling State University. She wrote *Our Mothers, Our Powers, Our Texts: Manifestations of Àjẹ́ in Africana Literatures* (2005).

JEFFREY ANDREW WEINSTOCK is associate professor of American literature and culture at Central Michigan University. He is the author of *The Rocky Horror Picture Show* (Wallflower Press, 2007) and *Scare Tactics: Supernatural Fiction by American Women* (2008). He has edited academic collections on topics including *South Park*, *The Blair Witch Project*, and the ghostly in American life.

REGINALD WATSON is associate professor of English at East Carolina University, where he is the first African American male ever to receive tenure in his department. He wrote *The Changing Image of the Mulatto from Harriet Beecher Stowe's* Uncle Tom's Cabin *to Francis E. W. Harper's* Iola Leroy *and Zora Neale Hurston's* Their Eyes Were Watching God (1991) and *Literary Images of the Mulatto in Nineteenth and Twentieth Century American Literature* (1998).

DEAN FRANCO is associate professor of English at Wake Forest University. He has written *Ethnic American Literature: Comparing Chicano, Jewish and African American Writing* (2006).

LARS ECKSTEIN is a lecturer in contemporary American literature at the University of Tübingen. His publications include *Re-Membering the Black Atlantic: On the Poetics and Politics of Literary Memory* (2006), *Reading Song Lyrics* (2008), and *English Literatures Across the Globe: A Companion*, which he edited in 2007.

CHRISTOPHER PETERSON is visiting assistant professor of literature at Claremont McKenna College. He has written *Kindred Specters—Death, Mourning, and American Affinity* (2007).

ANITA DURKIN is a doctoral candidate in the English Department at the University of Rochester.

CYNTHIA LYLES-SCOTT is a freelance writer and editor employed at Florida Atlantic University. She has written articles on the rising popularity of Southern horror fiction, the tragedy of the mulatto character, and images of the antiheroine in popular culture.

Bibliography

Crouch, Stanley. "Aunt Medea," *New Republic* (October 19, 1987): 38–43.

Davis, Cynthia. "Self, Society and Myth in Toni Morrison's Fiction," *Contemporary Literature* 23:3 (1982): 323–342.

Eckstein, Lars. *Re-Membering the Black Atlantic: On the Poetics and Politics of Literary Memory*. Cross/Cultures: Readings in the Post/Colonial Literatures in English 84. Amsterdam, Netherlands: Rodopi, 2006.

Goldman, Anne E. "'I Made Ink': (Literary) Production and Reproduction in *Dessa Rose* and *Beloved*," *Feminist Studies* 16 (1990): 324.

Henderson, Mae G. "Toni Morrison's *Beloved:* Re-membering the Body as Historical Text," *Comparative American Identities: Race, Sex, and Nationality in the Modern Text*. Hortense J. Spillers, ed. New York: Routledge, 1991. 62–86.

Horvitz, Deborah. "Nameless Ghosts: Posession and Dispossession in *Beloved*," *Studies in American Fiction* 17 (1989): 157–167.

Keenan, Sally. "'Four Hundred Years of Silence': Myth, History, and Motherhood in Toni Morrison's *Beloved*," *Recasting the World: Writing after Colonialism*. Jonathan White, ed. Baltimore: Johns Hopkins University Press, 1993. 45–81.

Kella, Elizabeth. *Beloved Communities: Solidarity and Difference in Fiction by Michael Ondaatje, Toni Morrison, and Joy Kogawa*. Acta Universitatis Upsaliensis, Studia Anglistica Upsaliensia 110. Uppsala, Sweden: Uppsala University, 2000.

Kubitschek, Missy Dehn. *Claiming the Heritage: African-American Women Novelists and History*. Jackson: University Press of Mississippi, 1991. 174, 177.

Mandel, Naomi. *Against the Unspeakable: Complicity, the Holocaust, and Slavery in America.* Cultural Frames, Framing Culture. Charlottesville: University of Virginia Press, 2006.

Marks, Kathleen. *Toni Morrison's* Beloved *and the Apotropaic Imagination.* Columbia: University of Missouri Press, 2002.

Morrison, Toni. *Paradise.* New York: Knopf, 1987.

———. *Beloved.* New York: Knopf, 1987.

———. *Tar Baby.* New York: Knopf, 1981.

———. *Song of Solomon.* New York: Knopf, 1977.

———. *Sula.* New York: Knopf, 1973.

———. *The Bluest Eye.* New York: Holt, Rinehart, & Winston, 1970.

———. "The Pain of Being Black: an Interview with Toni Morrison," with Bonnie Angelo. *Conversations with Toni Morrison.* Danielle Taylor-Guthrie, ed. Jackson: University Press of Mississippi, 1994. 255–261.

———. "In the Realm of Responsibility: A Conversation with Toni Morrison," with Marsha Jean Darling, *Women's Review of Books* (March 1988): 5–6.

———. "Unspeakable Things Unspoken: The Afro-American Presence in American Literature," *Michigan Quarterly Review* 28 (1989): 32.

Otten, Terry. *The Crime of Innocence in the Fiction of Toni Morrison.* Columbia: University of Missouri Press, 1989. 82–83.

Page, Philip. "Circularity in Toni Morrison's *Beloved,*" *African American Review* 26:1 (Spring 1992): 31–40.

Peterson, Nancy J. *Beloved: Character Studies.* Character Studies. London, England: Continuum, 2008.

Plasa, Carl. *Toni Morrison: Beloved.* Columbia Critical Guides. New York: Columbia University Press, 1998.

Ramadanovic, Petar. *Forgetting Futures: On Memory, Trauma, and Identity.* Lanham, Md: Lexington, 2001.

Sale, Maggie. "Call and Response as Critical Method: African-American Oral Traditions and *Beloved,*" *African American Review* 26:1 (Spring 1992): 41–50.

Samuels, Wilfred D., and Clenora Hudson-Weems. "'Ripping the Veil': Meaning through Rememory in *Beloved,*" *Toni Morrison.* Boston: Twayne, 1990. 94–138.

Schreiber, Evelyn Jaffe. *Subversive Voices: Eroticizing the Other in William Faulkner and Toni Morrison.* Knoxville: University of Tennessee Press, 2001.

Simpson, Ritashona. *Black Looks and Black Acts: The Language of Toni Morrison in* The Bluest Eye *and* Beloved. New York: Peter Lang, 2007.

Sitter, Deborah Ayer. "The Making of a Man: Dialogic Meaning in *Beloved,*" *African American Review* 26:1 (Spring 1992): 17–30.

Smith, Valerie. "'Circling the Subject': History and Narrative in *Beloved*," *Toni Morrison: Critical Perspectives Past and Present*. K. A. Appiah and Henry Louis Gates Jr., eds. New York: Amistad, 1993. 340–354.

Valade, Roger M., III, "Post Aesthetic Movement," *The Essential Black Literature Guide*. New York: Visible Ink Press, 1996. 299.

Acknowledgments

Steven V. Daniels. "Putting 'His Story Next to Hers': Choice, Agency, and the Structure of *Beloved*," *Texas Studies in Literature and Language*, Volume 44, Number 4 (Winter 2002): pp. 349–367. Copyright © 2002 The University of Texas Press. Reprinted by permission of the publisher.

Nancy Kang. "To Love and Be Loved: Considering Black Masculinity and the Misandric Impulse in Toni Morrison's *Beloved*," *Callaloo: A Journal of African-American and African Arts and Letters*, Volume 26, Number 3 (Summer 2003): pp. 836–854. Copyright © 2003 The Johns Hopkins University Press. Reprinted by permission of the publisher.

Teresa N. Washington. "The Mother-Daughter *Àjẹ* Relationship in Toni Morrison's *Beloved*," *African American Review*, Volume 39, Numbers 1–2 (Spring–Summer 2005): pp. 171–188. Copyright © 2005 Teresa N. Washington. Reprinted by permission of the author.

Jeffrey Andrew Weinstock. "Ten Minutes for Seven Letters: Reading *Beloved*'s Epitaph," *Arizona Quarterly: A Journal of American Literature, Culture, and Theory*, Volume 61, Number 3 (Autumn 2005): pp. 129–152. Copyright © 2005 Jeffrey Andrew Weinstock. Reprinted by permission of the author.

Reginald Watson. "Derogatory Images of Sex: The Black Woman and Her Plight in Toni Morrison's *Beloved*," *CLA Journal*, Volume 49, Number 3

Index